Contents

John Rogerson

The Dog Vinci Code

Unlock the secrets to training your dog

metro

Published by Metro Publishing
an imprint of John Blake Publishing Ltd
3 Bramber Court, 2 Bramber Road,
London W14 9PB, England

www.johnblakepublishing.co.uk

First published in hardback in 2010
Published in paperback in 2011

ISBN: 978 1 84358 307 3

British Library Cataloguing-in-Publication Data:
A catalogue record for this book is available from the British Library.

Design by www.envydesign.co.uk

Printed and bound in Great Britain by CPI Group (UK) Ltd

3 5 7 9 10 8 6 4

Papers used by John Blake Publishing are natural, recyclable products made from wood grown in sustainable forests. The manufacturing processes conform to the environmental regulations of the country of origin.

All internal images courtesy of Judy Rogerson. Training sequence photos courtesy of Redgy Vergracht. Special thanks to Frosty for posing for Judy to draw the front cover.

Every attempt has been made to contact the relevant copyright-holders, but some were unobtainable. We would be grateful if the appropriate people could contact us.

For Judy, my wife and best friend

Acknowledgements

I have been privileged to have been helped and influenced in my life with dogs for the past 50 years by some great trainers who freely gave their time to answer my growing list of questions, and without whose help and encouragement it would have been impossible for me to learn 'the code'. Sometimes a great teacher is one who does not give you the answer you are seeking but the means to find your own answers. So a big thank you to John Holmes for getting me to look at things from the dog's perspective, to Roy Hunter for daring to be different in his kind approach to dog-training, and to Ian Dunbar for uniting trainers worldwide to the benefit of dogs and their owners. Three truly inspirational figures, for without whom the dog world would be a much sadder place.

The Dog Vinci Code

DOG BISCUITS

Introduction

I always said that I would not write another book. The danger of using the written word is that it can so easily be misinterpreted, which sometimes means that an idea put down on paper with the best intentions can be a trap for the unwary. You cannot train a dog by reading a book; nor can you modify a dog's behaviour by merely reading words on a page. When you, dear reader, cast your eyes over the words that I write you cannot feel the emotions that lay behind my words or see the images in my mind. So you must not view this book as a manual on how to raise, train or modify your dog's behaviour. You should view it as a philosophy of thoughts and emotions that may better help you understand your dog, as a way of bridging the sometimes immense and widening gap between man and dog.

In an age of technology, where it is possible to communicate almost instantly with someone on the other side of the world, we humans seem not only to find it more difficult to communicate with one another on an emotional level but we are also losing the ability to communicate with our canine friends. The world we live in bears little resemblance to the world our forebears lived and worked in, and gone are the days when dogs lived a life with freedom to exercise most of their natural behaviours. The role of the working dog has changed little but now there are fewer jobs to go around and many of the breeds born to do a job now find themselves in the almost impossible position of having to adapt to a life in permanent retirement. Even the humble family pet is rapidly becoming a thing of the past as our busy lives leave precious little time for family life. We are able to get things done now with the push of a button on a computer but we are losing our ability to understand the animals that we share our lives with, even at the most basic level.

Today we have more trained behaviourists than ever before, more professional dog trainers and more pharmaceutical companies have realised there are profits to be made by giving dogs mind-altering drugs. Yet dog behaviour in general is now rapidly getting worse – just ask anyone who works in a rescue centre. Culturally, we are losing our rights to exercise our dogs off-lead in public leisure areas. We are also slowly but surely segregating dogs from children and it is sad that many children in the not too distant future will only ever see dogs in a segregated dog park. Do we really want our children, the next generation of dog owners, to grow up only being able to see a nicely trained dog within the confines of a dog-training facility or in an obedience ring? The days of dogs enjoying a day out with their families are numbered as more and more legislation is brought in by more and more countries to restrict ownership (banning breeds) and reduce the opportunities for good physical and emotional exercise in public areas.

Why is this happening? Because we are failing to understand, communicate with and train our family pets. Guide dogs are allowed access to public areas because they are well-trained and have to pass tests of outstanding social behaviour, not because they are necessarily any healthier or cleaner than our family companion. I have eaten in restaurants in Belgium and France where it is not uncommon to see a family enjoying a meal with their pet beside them at the table. This sight is very rare indeed in countries like Great Britain and the USA. There are also huge cultural differences in not only the attitude of dog owners but also in the behaviour of their dogs. Basically, if you look at any culture in the world, the behaviour of pet dogs is mirrored in the behaviour of its children. Why? Because they have the same role models for the way they behave.

Ask any breeder and they will tell you they can tell how a puppy will grow up based on the parents that want to buy it and the way their children behave when they come to view the puppy.

Take England as an example. England is a very small country, so if there is a change in the behaviour of a population then it will be more noticeable. In England, we have a tradition of companion dog ownership. When I was growing up in London, all my school friends had a dog. Where did these companion dogs come from? Generally, the puppies were bred in someone's home and advertised in the local area.

Thus even before a puppy arrived in its new home, it would have built up a model of the world at the breeder's that was not too dissimilar to what its life would be like when it went to its new family. Then we had the first change in culture. Prompted by animal charities and, I might add, professional breeders, the government decided to bring in the Breeding of Dogs Act 1973. This required breeders to obtain a licence from their local authority. Because the law was hastily drafted, it contained almost word for word the licence requirements for a boarding kennel! This started to signal the death knell for the pet dog breeder and, to the delight of puppy farms, large-scale dog breeding started to take place where emphasis was placed on breeds and marketing. Dog-breeding became, and has remained, big business.

But there is a way of changing attitudes in any culture by presenting good role models for behaviour. It starts with every dog trainer, behaviourist, groomer, breeder, dog sport enthusiast and companion dog owner understanding their responsibilities towards their community by learning how to communicate with and train their dogs. It requires everyone involved with dogs to understand that if breeders get it wrong, we all pay the penalty.

The Dog Vinci Code aims to get everyone back on track, the way it used to be: breeders producing nicer pet dogs, trainers learning the practical training skills by working with dogs rather than sitting in a classroom listening to a lecture on dog-training, and owners able to communicate with their dogs by understanding the almost forgotten code.

The art of raising and training a family pet is rapidly being turned into a science where the student is required to learn a new and complex vocabulary. Many of the people involved in this new science seem to understand more about statistical analysis than the emotions involved in raising a well-behaved pet dog. The emotional relationship that leads to a once-abandoned dog eventually becoming the ears of a deaf person cannot be defined by any scientific formulae. The mechanism by which a dog would willingly place its own life at risk in order to protect the life of its handler defies scientific analysis.

In my lifetime I have been privileged to work with thousands of dogs and with many organisations connected to dogs and their training. I have met some remarkable people who have the ability to communicate with the dogs that they work with, not by teaching words of command but by expressing their emotions. I have also watched some of the more modern scientific and mechanical training systems using words of command rather than expressions of emotion fail spectacularly.

When I watch an outstanding trainer working with a dog, it is like watching a great artist working with a canvas and palette of colours. The artist uses the palette to bring life to the canvas, creating light and shade and above all weaving his emotion into the very fabric of the canvas. Compare this to painting by numbers… need I say more?

Words are very specific to a culture. Even cultures that share the same language do not necessarily use the same words to express ideas. Coming from England, I have to change many of the words I use when I lecture in the USA, to avoid not only causing confusion but sometimes saying something that may be offensive. When I lecture in India through an interpreter, many words lose their impact because of the way they are translated into a different language. Written words are an attempt to record thoughts but the written word alone seems a poor substitute for the spoken word expressed with emotion.

This book is more of an expression of the emotions involved in raising and training the dog of your dreams as opposed to the use of mere words on a page. Dogs can't read words but there is no doubt that they can read emotions. In the days of Leonardo da Vinci, when dogs were appreciated for their skills as well as their companionship, ordinary people were better able to decode their dog's behaviour and truly understand and communicate with them. In this day and age, that understanding seems to be lost. Good dog trainers are born with the ability to communicate with their companions and cannot learn this ability in a classroom. Just like learning to play a musical instrument, anyone can learn to be a good dog handler. But, just like great musicians have immense passion for their craft, a great dog trainer needs to draw inspiration from within.

Section 1

Raising and Training a Puppy You Will Want to Keep for Life

'Knowing is not enough, we must apply.'
– LEONARDO DA VINCI

1
The Background to a Philosophy

Picture the scene: a class where students have come to learn about training dogs. All are highly motivated because not only do they have a passion for working with dogs, for many it is their livelihood. Many of the students are already professional trainers. Each student has chosen a dog from a rescue kennel and is trying, under instruction, to train the dog to do various exercises. The dogs have been carefully selected as being moderately easy to train. All the students have exactly the same amount of training time available to them, and all are armed with various rewards that the dogs are prepared to put in some effort to obtain.

The instructor demonstrates how to get each dog to carry out a very specific behaviour and uses a logical, step-by-step approach. The instructor uses a word of command, gets the dog to respond in the correct manner and then rewards the dog. All the students watch and are given the opportunity to repeat the exercise. Their actions and timing are flawless and perfectly mirror what the instructor has shown them. The rewards used are the same and given at the same point in the training process. Several training sessions come and go but hardly any of the students seem to be able to get the dog to respond to their commands. So where are the students going wrong?

The answer lies in the way the instructor is able to read the dog's emotions and in the way a pathway of communication is opened up between the two of them, based on how the instructor uses emotions in voice, movement and facial expression. The instructor not only understands the dog but the dog understands the instructor.

Let's look at another scenario, this time in an animal shelter. A visitor to the kennels walks around to have a look at the dogs up for adoption. He is walking around with the manageress who has worked at the kennels for over ten years. As they walk around, the visitor remarks that the dog in the second kennel would not make a very good family pet because it would quickly over-bond with new owners and possibly become overprotective of them. At the third kennel the visitor mentions that this dog suffers from separation problems and would be difficult to leave by itself. Two kennels later the visitor observes that this dog has not been raised in a family home but has lived mostly by itself with little emotional contact with an owner. In the next kennel he identifies a dog that has quite definitely been raised with another dog, even though it is in a kennel by itself.

The manageress is astounded by how accurately the visitor has managed to describe the character and background of each of the dogs. The visitor, for his part, cannot comprehend why the manageress, who has worked there for over ten years, cannot see what he sees! The visitor happens to be someone who has been involved in training dogs to the very highest standard for more than 20 years, while the manageress has simply been taking care of the dogs without really taking much notice of them. All the dogs arrive at the shelter with amazing tales to tell but sadly no one seems to know how to listen to what they are saying.

Dogs are a product of their five senses and five basic emotions. Taking them in turn we have:

SENSES

SMELL

This is often said to be around a million times better than our own. From my own experience, I believe this to be a gross overestimate but even so, a dog's sense of smell is truly remarkable. A dog can very easily be trained to follow the path that a person has walked, without having to be given a whiff of their scent. It can follow this trail for miles, across changing terrain and in difficult weather conditions, even many hours after the person has left the scene. A dog's nose is often described as being able to detect individual molecules of scent that make up a compound. Give a dog a sniff of perfume and it could probably tell you not only what ingredients make up the perfume but in what proportions!

HEARING

A dog can hear sound frequencies much higher and lower than we can, so it is possible to train a dog to respond to a whistle that a person cannot hear. Because of this remarkable sense they can detect the sound of a small prey, such as a mouse, from a dozen or more yards away and correctly pinpoint where it is. They can also detect even the minutest change in the emotions of the human voice. Look at the shape of your dog's ears and you will get a clue as to how their hearing memory works. Breeds with naturally erect ears usually hear sounds much better at all frequencies than dogs with drooped ears. A German Shepherd has an amazing sound memory and will easily identify its owner's car when it is still a couple of blocks away from home. Actually this is not quite true: many cars of the same make and model can drive past without the dog being able to link them to the presence of its owner. What the dog identifies is the *way* its owner drives this particular car as they approach home.

SIGHT

A dog's vision seems to be black, white, shades of grey and maybe some colour but a dog lacks the colour recognition associated with human eyesight. It does seem as though dogs can recognise colour, though maybe not by using their eyesight. When some of my students on dog-training courses work with shelter dogs at the Battersea Dogs and Cats Home in London, it seems the dogs there can indeed pick out colours. Anyone walking past in a light-blue sweatshirt always attracts a lot of excitement from the dogs, while anyone in a green sweatshirt immediately produces avoidance behaviour. The kennel staff responsible for the day-to-day care and welfare of the dogs – the ones who feed and befriend the dogs – all wear light-blue sweatshirts, while the veterinary staff all wear green ones. Is it the colour or is it the smell? Certainly the veterinary staff will smell very different from the kennel staff to a dog, but this does not explain why a student who arrives wearing blue is greeted very differently from one who arrives wearing green. But maybe it is the smell: it is possible that the dogs smell the chemical used to dye the clothes and not the occupational smell that impregnates the cloth! This just serves to illustrate what a different world our dogs live in compared to the world that we see with our eyes.

Some breeds, notably some retrievers and spaniels, have the most amazing visual memory. Throw a ball into long grass and let your Springer Spaniel see it land 50 yards away. Then obscure the dog's eyes and wait for a while before releasing the dog to go and fetch it. Incredibly, some have been able to pinpoint the exact spot where they saw the ball land twenty minutes earlier. Border Collies, on the other hand, seem to have a really poor visual memory. Throw a ball into long grass and obscure its eyes for even a few seconds and when you release the dog it will run where it wants, not where the ball was thrown!

If you look at the way breeds have been developed, what you learn about their senses should be of little surprise, along with the fact that some dogs appear to have certain memories built into their genetic code. When out on a shoot, a Springer Spaniel is required to mark the spot where the shot bird has landed and then remember it until sent to retrieve by the handler. Maybe that is also why a Border Collie never takes its eyes off its sheep: its visual memory is so poor it will forget where it last saw them!

TOUCH

Some breeds have been developed to be very insensitive to being touched, which some believe makes them more suitable to have around young children who may be a little rough in the way they handle their pets. But the reason that they are insensitive to touch is because they were originally bred for fighting! A dog would not be a very efficient fighter if he screamed and gave in the minute he felt a tooth touch his skin! There are dogs, notably Bull Terriers, which continue to fight despite the most appalling injuries.

TASTE

Taste and smell are undoubtedly linked, so it is surprising that many pet owners, seduced by the major pet food manufacturers, feed their dogs the same food every day for most of its life. Dogs can develop taste preferences in the same way that we can, so to deny a dog the opportunity to sample a varied diet would be the same as giving a child chicken and rice every day of its life. Building a repertoire of tastes in a dog also makes it so much easier to use food as a reward in training. There is a possibility that if you feed your dog the same diet day in and day out, when you offer it a new food it will eat too much and become ill. If this happens, the dog may reject this food in future. This works in the same way that it would if you ate something that made you ill – you would naturally build an aversion to this food.

There is no doubt that if a dog eats a varied diet then, all things being equal, it will outperform a dog fed the same food each day in exercises requiring discrimination in its sense of smell. A sniffer dog fed the same diet every day will never be as good as a sniffer dog given a very varied diet. Usually, however, the performance of the dog is dictated more by the quality of training it receives! A well-trained dog fed a repetitive diet will still perform its job better than a poorly trained one fed a varied diet.

Joy

EMOTIONS

The five basic emotions are sometimes difficult to describe but I think we would all agree that any dog raised in a human pack is capable of showing and understanding the following emotions:

JOY

Look at your dog wagging his tail when you arrive home and you cannot fail to recognise the expression of joy in his body language, facial expression and sometimes even in his vocalisations. Joy in a dog, like the other basic expressions of emotions, is a universal expression not tied to culture or upbringing. It seems to be an important inherited characteristic.

SURPRISE

Many owners have seen this expression in their dogs when caught in the act, or when the owner turns up unexpectedly when the dog is engaged in some all-absorbing behaviour. The look on a dog's face is a mixture of bewilderment, sometimes accompanied by a freeze or temporary startled behaviour. Pretend to go out and leave the dog by itself in the house. Open the front door and then close it again without actually going out and get a friend to drive your car away. Wait for a few seconds as the car disappears down the road and then calmly walk back in to the room where your dog is and you should see a degree of surprise on his face.

ANGER

Anger does not necessarily mean aggression but, like aggression, it is often the result of frustration. Aggression is the intention to do harm. Anger is an expression of emotion and not an expression of aggression. A young dog that is being teased may well become frustrated and angry with its antagonist, make a vocalisation and then simply walk away. Sometimes anger can build up to the point where the dog has a temper tantrum or even begins to exhibit aggression. Some breeds are good at expressing anger. Rottweilers will tell you when they are feeling angry because something may have upset them. The good thing about Rottweilers is that they are so expressive that they communicate their emotions really well compared to, say, the Japanese Akita.

FEAR

I only have to mention two words – fireworks and thunderstorms – and every dog owner can visualise a dog expressing fear. When fear grips a dog there are many physiological symptoms that accompany the emotion. For

Disgust

more information on fear, please refer to Chapter 39, page 232.

DISGUST

Disgust is an emotional expression when something offends one or more of our senses. Bill Ryan, the husband of leading American dog behaviourist and trainer Terry Ryan, tells of the night he woke in the early hours to a really offensive smell. Suspecting the culprit was their Cocker Spaniel who needed to go out, he stepped out of bed and his bare foot squelched into a pile of very soft dog mess. To avoid treading this mess across the carpet, he decided to hop on one leg to the shower. One hop, two hops and then a third hop into another soft and still warm pile. Whenever Bill recounts this story, not only does the smile on his face fail to disguise the expression of disgust but his emotions are almost always reflected in the facial expressions of his audience! We can be disgusted by things we hear, feel, see, taste or smell and so can dogs.

These then are five of the fundamental expressions of emotion. Are there more? How about sorrow – do dogs understand this concept? Do they get sad when they are parted from a loved one? Are they able to comprehend their owner's sadness? Many owners believe that they are.

How about the emotion of guilt? Do dogs understand and express that emotion? How about the dog that has ripped up a book from the bookshelf when its owner is out of the house? When the owner returns and enters the room, even though the dog chewed up the book several hours ago, the owner still believes that because of the dog's expression of emotion, he looks guilty. Or is it just that the dog is reacting to the owner's expression of anger?

Sorrow

Is it possible that a dog feels the emotion of embarrassment when caught in the act of eating a biscuit it has stolen from the coffee table? How about love? Is a dog capable of giving only companionship to its human partner, or is it also able to love its owner and receive love in return? And jealousy? Do dogs really get jealous when the owner tries to pet another dog, or is the dog merely protecting its own interests and the resources that the owner represents?

It is when discussing the emotions of a dog that the modern, science-based training and behaviour-modification specialists really do come unstuck. They simply fail to recognise that your pet dog can not only understand your emotions but also express many of its own.

Learning experiments where animals are trained under laboratory conditions, or marine mammals kept and trained in the most sensory-deprived environments, where both animal and trainer are devoid of emotions, teach us precious little other than how not to do it. A pet dog lives its life as part of the family. The owners cannot walk away at the end of a training session, leaving the animal in an emotionally and environmentally deprived state. Above all, both dog and owner will communicate with one another on a much higher emotional level.

So to understand the basic philosophy of the code, throw away any preconceived ideas you may have on how to train a dog using words of command, mechanical clickers, whistles and hand signals, and understand the universal language of emotions. It is your emotions, when coupled with the giving or withholding of rewards, that will enable you to communicate with your dog better than most academically trained behaviourists ever could. Welcome to the real world of dogs.

2

Dogs & Human Language

In writing about a philosophy, I need to use words to express ideas and emotions. Sometimes these words may be misinterpreted, giving a totally different meaning, so sometimes I have to use more than one word to describe an idea or action. The problem is that if you have already read a few books on dog-training or behaviour, you may think that some of my words are wrong. If you belong to a particular school of thought, you probably use a unique vocabulary to describe behaviour, and the more academically based the school, the greater number of letters your words will contain.

For example, 'fear aggression' may also be called 'nervous aggression' but many service-dog organisations refer to it as 'apprehensive aggression'. The word that precedes 'aggression' is therefore related to a particular culture, yet I believe all three words – fear, nervous and apprehension – actually describe the same behaviour. When I see a dog behaving aggressively and that aggression is rooted in fear, nervousness or apprehension, I understand the emotion that the dog is feeling, even if the word I use to describe this expression of emotion may be different from that used by others. (Don't worry – I will try to use words that use the minimum number of letters!)

The final part of the philosophy is to understand that 'behaviour therapy' simply means retraining a dog. A behaviourist should have an outstanding ability to train dogs, because being able to retrain is much harder than training correctly in the first place. Being a behaviourist means that you have to be a trainer – it simply does not work any other way!

Imagine, for example, that your dog's mind is like a container full of wax. An impression can be formed on the surface of this wax by dropping a hot pebble on to it. Once the first pebble hits the surface it will form an impression. Once an impression is formed in a dog's mind, it will retain that original impression, sometimes for the duration of its life. Training can create new impressions to replace the old ones but remember that the old ones cannot be removed. Retraining a dog often means creating a brand new set of impressions. Only once these new impressions are formed might it be possible for the dog to shelve the old ones.

3

Dog Behaviour: In the Beginning

The behaviour of your dog starts even before your dog is born. It begins with the genetic code that makes up your dog's breed type, physical stature, coat type and colour, and also some of its inherited behavioural and temperamental characteristics.

The genetic code of the Golden Retriever, for example, includes the distinctive colour of its coat and the dog's instinctive desire to pick up objects and take them to its owner. Thus the correct genetic trait to breed in is a desire to share (that is what retrieving is all about). The Dobermann, however, can be coloured black, tan, red, fawn etc., and should have an instinctive desire not to want to share anything with anyone (other than perhaps the owner). It is a guarding breed and these normally do not want to share.

Breeders can change the inherited characteristics of a breed by selecting for specific traits. Many breeders curiously produce Golden Retrievers that are white. They also breed these white dogs with an instinctive desire to share nothing at all, even with their owners. Maybe they should be called White Non-Retrievers, which would be a much more accurate description!

So the dog that you own will have certain genetic traits or tendencies. These are generally considered immune to any kind of removal or even modification. Let's imagine you own a Dobermann and arrive at a training class. You tell the instructor you do not care for its black short-haired coat and want to know if he can change it to a lighter longer-haired one. You also ask if he can make your dog's nose a little shorter and reduce the dog's height a little. Of course no instructor, behaviourist or even veterinarian would be able to carry out your requests. At best you would be advised that if you did not like the genetic traits your dog was born with, you should look for a different breed of dog.

What a great many people also do not realise is that if you turned up at a training class with your Dobermann and told the instructor you needed help with its behaviour, then the same is true. Suppose you asked for help to stop your ten-month-old dog barking at people that walked past your property. I am afraid the same rules apply for genetically derived behaviour as for coat colour etc. A ten-month-old Dobermann *should* bark when anyone approaches your property. That is exactly what the

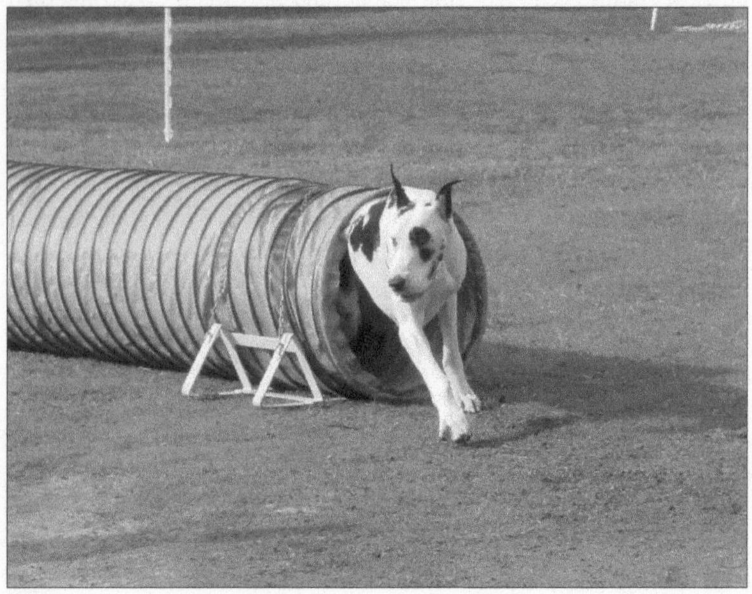

A Great Dane running an agility course

breed was developed to do – guard people and property. So no training instructor or behaviourist can turn your Dobermann into a Labrador Retriever, either in appearance or behaviour.

Herein lies the basic reason that many people who get a puppy eventually get rid of it. This happens typically at around the age of ten to eighteen months, simply because they purchased the wrong breed for their circumstances. Just go and have a look around the many dog shelters and you will get an idea of the scale of the problem. You can *train* your breed of dog to do anything that any other breed can do (apart from those behaviours that have physical limitations for your breed) but it will never actually be that breed.

Can you train a Great Dane to run an agility course designed for Border Collies? Definitely. Can you then train a Husky to walk properly on the lead without pulling? Yes, you can. Can you train an Afghan Hound to return when off-lead? You bet. Can you train a West Highland White Terrier to track? Certainly. And can you train an Airedale Terrier to retrieve? No problem.

These are all functions of training, not of genetics, so you cannot use your dog's breed as an excuse for not being able to train it, I'm afraid. You can certainly control a Dobermann's guarding instincts by careful early training. Will it be as easy to train a West Highland White Terrier to track as it would a Bloodhound? No, as the Bloodhound is better equipped to follow a track because the breed has more olfactory cells in its nose than West Highland White Terriers. But a really well-trained Westie will always beat a really badly trained Bloodhound in a tracking competition!

Genetics, then, give the dog the possibility, the environment gives opportunities for the instinct to develop, and training puts the instinct under the influence of the trainer. Imagine it this way: buying a dog is like buying a book. On the front cover is the book title (in the dog's case the breed). The foreword is the genetic code and is made up of mother, father, grandparents etc. The introduction is the early learning environment, plus the influence of the mother's behaviour, littermates and the breeder.

At around six weeks the contents and chapter headings will also be

A Westie tracking in Alaska

written, but the rest of the book is blank for you to write in. You can therefore shape and mould your dog's behaviour (within reason) to how you want it to be. Remember that the chapter headings are already there, so with our friend the Dobermann, chapter ten (ten months of age) will say it starts to bark when people walk past the house! By buying this dog as a puppy and with careful training you can write in how much it barks and whether you are in control of the barking.

If you get your dog around the age of 16 weeks then I am afraid that most of the book has already been written for you, with little room for you to add more. At around six to seven months the book is virtually complete and if you want to write something then, you had better have a good eraser! (For the word 'eraser', substitute 'dog trainer' or 'behaviourist'.)

The two types of behaviour of interest to us are genetic (instinctive or innate) and learned. Genetically based behaviours are generally considered inflexible to modification. Of more interest to us, once the right breed of puppy has been acquired, is learned behaviour. Learning starts with the development of the five senses – touch, taste, sight, smell and hearing – and the early stages of development follow the same pattern regardless of breed.

There is very little we can do about genetically derived behaviour other than to control it with careful breeding programmes, so the responsibility falls on the shoulders of every breeder. Sadly many breeders produce dogs that, while they may look beautiful, are seen as ugly by the community because of the way that they behave. Some breeders place more importance on looks than they do on behaviour.

One of the greatest authorities on the Labrador was JH Walsh who wrote in his book *Retrievers* in 1887: 'Mr Bond Moore who is considered to be the highest authority on the breed (in Great Britain) would disqualify a dog for a white toe or a white spot of the smallest kind on the breast or forehead. This is very absurd for a dog intended for use. Fancy dogs may be measured by any rule however artificial, but a shooting dog should only be judged by points which are relevant to his work.'

So clearly our first job is to find a breeder who is breeding for temperament, with looks being of secondary importance. Genetically driven behaviour can be controlled by careful early training, so now we are more interested in learned behaviour, which is shaped and modified by the environment from birth to ultimate death.

The most vital time in a puppy's life is between the age of three and seven weeks. During this period of development problems are sometimes caused at the breeders that will have a life-long effect on the behaviour of that puppy, almost regardless of how it is subsequently raised. Getting the right material to work with is part of the battle that pet owners face when selecting their dog.

When a puppy is born, it will use all its senses to explore the world in which it lives. The more opportunity it has to use its senses, the better it will develop and the better able it will be to make good decisions about new or novel situations. So if we start by looking at some typical patterns of early behaviour, and the effect they are likely to have, it will give us an insight into some behavioural problems that can emerge later.

4

Early Behavioural Development

First, let's take a look at behaviour in a litter and at the whole early learning environment. It can never be overstated just how much of a role model a mother is to her puppies. Much of what they learn in the crucial early weeks of life will be down to what she is able to teach them about the world in which they live. These are the factors involved in raising a well-balanced litter of puppies:

LITTER SIZE

The greater the number of puppies in a litter, the harder the mother will find it to teach and control her offspring. This presumes that the father of the litter will not be present to help raise and educate them. It is rare that a father gets to even meet his offspring these days!

If we were only concerned with behaviour then the optimum number of puppies in a litter would be around five. For each additional puppy, the mother's control is diluted. When the litter is double the optimum number – around ten or more – then a few things begin to happen. First of all, it would be nearly impossible for a bitch to correctly raise more than ten puppies without external assistance, which is usually forthcoming in the shape of a breeder who will supplement the milk supply with artificial feeding.

It has been suggested that the act of competing over food at a very early age, thereby placing the puppies under very mild amounts of stress, is good for their development. There is also a related theory, which seems to be borne out in practice, which suggests that bottle feeding (where the milk supply does not really have to be worked for) allows puppies to get their meal too easily. Such puppies are said to grow into young dogs that are unable to handle frustration well and often throw a temper tantrum when they cannot get what they want. It bears repeating here that frustration is one of the major components of aggression.

DISCIPLINE

There is also the question of discipline. At around three weeks the mother will begin the weaning process to convert her puppies from milk to more solid food. This seems to coincide with the eruption of sharp teeth in the puppies' mouths. Mum will use several strategies when puppies now come and try to feed at inconvenient times. The first is for her to freeze and curl her lip with her head slightly turned towards the offending puppy. The second is a low growl, again in the freeze position. The third is for her to air-snap at them. The final solution is an air-snap followed by a head butt, which send the puppy reeling backwards across the floor.

This form of discipline is vital, as it teaches the puppies that they cannot always have what they want, when they want it. In human parenting terms it is the use of the word 'no'. For many children 'no' seems to be interpreted as 'try harder' – the same goes for puppies! And of course breeders, when producing a bottle to feed the puppies, would never even think of doing what nature has equipped the puppies' mother to do.

FEEDING

For food treats to work more effectively in training, it would be wise to select a puppy from a litter that has been fed a very varied diet. Modern feeding methods mean that fewer puppies experience many tastes and textures of food early enough in life, which may be the principal reason that many young dogs go on to suffer from food intolerances. Again it comes down to providing the puppies with the right experiences necessary

Puppies eating from separate bowls.

for them to be able to cope in later life. Taste and smell are linked, so it should make perfect sense to feed a puppy a very varied diet.

It is also important to understand the concept of food aggression, sometimes known as food bowl guarding. If there are six puppies in a litter and the breeder presents them with food in a single bowl, this can easily set up competition over this valuable resource. The law of nature says that there will always be one or two puppies that want to eat more than their share. This means one or two puppies will get less than their share and this results in more competition over the food at the next meal. Feed six puppies out of nine food bowls and food aggression is usually reduced to zero. It's common sense when you think about it.

If a litter feeds out of just one bowl, the puppies learn to gulp the food down as quickly as they can to get their fair share. They will push and shove to get at the available supply, and the stronger puppies will push the weaker ones out of the way. Weaker puppies now have to gulp down what they can. When one of these puppies goes into its new home it will not forget the lessons learned in the litter. The first thing that the new owner will notice is that when they approach their puppy when it is eating, it suddenly starts to eat faster. This is the first stage of food guarding.

Now let's take a look at a litter where there are one-third more bowls than there are puppies. Each bowl contains the correct amount of food for each puppy and the breeder is there to supervise. The puppies tend to distribute themselves randomly around the bowls. If one puppy approaches another that is eating out of another bowl there are a number of possible outcomes. Number one is that the feeding puppy is displaced by the approaching puppy but gets rewarded for leaving the food bowl by finding another food bowl of equal or greater quantity. Outcome number two is that the approaching puppy, on seeing that this bowl is occupied, gets rewarded for walking away and finding an unoccupied bowl of equal or greater quantity. Outcome number three is that the two puppies will happily share the food bowl in the knowledge that there are more available. In other words, they learn not to compete over the available food supply. When each puppy has eaten their fill, the breeder removes the puppies one at a time from the feeding area.

GROOMING

The mother's ability to restrain and groom her puppies will also have a direct effect on the frustration that they may feel later in life when they are restrained, touched, handled and groomed by their human owners.

Grooming serves two functions: helping to keep the dog clean and to cement individual bonds between group members. A mother will use her tongue on her puppies both to stimulate the elimination of urine and faeces, and to keep their coats clean. A second type of grooming seems to be more geared towards showing affection than personal hygiene. One advantage of puppies in a large litter is that they will have experienced more in the way of close body contact and should therefore be slightly more tolerant of this than a puppy born in a very small litter.

Large litters, however, are more likely to be deprived of the restraint element of the grooming process. Imagine a bitch trying to clean a puppy that simply does not want to be kept still. Mum will usually pin the puppy to the ground with her front paw and insist that it is cleaned properly. When a young human mother does the same with a child that objects, the child is usually held firmly with the mother's free hand. If you watch owners trying to restrain some young dogs by the collar and groom them with a brush, it is similar to watching a parent trying to brush the hair of a really badly behaved child. Neither child nor puppy has learned to cope with the frustrations of being restrained and groomed, and the result is often a display of aggression. When you buy a puppy, ask the breeder to show you it being groomed before you part with your hard-earned money!

This alone should make everyone realise there is a greater statistical probability of a short-coated puppy being more difficult to restrain and handle than a long-coated breed. Why? Because breeders of puppies with long coats are more likely to brush long-coated puppies when it is approaching the time that they are sold. During one course at a shelter where pupils came to train some of the resident dogs and puppies for five days, three 14-week-old, short-coated puppies had drawn blood by the end of the second day when being restrained, while the same number of long-coated puppies were all really pleasant to restrain and handle. The short-coated puppies can only be described as throwing a temper tantrum because they could not wriggle free from the grooming session!

PLAY

For any litter of puppies of any breed at around the age of five weeks, their day consists of feeding sleeping and playing. But why do puppies play so much?

1. Play is a way of measuring or comparing yourself against others around you.
2. Play is a way of building or cementing a bond between two individuals.
3. Play is a way to release stress and is sometimes an aid to relaxation.
4. Play is a way of stimulating body and mind.
5. Play gives opportunities to practise strategies that may be useful for survival.
6. Play can remove inhibitions.

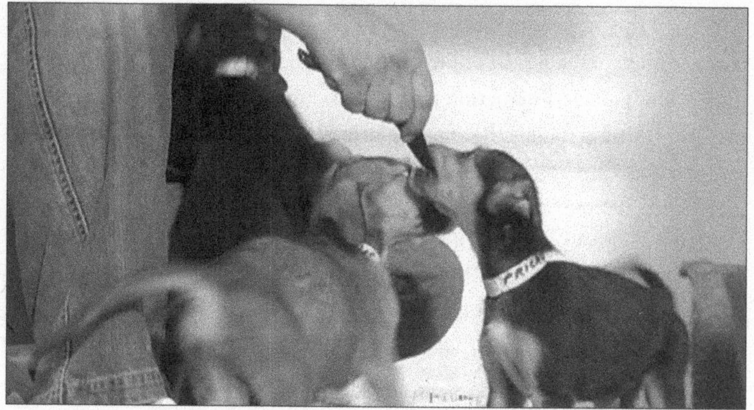

Puppies playing with a person.

There are two basic types of play. One is where the dog plays an individual game with a novel object as a way to explore and make sense of its world and sometimes to alleviate boredom, stimulate body and mind, and to relax. The second type of play is where the dog plays and interacts with another playmate to build or cement a bond. For humans this might be a game of tennis or golf where there is no actual physical contact – they simply play an interactive game with a set of toys. There are also physical games against an opponent such as wrestling, boxing or running, where no tools or toys are used.

Because we don't want our dog to play physical games using us as a toy, it makes sense that the best environment for a young puppy to be raised in is one where there are plenty of novel toys readily available from the age of three weeks. This way, most young dogs will have already been conditioned to play with one another using a toy, rather than using one another as a toy. Ever wondered why a puppy prefers to play with your fingers rather than the toy in your hand? Surprisingly, puppies raised in a litter with daily access to lots of novel toys that change daily almost never develop into finger-nipping monsters in their new homes. This alleviates the necessity to take drastic measures to stop it biting your hands and arms every time your puppy wants to play and interact with you.

Also, if the puppies in a litter are already playing games with toys, then it is easy to take a toy from the litter when you buy your puppy. That way you have a ready-made interaction available to build more play sessions. Think of it like learning to play the game of tennis. When you have learned to play, you can go to any tennis club in the world and have something in common with every member of that club, even in very different cultures, because you all play the same game with the same basic set of tools (toys).

But what about bite inhibition? Is it not true that puppies have to play and bite one another to learn how to inhibit their bite? Well, I know of no court in the world where they will accept bite inhibition as a defence when a dog bites someone – 'It was an inhibited bite that only caused minor lacerations, your Honour, as he could have ripped the person's arm off if he had wanted to!' Dogs should be raised not to bite. Full stop (or period if you are reading this in America).

DISCRIMINATION/HOUSETRAINING

A puppy kept on just one floor surface from the age of three weeks will be harder to house-train than a puppy that has access to two separate surfaces. If there is only one surface available, discrimination cannot take place. If a litter of puppies has a food bowl, water bowl, toys and beds on one surface, and another contrasting surface is available, then the mother can do a good job of housetraining. She will teach her puppies to discriminate between the surface they live, sleep, play, eat and drink on and an alternative surface they can go to the toilet on. Ideally the separate surface should be as close as possible to the ultimate toileting surface, such as grass.

Remember that if there are two surfaces available but the food bowl, water bowl and toys are on one surface and the bedding is on the other, they will have problems in discrimination! I remember going to a large animal charity in England and being shown their new puppy block. There was a large play area at one end where all the puppies spent most days together playing, but newspaper covered the entire floor! Teaching a puppy to discriminate between two surfaces by using its senses is only possible if those surfaces are available.

5

Mother: The First Role Model

How does the temperament and behaviour of the mother of the litter impact on the future behaviour of her puppies? Because she is their first role model, much of the puppies' behaviour will follow how she behaves in the environment in which they all live. If I arrived at a breeder's home, rang the door bell and heard the mother explode into a frenzy of barking, I shouldn't really be surprised if one of her offspring, after relocating to my house, eventually displayed the same behaviour as her mother did when visitors arrived.

SEPARATION: THE FIRST STAGE TO INDEPENDENCE

At just a few hours old, it takes a lot of persuading to get the mother to leave her newborn litter even for a few minutes. At three weeks, which coincides with the eruption of very sharp puppy teeth, she will start to actively reject her puppies when she wants some time to herself by walking away from them, growling or even snapping when they bother her. By four weeks she will start to physically remove herself from the puppies while still remaining within sight, often by climbing on to something out of their reach. By the age of five weeks she will start to visually remove herself from them as part of her enforced separation programme. At six weeks she should be writing out the advertisements for the puppies herself!

As the mother goes through her slow separation programme, the puppies become mildly stressed but learn to cope, and their emerging interest in play gives them opportunities to build relationships with one another.

Puppies from a breeder where the mum has not been able to physically remove herself from their attentions at will are likely to become over-bonded to her. When the new owner then takes one of them home, it will quickly bond to this person and scream in distress every time he or she attempts to leave it by itself. This condition is often known as separation anxiety – becoming distressed when it can't make physical or visual contact with its attachment figure.

However, if the mother is physically and visually removed from her puppies by the breeder but only isolated in close proximity, another behaviour problem can easily occur. When the mum hears her puppies cry out for attention she becomes disturbed because she cannot get back to them and begins to respond with vocalisations of her own. This can easily start attention-seeking barking when any of her puppies go to their new homes and are left by themselves. So it is important to choose breeders who allow nature to dictate how a mother teaches her puppies to become more independent in order for social skills to be learned.

COMMUNICATION

All groups of social animals have a way to communicate with others within the group. For example, they all have an alarm call (or calls) to communicate the presence of a predator. The members of the group have to understand instinctively that the alarm call means danger, as it would be detrimental to survival if they had to learn its meaning by trial and error! Dogs are no exception to this and have a distinct alarm call that warns of the presence of a predator. This usually takes the form of an explosive bark that suddenly raises an octave or two.

Let's look at a litter of puppies at the age of six weeks. When the breeder walks in to where they are, the mother approaches the breeder and wags her tail enthusiastically. The puppies observe this behaviour from their role model and follow suit. Mum is saying to trust and enjoy the company of this human being who shares the property and its resources with them: this is a good human being.

Now a visitor arrives who does not live in the house and is a complete stranger. Mum responds to the intrusion of a visitor by doing her explosive bark to warn the litter of the presence of a possible predator. Because of her behaviour she is now removed by the breeder and put into isolation. Imagine that you are one of those puppies. Your mum has warned you that the human being who has just arrived is very different from the one you share your environment and resources with. This one is different by nature of their smell, the sounds they make, their appearance and possibly even the way they touch you (they pick you up and caress you). Now this predator leaves with one of your brothers or sisters! When your mum comes back you will see that she is disturbed – one of her offspring has been taken.

After being in its new home for a few days the first puppy to leave the litter will have a distrust of anyone that does not live there. Remember the lesson taught by Mum: only trust the people that live in the house that you share your resources with. However, with careful socialisation this puppy has a chance of recovering from its fear of strangers. But how about puppy number two that leaves – it will have witnessed this disturbed behaviour from its mother twice when visitors arrive, and the third to go will have seen it three times and so on. Each puppy that remains receives more information from its mum about the presence of strangers. By the time we get to puppy number five and up, the behaviour of not trusting anyone who does not live in the environment has been indelibly etched on the puppy's mind. There is no known cure for this form of fear-imprinting. It will exist for the entire duration of the puppy's life. Only trust the humans that you live with – everyone else is a potential predator.

6

Questions for the Breeder

Even before you get a puppy it will already have learned a great deal about life from the environment it lived in, from its mother, from its littermates, from the breeder and hopefully the breeder's family. Many behaviour problems can be traced back to the breeder who produced the litter because what they sold was fundamentally flawed. Even when buying a puppy raised by a really expert mother and breeder in a perfect environment, it is still possible for the new owner to get things wrong, but for many behaviour problems it is unlikely. Buy a puppy that already has fundamental flaws in its behaviour and you will almost certainly have problems with it.

If you are going to hand over some of your hard-earned money to a breeder, you may as well get some good material with which to work. Would you go out and buy a car that had defective transmission and brakes that did not work? Or had a fault in the engine that required you to go through a complex procedure before it would start? So why take on a puppy that then requires a behaviour-modification programme to get it to behave acceptably? For the same amount of money it is possible to get something that you and your family will enjoy without the need for expensive maintenance.

Before you even think about going to a breeder, do as much research as you can on your chosen breed and sit down with your family to discuss what you want your new family member to provide you with. Remember that if the presence of a family dog does not enrich your life in some way, it is better not to get one in the first place.

Maybe you want your dog to be a great agility champion, in which case you will probably be buying a Border Collie. Or how about the first Bassett Hound to get an agility title? Maybe your new dog is destined to become a therapy dog, or maybe a great companion and playmate for your children. Perhaps you like to go out walking and a good walk is wasted without a dog with you. Perhaps the presence of a dog in your house will give you a greater sense of security or the chance to meet more people socially. In other words, there has to be a reason for wanting to own a dog. I have never met anyone who has purchased a puppy with the express intention of 'donating' it to an animal shelter between the age of ten to 18 months! Yet every year tens of thousands of dog owners do just that, simply because their choice of breed was poor or the puppy came with problems.

Once you've decided on the breed, phone a breeder and ask a few questions before deciding to go and view a litter. Here are some of the things to look out for:

- The mum. What is her temperament like? How friendly is she towards visitors? Why did the breeder want a litter of puppies from her? Has she had litters before and if so, how many? Ask for contacts so you can make enquiries about her offspring. How about the dad? The same questions apply.
- The breed. What is its country of origin? What were they originally bred for? What are the breed's typical behaviour traits? (All breeds must have some particular trait that resulted in the breed being developed.) Are there people who still use the breed for their original purpose? What, if any, hereditary problems does the breed have? (Do you want to pay lots of money for a breed that has heart problems, eye problems, hip dysplasia, will cost you ten times the purchase price in veterinary care and will die before it reaches the age of six?) The answers you get should match the research that you

have carried out. If the breeder does not appear to know the answers then I would certainly not advise you to invest in one of their puppies. There is no point in even viewing a litter if you have concerns about the breeder's intentions in bringing these puppies into the world. Remember that for the same amount of money you can get a good puppy!

- Now go and have a look at the litter. Take your whole family along and insist that the mother is present with her puppies when you arrive. It is normal for a dog to bark when a visitor arrives at the front door, but is it acceptable, and how much can the breeder control the barking? When you enter the house, does the mother have to be restrained? If so, you have to ask yourself why. Mum should be proud to show you her litter. If she appears to be suspicious or even aggressive, or has to be removed, then leave and look elsewhere for the puppy of your dreams.
- Now look at the floor surface and the toys they play with. Pick up a toy and you should have the whole litter surrounding you wanting to play.
- Ask the breeder to groom one of the puppies for at least ten minutes. Does the puppy wriggle around and try to escape? Does it start screaming? Does it try to bite? By six weeks of age the puppies should be used to being touched, restrained and groomed by the breeder. If the breeder can't do this, I would be unwilling to buy one of their puppies.
- Now ask the breeder to feed the puppies. If you see any signs of food aggression then reject the whole litter. You can also ask the breeder to stroke each puppy as it is eating. Again, if you see any signs of food aggression then move on.
- Remember that any display of aggression in a puppy under the age of nine weeks should result in the puppy being left at the breeders, or returned to the breeders if it has already been purchased. Remember, if you purchased a new car with a fault on it, you would take it back, right?

If all is well, the paperwork is checked and found to be right, decide if you want a dog or a bitch and then shut your eyes and make a choice, because if the breeder has got it right then any puppy has the potential to be a great dog.

Now we are driving home with the new family member in the back of the car. We may dream of it being a great family companion. It may be a particular breed and we may want it to take out hunting or to engage in some dog sport. It is a bonus if it grows into a really good-looking example. We want it to be the sort of dog that people in the community will admire because of its good behaviour. No matter how beautiful your dog looks, your friends and neighbours will think it ugly if it behaves really badly. Conversely, any dog that is visually unattractive will be deemed one of the most beautiful dogs they have ever seen if it behaves impeccably.

7

New Family Member or Temporary Lodger?

What is going through the puppy's mind on the exciting drive to start a new life in a new home? The puppy will have hopes and dreams. Does any puppy dream of ending up at a shelter, unwanted by the owners that had promised it a good life? Does any dog really dream of eating the same manufactured dog food day in, day out? Does any dog hope to be kept on a leash and never allowed to run free to exercise? Does any dog dream of being put into a cage so small that it can't even turn around without making contact with the sides? Does any dog ever dream of living in someone's back garden or yard when it craves social attention and the rest of the family living inside? Does any dog ever dream of never being allowed to express any part of its natural behaviour?

Now you get the idea of where lots of behaviour problems come from: a failure to understand the dog that we ask to live with us. Almost all the dogs I see in shelters end up there because of this failure and the owners' inability to communicate with their dog.

How will your puppy learn to communicate with you? In children the basics of language have to be present by the time the child is around five. In dogs it seems that the basics of language have to be present by the age of 16 weeks.

Only a small proportion of people reading this book will have the ability to speak more than one language but, to be able to get through life easily, all dogs need to understand two different languages. The first one is canine language and this will be learned from their mother and practised on their littermates. This language is very useful later when a dog meets another dog and can communicate effectively with it. However, every dog also has to have human language as its first language because it has to be able to communicate not only with its owners but also with other people in the community. Too much exposure to canine language for too long in early life means a young dog's ability to learn and understand human language decreases dramatically. Similarly, when a single puppy has been raised from birth by a human mother, it dramatically decreases a young dog's ability to be able to communicate with other dogs.

In an ideal world your young dog needs to have a 'tourist' understanding of canine language but should be fluent in understanding human language. So when you exercise your dog in the park and it meets another dog, it should be able to politely hold the following conversation: 'Hello there, I don't believe that we have met before, but my name is Rover and I live just a short distance down the road. What is your name and where do you live?' 'Oh, you must excuse me – my owner has just called me so I must go, but it was nice meeting you.'

What you don't want is the following conversation: 'Hi there, what a great day to meet you in the park. Are you up for a game of chase? Actually, there are another group of dogs just over there – why don't we run up and surprise them? I know all their names and most of them just love to play chasing and wrestling games.' 'There are a couple of really cute-looking girls there as well – pity you've had the snip.' 'What was that? Someone shouting Rover? Anyone here called Rover? No? I can't understand what these people keep shouting. Anyway it's of no concern to us – let's play!'

Teaching a puppy our language is incredibly important in terms of social development and education. But there are two types of human language. There is spoken language, which is specific to the country and region that you come from. When I am asked to speak in non-English speaking countries I am given an interpreter to translate my spoken English into words my audience will understand. Sometimes the meaning of my words is lost in translation and some of my best jokes are not funny at all!

When lecturing in Cuba for the military, I was given a government interpreter. We met up the day before the five-day training and behaviour workshop and, being non-doggy, my interpreter wrote down some of the words that I intended to use. Sometimes words like 'fixed reinforcement aggression', unless you know it means temper tantrum, make translation difficult. But my interpreter was having a problem understanding how it would work for the practical training sessions. Would I give the dog a command in English and was he to repeat it to the dog in Spanish? How was it going to work? I assured him there would be no language barrier and every one of their dogs would immediately understand me with no translation required! He was now even more confused. That was because most of the real communication we have with our dogs uses a different type of language: emotional language. So when I use my hands, facial expressions, tone of voice and body posture, every dog that has been raised to understand human emotional language will immediately understand everything that I am trying to communicate.

Understanding that your dog can recognise emotionally expressive tones in your voice rather than the words themselves will get you closer to understanding the code. Try the following test with your own dog to see just how much of your language your dog understands.

Leave your dog in the house by itself for about an hour. When you return to your dog, think about something that makes you really happy. You cannot fake it! Don't just go to where the dog is and smile; you must think happy thoughts. Don't say a word when you go in but just look down at your dog. It should be standing there wagging its tail and almost smiling back at you.

Now repeat the experiment but when you return after your short absence think of something that absolutely disgusts you. Remember you are showing disgust, not anger, and you must not fake it! Think the thought and glance down at your dog. It should glance up at you and then turn away, almost mirroring the disgust in your emotional expression.

Now try entering while you are thinking of something really sad that makes tears well up in your eyes. Glance down at your dog and he should look at you and offer emotional support, maybe by offering a paw, licking your hand or generally trying to reach out and touch you. I have had people in tears when they realised just how much of their emotions their dog is able to pick up on. I have also had people realise that their dog has absolutely no understanding of their language at all!

The good thing about a young dog learning human emotional language is that they are then able to communicate with everyone in the world. If you only teach your dog verbal language, usually in the form of commands, then your dog may be able to understand you, but it would never have the ability to understand anyone from another region. For example, at home I have some working trials champions. The dogs are trained to a very high level of competition and all understand a list of commands (more on this later). So if I wrote down the list of commands for a particular competition, could you then enter the competition and win with my dog? Impossible. Why? Because my dogs are trained on words with specific tones of voice and unless you could reproduce them exactly (and you couldn't) then my dog would only have a very vague idea of what you wanted it to do. If you trained with me for a few months and worked with my dog it would hopefully learn your words have a completely different accent, but it might not then be able to translate them into the desired actions.

You have to accept that verbal language is very restrictive when applied to training a dog but emotional language is universal. It is mainly emotional language that you are going to use to train and socialise your new puppy.

Having acquired your new puppy, how do you go about teaching it all the things necessary to end up with a well-socialised and easily controlled adult dog? One thing is for sure: without any formal education, your pride and joy will end up being out of control and a liability to you and your family. Puppies have no concept of how to interpret and obey instructions as they mature and, like children, must have some formal education if they are to realise their full potential. So to understand how we can train a puppy, let's examine how it learns.

Your puppy came to you with some behaviour already programmed at birth, but you are responsible for all learned behaviour that it is acquired as the result of personal experience. We can manipulate this learning process so we end up with a well-trained dog that has learned to display only appropriate behaviour within its environment. For training to begin you will need two basic ingredients: one is a reason for your dog to adopt a particular behaviour, and the other is your ability to influence how your dog reacts to certain situations.

This is where we come to Thorndyke's Law of Effect, which basically says that behaviour changes because of its consequences. If a behaviour has a pleasant consequence then that behaviour will be likely to be repeated. If a behaviour has an unpleasant consequence, it is less likely to be repeated. Simple, isn't it? Well, it would be apart from one significant point: the dog must *associate* its actions with something pleasant to want to repeat the behaviour, or with something unpleasant to avoid the behaviour on the next occasion. Thus punishing a dog more than two seconds after the event will be doomed to failure as the punishment cannot be linked to the crime in the dog's mind. Similarly, rewarding the dog more than two seconds after a desirable behaviour will not increase the likelihood of the behaviour being repeated. For a dog to make an association between two events they have to be linked by less than two seconds and this is called the *association time.* Promising a reward in the future or threatening punishment is therefore unlikely to result in the desired behaviour!

Rewards have to be given immediately to be effective, and the type of reward given will have a bearing on how strong the behaviour becomes. A nice smile, a pat on the head and the words 'good boy' will be sufficient for most simple behaviours, such as sitting on command. But calling a dog away from other dogs when it is playing will need something much more rewarding, such as a game with a favourite toy or a tasty food treat, in addition to the pat on the head, a nice smile and the words 'good boy'.

Most owners are totally unaware of the multitude of rewards available to them for use in training. If you have raised your puppy to enjoy playing with toys, going for walks and outings to different areas, eating a varied diet and being touched stroked and caressed, then by the time your puppy has reached the age of 16 weeks you should have acquired a list of rewards you can use in training your puppy and be able to answer the following questions:

1. Name five things, in order of importance, that your puppy would choose to play with if he or she were given a free choice in the matter.
2. Name five foods in order of preference that your puppy would like to eat if given a free choice.
3. Which of these forms of physical attention does your puppy like most? Place them in order of his preference: stroking, cuddling, patting, tummy tickling, scratching.
4. Name five places your puppy would choose to go if a free choice was given and what would he choose to do when he arrived there?
5. Which words or phrases start your puppy's tail wagging happily and which words or phrases cause a tail lowered, ears back, looking sorry for itself expression?

If your puppy's favourite thing to play with is another dog, if he has no real desire to be stroked etc., and would choose to go somewhere by himself and do something independently of you when he got there, you do not really have much chance of influencing his behaviour. You will have to resort to using food for the time being until you have built up a better relationship with your pet.

If your puppy's favourite toy is the one that you supplied for him to play with, if he likes to be stroked and touched and would choose to go somewhere with you and wanted to be around you when he got there, then you will have a major influence on how his behaviour develops.

8

Early Training: The Basics

There are basically three ways that you can control and influence your dog and the instincts that it came programmed with. One way is by training it to obey a few simple commands such as 'come', 'stay' and 'no'. The second is by restraining it physically – keep it on a lead for the rest of its life and you will never have to teach your dog to come when called. The third way is to build up an emotional working relationship with your dog.

In practice, almost everyone involved with dogs makes use of all three ways to control their dog to a greater or lesser extent. But many, including myself, believe the most important way to educate and control your dog is by building an emotional relationship with it.

This can usually be achieved within six days but with some breeds – hounds, for example – it can take up to ten days. During this period you should spend as much time as possible each day simply talking to your dog. When you talk you will express emotions. You are going to be your puppy's principle caregiver – the one who feeds it, plays with it, reassures it, comforts it, strokes and interacts with it. Make a list of what your puppy enjoys as you learn about it, and always make a point of smiling, stroking and speaking to your puppy in a really happy voice just before you give it what it wants.

What about teaching it other emotions? If it does something you do not want (providing you can do so safely), simply stand up, give an expression of disgust such as 'I can't believe that you just did that,' storm out of the room – and I mean storm – and slam the door behind you, leaving your puppy on its own for at least five minutes before returning in a matter-of-fact way. This is the best procedure to adopt in situations such as your puppy barking for your attention or jumping up in an inappropriate greeting, but it does not work well for behaviours that are self-rewarding, such as chewing.

You can also teach emotional language by holding a food treat in front of your puppy so that it can see your face in the background. Always start this off using a very low-interest food treat. Smile and talk to your puppy and let it eat the treat. Repeat this with a second, third and fourth food treat. For the fifth treat you should dramatically change your facial expression to disgust as you turn your face away from your puppy, this time clamping your finger and thumb on the treat so that your puppy cannot get it. You see now why you had to use a very low-value food treat! Your eyes should not be staring at your puppy as this may be considered threatening. The idea is to show disgust. When your puppy turns its head away, soften your expression back to a smile, turn to look at your puppy, quickly tell him 'good dog' and give him the treat. Do this by putting it right to his nose; don't make him come towards you to get it.

After a few repetitions he should get the message – smile equals acceptable behaviour, good things happen and everyone is happy. Disgust and turning away means nothing good is going to happen. It follows naturally from this simple lesson that your young puppy should learn to try and keep you smiling and avoid disgusting you because of the consequences of both emotions. If you wish you can even pair your expression of disgust with a word of command such as 'no', 'leave' or 'off'. Do it every time you play the food game and your puppy should master the lesson quickly. If you wanted to, you could teach your puppy the concept of food refusal – teaching him not to take food from strangers or pick it up off the floor. Just teach him the commands of 'take it' and 'leave it' using your emotional expressions.

When you have mastered this using food, you can apply the same lessons to get your puppy to play with you using a toy. Retrieving is one of the best games to play with a puppy and it is incredibly easy to teach. There are two reasons it is so important to teach your puppy to retrieve. First, it is the only game that will teach the concept of sharing. In teaching this idea you will remove at a stroke the possibility of your dog growing up being possessive over 'trophies' it has taken. The second reason for teaching your puppy to retrieve is that it will become a much more useful companion as, later in its training, you will be able to teach it to fetch your car keys or find and retrieve your mobile phone! It is never wise to teach a young dog to play tugging games unless you have a good retrieve, as tugging games, played incorrectly, can make a dog spitefully possessive and aggressive.

TEACHING RETRIEVE

First find something that your puppy is interested in, perhaps a sock, a glove or a toy you have bought for him. Don't be tempted to use a toy that is really exciting as you will have a more difficult time getting him to want to share it with you. Choose one that is interesting but not wildly exciting. Don't use a squeaky toy with a terrier – they have been genetically programmed to take the toy (rat) away and kill it quickly. Unlike with the Golden Retriever, we never wanted terriers to bring us what they had killed so that we could eat it! With some breeds – hounds and terriers usually – you will need to keep switching toys to retain some degree of novelty.

When your puppy is wide awake and looking for mischief, get the toy or article and tease him with it. Throw it a short distance and allow him to run and pick it up. *Do not chase after him.* That will make him think you are competing for the toy and force him into taking evasive action. Wait for a minute and you will see that he takes it to a particular spot and lies down with it to chew. This location is often either underneath or behind something. Now slowly get up and move towards him without looking him in the eye, then sit and extend your arm, stroke him and gently reassure him with your voice. Do not attempt to take the toy from him at this stage.

When he finally releases the toy, quickly tease him with it, return to the spot you originally threw it from and allow him to pick it up and take it to his safe spot. Again, go quietly over and sit with him and stroke him as before. Repeat the whole process for as long as he retains an interest in playing the game. Play in this manner for a couple of sessions then change the game slightly. Now throw the toy but when your pup runs to pick it up, go and sit in the spot where he usually takes it to. Guess what? He will probably bring it right to you and lie alongside or behind you to be stroked.

Repeat this several times, then move your position two yards or so in any direction. It is quite possible that your puppy will still take the toy to the old location and lie down with it, so just ignore him for a few seconds then use your voice to encourage him to come closer to you. Scratching your nails on the carpet will usually do the trick. When he comes to you, remember to praise him well with your voice and hands before you even think about taking the toy away to throw it for him again. After a couple more sessions your puppy should bring the toy to you wherever you are sitting.

All that remains is to use several toys, so he releases the one that he has to chase and retrieves the one you have. Remember that if he picks up anything he should not have, it is easier (and safer) to call him to you with 'good boy, fetch' rather than 'bad boy, leave.'

When your puppy has learnt to retrieve correctly for you then you can introduce him to all your friends that visit by simply throwing the toy for him to retrieve. Do this a couple of times and then give the toy to them to throw while you exit the room for a short while. If you were to stay in the room then the puppy would ignore your friends and want to play with you, but for the few minutes you are absent they become a welcome playmate. This is far better than allowing your puppy to use your friends as though they were toys or, worse, growing up in fear of people who visit.

9

Training Specific Breeds

In this chapter we'll consider why it is so important to have a basic understanding of breeds before attempting to train or socialise your young puppy. As we saw earlier, different breeds have evolved to be used for specific tasks, so in general terms these breed traits will influence our training programme. Some breeds, like the German Shepherd, tend to form very strong personal bonds with their owners, to the point where they sometimes start developing protective behaviour over them at around ten months of age. So let's look at the variations involved in first training and then socialising various types of dogs.

GUN DOGS

Examples: Golden Retriever, Cocker Spaniel, English Pointer, Standard Poodle, etc.

These dogs are used for finding, flushing and often retrieving game, and work in close cooperation with a hunter who kills the game. Many of these breeds therefore have a highly developed predatory instinct around game, and this has to be controlled at the earliest part of the young dog's education. To do this, the puppy is exposed to game under very controlled conditions, usually in an enclosure known as a rabbit pen, where showing a desire to chase is controlled and partially inhibited by the trainer. The young dog learns that while showing an interest in game is permissible, chasing is definitely not. There follows a period of training that then utilises the dog's natural instincts with the addition of some control commands (or whistles) that mutually benefit both hunter and dog.

TRAINING

When teaching or encouraging a gun dog to retrieve, the choice of early toys can be of paramount importance. Choose a soft ball for your gun dog puppy to retrieve and you tend to encourage lots of mouthing behaviour, sometimes resulting in the dog becoming 'hard-mouthed' – that is, it self-rewards by repeatedly crushing the toy in its mouth. So a more acceptable toy for games of retrieve would be a canvas 'dummy' filled with sawdust. This provides a good texture, is solid enough and has enough resistance to reduce the amount of self-reward achieved by chewing.

A canvas gun dog dummy

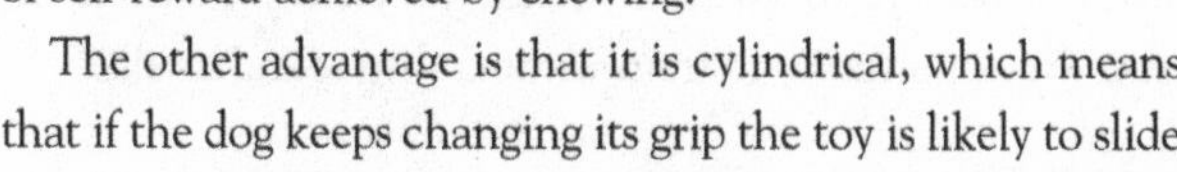

The other advantage is that it is cylindrical, which means that if the dog keeps changing its grip the toy is likely to slide out. This encourages a better holding behaviour than something like a ball, which will rest in the dog's mouth just behind its canine teeth and therefore not require the dog to think about holding it. Also, a soft, light ball is infinitely more difficult to get a dog to drop than a canvas dummy, most of which have a short length of string and a wooden toggle for you to hold on to when asking your dog to drop it.

Even how you throw the toy for your puppy to retrieve will be important in the early stages of training. Always throw the toy up in the air so that it arcs reasonably high before it lands. The type of toy you use should be one that stays put when it lands – another reason for not using a ball, which will continue to move. Hold on to your dog's collar to restrain him and wait for a few seconds before getting him to look at you then giving him permission to run out and fetch the toy.

Why? First of all, gun dogs have a good visual memory – they have been developed over centuries to see shot game fall out of the sky and mark the position they saw it land. Then after waiting patiently they would run to the area where they remembered the bird had fallen and finally locate it using their nose. Second, you would not want your young dog to run to the area where they remember seeing the ball land only to find it is not there because it has rolled some considerable distance away. Even in the early stages of encouraging a gun dog to retrieve, it should always be done when the trainer gives the dog permission to leave their side and run in the direction of the toy.

An early requirement for most gun dog breeds is to put the trainer in better control of the dog's inbred hunting instincts. Early recall training should be carried out where the dog will not be distracted by the smell of animal tracks, otherwise their noses usually overrule their ears when they are called. Where it is not possible to avoid game smells, training can be made easier by taking out a small jar of Vicks vapour rub. Before letting your dog off the lead, unscrew the lid and lightly touch the top of the jar with your finger. Now rub your finger gently on the dog's upper lip hair, just below the nostrils, and it will not be able to smell anything but Vicks for around 20 minutes, giving you the opportunity to train without distracting smells.

SOCIALISATION

With most of the gun dog family this is usually not too difficult. These dogs were bred to work in close cooperation with their owner and sometimes the training was carried out at specialist training kennels before the trained dog was handed back to the owner. The essential thing to remember is to take your gun dog everywhere you possibly can to let it experience most of what life has to offer and you will be fine.

The other very important aid to socialisation is to find an activity that will allow your dog to exercise some of its natural behaviours. Buying a dummy launcher, teaching him to find a toy thrown into long grass, swimming excursions, teaching him to track or use his nose to find specific odours will all help to occupy his mind and build a bond with you. Once you have compiled a list of his interests, socialisation is simply a case of getting other people involved in some of the activities he loves.

PROBLEMS

Other than chasing after game, the next most common problem is destruction when left alone. This is usually due to boredom and lack of stimulation or a proper outlet for their instincts. It usually occurs at around eight to ten months and is often linked to limited or no off-lead exercise. Getting a good reliable recall, so that the dog can be allowed more freedom, or any of the measures listed in the behaviour problem section under destruction when left alone (page 213), should work.

With some of the spaniel breeds, notably the Cocker and Springer, there are many reported cases of the dogs becoming possessive and aggressive when their owners try and take something from them. This is often because when the dogs start to show their instincts to pick things up in the house, the owner starts to chastise them for doing so. The result is that the dog learns to take the object away from the owner and then becomes defensively aggressive when cornered and threatened. So remember that if your young spaniel picks up something he is not supposed to have, use the words 'good dog, fetch it' rather than 'bad dog, drop it!'

HERDING BREEDS

Examples: Border Collie, German Shepherd, English Sheepdog, Welsh Corgi, etc.
Within this group we have dogs that we refer to as 'headers' and 'heelers'. These two distinct groups were used for either driving stock or herding them together. Welsh Corgis, for example, were basically dogs that would drive cattle and sheep from one area to another, whereas Border Collies were developed primarily to gather a flock of sheep together. Some dogs within a breed were developed to do both jobs, such as the German Shepherd, whose basic job was to keep a flock within a given area by patrolling its boundary but also to drive it to new pastures.

It follows that all herding breeds are going to have a highly developed chasing instinct, switched on either by movement or the lack thereof. Watch a good German Shepherd driving a flock of goats along a road and if one or more of the goats stop, the dog gets irritated and rushes at them to drive them on and continue the movement. Contrast this skill with a Border Collie who has gathered the sheep together and has them all held in a stationary position. This dog gets irritated if one tries to move away! So there we have it: headers and heelers, one driving the stock by getting behind and keeping it moving and the other by getting in front of the stock and keeping it stationary.

TRAINING

Training a herding breed involves finding a toy that will satisfy its natural instincts while allowing you to teach some basic control. The choice of toy will be one that bounces and skips when it hits the floor. It is also thrown at a very low trajectory so that the movement excites the dog's natural response to movement.

In the early stages of training you should gently restrain the dog while the toy is thrown, but release it before the toy becomes stationary. With a typical herding dog, unlike a gun dog, the youngster will quickly lose interest if the toy is stationary for more than a second or two. Once your dog has an interest in playing the game, you should increase your control by teaching it to stay while the toy is thrown. Make sure that right from the earliest stage you do not allow your dog to move towards the toy until you have given your permission to do so in the form of a command. This will help you to start to control the chasing instinct and prevent the development of chasing problems later on.

A kong toy

By the age of 12 weeks you should be able to throw a toy with a 'stay' command in the knowledge your puppy will not move until given permission. How do you achieve this? Simply restrain your puppy by placing your hands around its shoulders, and chest, tell him to 'stay' and throw the toy. Wait until the puppy completely relaxes before telling him 'good dog' and only then should you release an allow him to run after the toy. By the age of 16 weeks you need to expand your control so that you can throw a toy, give your dog permission to run after it and then call him back half way before he reaches it (see Coming When Called, Chapter 21, page 127). You will now have total control over his chasing instincts without suppressing this instinct. If you fail to do this, remember that every time you throw a toy and allow him to run straight out and get it, you are strengthening his chasing instinct but that now it is outside your control. So if he then starts to chase joggers, cars, bicycles etc., you only have yourself to blame for not controlling this early in his life.

SOCIALISATION

The good thing about most herding breeds is that it is easy to get them to play games with a toy. This makes exercising their minds and bodies really easy. Just stand at the top of a hill and throw a ball for your dog to run after for 15 minutes twice a day and you should have a tired dog as a result.

Because of the dog's instincts to chase, part of its socialisation programme should be to introduce it to lots of people by handing them its favourite toy and asking them to throw it. This is so much better than turning people into food containers by asking them to approach your young dog and offer food. Using instincts to run and chase a toy requires that there is no physical contact in early relationships with people that the dog is unfamiliar with. Thus the young dog will learn to stand a short distance away from people, waiting for the chance to run after a toy, rather than rushing up to people in the expectation of food.

PROBLEMS

Top of the list is the undeniable fact that these breeds are often too clever for their owners and learn repeatable patterns of behaviour really easily, almost to the point of obsession. While this is a distinct advantage in a sport such as competitive obedience or agility, it is too much for many owners. The root of most behaviour problems with herding breeds is that they find themselves unemployed very early in life. They are dogs without a job and as such will get themselves into all kinds of mischief, including extremes of aggression. Early training is essential if these problems are to be avoided. Obedience classes, agility classes, tracking, flyball, rally and various other dog sports are now considered almost essential components of a young herding dog's education to help prevent later problems.

GUARDING BREEDS

Examples: Great Dane, Dobermann, Boxer, American Bulldog, etc.

By nature these dogs have evolved to be very territorial and possessive, so very specialised upbringing and training are required to avoid many of the problems associated with these breeds. The selection of early interactive toys is of vital importance. The very first game to introduce to any guarding breed is retrieving. This is the only game that will give it the concept of sharing things with you. Teaching tug of war and other possession games before it learns the idea of sharing can unfortunately make your dog spitefully possessive because he comes with this pre-programmed in him via genetics.

TRAINING

Take a look at the section on play (page 111) and find a toy your dog is not crazy about. I would definitely rule out balls, kong toys etc. and go for something that would keep my fingers away from the dog's mouth and favour easy control over the toy. Suitable toys would include anything that is cylindrical and has a length of string or rope attached.

A cylindrical tug toy

You will need two toys that are exactly the same, so that when your dog returns with the first one, you can tease him with the second to get him to release the one that he has in his mouth. If necessary, the early games should be played with a long line attached to the dog's collar. This at least prevents the dog from following its instincts to take the toy away and become possessive over it.

Only when the dog has learned to retrieve would I ever suggest playing tug-of-war games with a guarding breed. It is safe to do so if the dog has already learned the concept of sharing, as long as there are some rules to the game. Rule number one is that the dog should only start the game at the owner's request. Rule number two is that if the dog becomes over-excited then a time-out is called to allow the dog to cool off. Rule number three is that the dog should only ever pull at the toy by thrusting away from your hand as he pulls. On no account encourage him to shake his head during the game as this can very quickly lead to him becoming so over-excited that you lose all control of him and he of himself.

Rule number four is that these early tugging games only ever take place when he has a lead or line attached to his collar, to prevent him from running away with the toy. After playing tugging games with a young dog for around a week, it is time to try the test of possession. During a game of tugging, let go of the toy and stand still. Your dog should now either drop the toy and look at you, or better still, try to put the toy back in your hand. Either result tells you that your dog now only thinks it is a fun game if you are participating in it with him. If he runs away with the toy when you let go of it, this tells you he does not want you to have it and you are now encouraging him to be possessive.

SOCIALISATION

Socialising a guarding breed involves everything that was required for other breeds but with some additions. Make sure you have as many visitors to your house as you possibly can when your puppy is still very young. Provide him with plenty of resources – two water bowls, two beds, lots of pairs of identical toys – and make sure your early guests to the house bring lots of presents for him in the form of food treats and toys.

PROBLEMS

Guarding breeds are traditionally not good with frequent visitors who do not enter the house, such as the postman. For this reason, if you want to avoid trouble as your young puppy grows, it is important that you ask your postman to greet your new puppy at the entrance to your house on frequent occasions. This is best achieved by having a small container of food treats just outside your front door. When your postman arrives, ask him to pick up a food treat before knocking on the front door. Open the door and allow your puppy to greet the visitor and the food treat to be given.

Alternatively, if you do not want to go through an actual greeting, ask your postman to take a treat from the container, push it through the letterbox (or leave it in the mailbox in the USA) and then deliver the letters. This procedure changes the dog's perception of the postman and, although there may still be a small amount of barking out of excitement when he arrives, it should eliminate any possible aggression.

TERRIERS

Examples: Jack Russell Terrier, Wire-haired Fox Terrier, English Bull Terrier, Yorkshire Terrier, etc.

The name terrier is derived from the Latin *terra firma* (solid earth) so many breeds of terrier are known collectively as 'earth dogs'. They were developed principally for the eradication of vermin, sometimes as lone hunters and sometimes with a pack of hounds to bolt an animal that had gone to ground. With this in mind we can see that training will need to be quite different from that required of other breeds.

TRAINING

As with most groups, you start by teaching some simple games so you become a playmate for your terrier. The worst toy to use for these games is a rubber toy that squeaks! Terriers were developed to kill rats, so if we try to play an interactive game with a terrier using a squeaky toy, the chances are that the puppy will get it, take it away from you, and repeatedly crush and shake the offending toy in its jaws. Any attempts to get the puppy to bring the toy to you will result in it taking the toy

A rope toy

further away. When the dog has successfully silenced the device that produces the squeak, it usually loses interest in the toy. Using soft plush toys will have the same effect – evisceration! So the best type of toy to start with is a short length of knotted rope.

All the rules that govern getting your dog to play are contained on page 111, but you will find that your terrier will start to lose interest in a toy very quickly. So during a typical early play session you will need a range of interesting toys such as ropes, raggers and even plastic bottles to ensure you maintain a desire for the games. By first gaining control of toys that do not over-arouse your young dog, you should easily be able to progress to more exciting ones. Once your terrier puppy has mastered the art of playing and retrieving the items you have selected, then you can progress to more exciting ones like plush or squeaky toys.

You will also find that your terrier has a shorter attention span than many other breeds so your early training sessions will have to be kept short – no more than five minutes – until your dog's attention span improves. The attributes we most associate with trainers who are successful with the terrier breeds are a good sense of humour and a great deal of patience.

SOCIALISATION

The downside of many terriers is their behaviour around other dogs. Some terrier breeds have a darker side to their history that has left them with something of a predisposition towards dog-to-dog aggression because of their use in (now illegal) dog fighting. This means that socialising your terrier around other dogs is going to be of paramount importance during the early stages of its upbringing. More than with any other breed group, attending a good socialisation class where puppies are not allowed to engage in exciting interactions with other dogs is vital to the owner being able to maintain control.

Allowing your young terrier to play rough-and-tumble games with other dogs is a recipe for disaster. The British Kennel Club breed standard in 2009 says of the Wire-haired Fox Terrier that it should 'be on tiptoe at the least expectation of provocation'. Roughly translated, this implies that although many terriers would not be the first ones to start a fight, they are usually the ones who want to finish it!

As with most of the breeds that have fighting in their history, they have been developed to be very insensitive to being touched. So when you are playing and interacting with your Staffordshire or English Bull Terrier you will easily raise their level of arousal by touching them in a way that a Yorkshire Terrier might find totally intimidating. For most short-coated terrier breeds, the rougher the game, the more they like it, but you must make sure that you are in total control over the dog's level of arousal and call a time-out if your young dog becomes too excitable. You should also ensure that all of your dog's energy is directed towards an acceptable toy.

Avoid games that encourage your terrier to use you as a toy or to bite at your sleeves or ankles!

PROBLEMS

Most of the people I have met who have been successful raising one terrier usually have few problems if they ever get another. So you could say that the major problems people tend to have are based on the fact that they are first-time terrier owners and did not know what they were getting into. I have already mentioned dog-to-dog aggression, for which the chapters on aggression, both prevention and cures, are appropriate (see section 7, page 301). The other big problem is usually destruction in the house if left alone or digging if left in the garden!

As mentioned earlier, terriers have a shorter attention span than most other breeds, but by giving your young terrier lots of exercise and finding games to play that will give it an outlet for some of its instincts, you should have very few problems. Games would include teaching your terrier to find a hidden food treat or to retrieve a small parcel that you then open to reveal food treats. Mini-agility is a very popular sport that the majority of terriers absolutely adore and there is also terrier racing. In the USA there is also a sport called earth dog trials, where the dogs have to run a labyrinth of tunnels to find and bark at a rat in a cage.

HOUNDS

Examples: Greyhound, Foxhound, Afghan Hound, Borzoi, Whippet, etc.
One of the oldest groups of dogs, hounds were used in the days before firearms on hunting expeditions, where they would chase down the quarry and do the killing. As a result, most hounds have a highly developed predatory instinct.

We can roughly divide hounds into two basic groups: those that hunted by sight and those that hunted by scent. Because some breeds worked in large packs, which had to live together in harmony, you tend to see less in the way of dog-to-dog aggression with them. Some breeds were developed to work just with the hunter, so good social behaviour around other dogs was not an issue.

Breeds such as the Greyhound, which were used to hunt for food as opposed to eradicating vermin (as were Foxhounds) tend not to be food-aggressive. Imagine a hunter taking his Greyhound out to hunt for rabbits for the pot but after chasing, catching and killing the rabbit, the dog ran off and refused to let the hunter have the catch. To avoid this, some of the hound group that was used to catch food had their behaviour genetically modified to allow a degree of trust and sharing between man and dog.

TRAINING

Most hounds are a product of either their noses or eyes, so they are generally reckoned to be difficult to train to come when called. Getting a reliable recall is thus of paramount importance in their early education. If owners do not have a reliable recall by the time their dog is eight months old, they are never going to get one.

The emphasis in early training is to find a reason for your young puppy to come to you. With most of the hound breeds this is easy to accomplish using food as a primary reward. Start from an early age by pairing a signal such as a whistle with the production of food. To do this you should prepare your puppy's daily food and blow a whistle before you feed him. You should also use food treats in the same way several times a day – blow your whistle and then offer your dog the treat. This establishes a connection between the production of food and the sound of a whistle, which makes it easy to progress to training your dog to come when called.

Something to bear in mind is that many of the hound breeds just love to run. This is what they live for, so to deny a hound the experience of running free to let off steam on regular occasions has to be one of the biggest cruelties in the dog world. You will sometimes be told that some hounds cannot be let off because they do not come back when they are called. Common sense tells us that this is just down to training and building a relationship with your dog. If breeds such as the Afghan Hound really do not come back when called then they would not exist today, as they would have all run away centuries ago. It would be more accurate to say that owners of some breeds do not possess the skills or understanding to train their chosen breed as this basic training code has been lost.

When you do let your hound off the lead as a young puppy, make sure you allow at least ten minutes before you call him back to you. This allows for a short burst of running energy, which then gives you more opportunity to get him to return. When he does return, reward him and then let him off to run again, repeating the procedure several times at each session before returning home. It is normal for most sight-hounds to run past you when you call them as they are often travelling too fast to stop. Sometimes they will run past you multiple times before eventually reaching you. Do not try to intercept them as they run past, as this will have the effect of making the dog avoid you by keeping at a greater distance. Just be patient and remember that it is often said about the Beagle that they do not fail a recall unless they have been gone for at least three days!

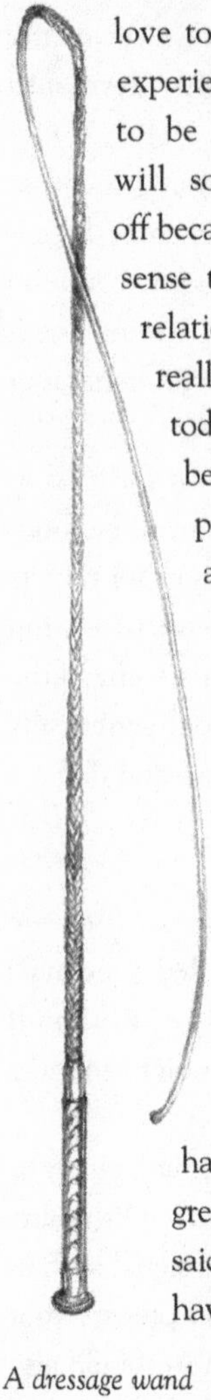

A dressage wand

The best games to play with your hound are ones that involve chasing. Start by buying a dressage whip. Actually, 'whip' is a bad word as it conjures up images of striking the dog, so I'll call it a dressage wand. Get some feathers and tie them to the end of your wand and flick them in front of your hound puppy. As it starts to show some curiosity, use the wand to flick them away. After a few seconds of this your dog should show signs of wanting to chase the feathers. You can now get your puppy chasing in a circle around you and by manipulating your wand, you can change direction to get your puppy turning left and right when engaged in the game.

When you start this game allow your puppy to keep getting hold of the feathers so he is successful but, as his skills improve, you can slowly make the game more exciting by adding a small amount of frustration in delaying the moment when you allow him to grab the feathers. This dressage wand can now be used for some of your outdoor exercise sessions and even incorporated into your recall training.

Lure coursing and agility are great sports for hounds as both allow physical and mental exercise and an outlet for their instincts.

SOCIALISATION

Socialising with people usually presents few problems for this group, but when considering a socialisation programme with other dogs, be careful to get the right sort of controlled exposure to some of the small or toy breeds. You do not want your Borzoi to think that a Yorkshire Terrier is a rabbit, do you? It is also important that you do not encourage your dog to exercise himself by chasing squirrels and other animals or birds, as it is only a short step from chasing squirrels to chasing toy dogs.

To put the situation a little more vividly, remember that almost all the hound breeds have been developed for the last part of the 'hunt, stalk, chase and kill' behaviour of predators, so if your hound does manage to catch a cat it is genetically programmed to administer a killing bite to the back of its neck. In this case, you need to find a training class that will have other breeds present, particularly some of the smaller ones, so you can correctly educate your hound puppy under the guidance of an accredited instructor.

PROBLEMS

Predatory behaviour towards cats or small dogs, squirrels or rabbits and bird-chasing are commonly reported problems but the main issue with hounds – which were developed to hunt in large packs – is that they are often really noisy when left alone!

Breeds like Beagles, Bassets and Foxhounds like lots of company. Often they do not take kindly to being left by themselves so they try to summon up the rest of their pack by baying and howling. Not a problem if you live in a remote area of the country, but not good if you live in close proximity to lots of neighbours. The problem is magnified if any of your neighbours also have hounds, as they will call to one another all day long if they find themselves deprived of social attention. To prevent this problem from occurring, use the strategies outlined in the section on chewing out of insecurity, but substitute barking for chewing (see page 222). To minimise the occurrence of unwanted barking, your hound should be raised to at least think that you are usually nearby, perhaps in another part of the house or in the garden, when he has actually been left by himself.

TOY BREEDS

Examples: Chihuahua, Maltese, Yorkshire Terrier, Toy Poodle, Rat Terrier, Italian Greyhound, etc.

This is where things can get confusing, as some toy breeds started life as working dogs while others were only developed to be human companions. There are even breeds that were developed purely for showing at dog shows. Some breeds were miniaturised by careful selective breeding, while others were created from two or more other breeds of small dog.

So do you treat your toy Rat Terrier as a working dog, as its name implies, or as a household companion, which is what it was developed to be? The answer to this question will more relate to the size of your puppy than any breed predispositions. Because of a toy dog's relative size, owners have a tendency to over-protect them. This results in the little dog lacking confidence or starting to become over-protective towards the owner that it adores. There is also the possibility of dog-to-dog aggression, which is bewildering to some because of the dog's lack of physical size and strength.

TRAINING

To train your young toy breed, first look at the breed history. Was there an original purpose for the breed and if so, what was it? If it was a breed such as the Italian Greyhound, which was only ever developed as a human companion, then the primary reward to use is affection and attention in both physical and verbal praise. It would be much more difficult (although not impossible) to use games with toys as a more effective reward. Many toy breeds are fairly delicate eaters, so food is probably not going to be particularly effective. On the other hand, with the Yorkshire Terrier we can use games with toys as a reward because of its ancestry of being used to kill rats in Yorkshire coal mines. Even though no Yorkshire terriers are still used for that particular purpose, most still retain part of their instinct for this type of behaviour.

Many young toy breeds receive little or no formal training or education from their owners, because all you have to do to control these little dogs is pick them up! The owner of a Standard Poodle is far more likely to spend some of the informative weeks and months training their dog than the owner of a Toy Poodle.

One of the problems with training a toy dog is that you could easily end up with a bad back because of all the bending down you need to do. Some people find it easier to carry out some of the early obedience training – such as commands to sit or lie down – with the dog on a raised platform, thereby bringing the dog closer to your face to see your facial expressions. Even training a toy dog to walk properly on the leash can be carried out by using a raised area or platform for early lessons.

With a toy breed that loves to sit on your lap and be stroked, you could add the following to your retrieving games. Get a small stuffed soft toy and set the rule that only when you have the toy on your lap is your little dog allowed to jump up for a cuddle. Place this toy on your lap and then invite your dog up, making sure that if the toy is not on your lap, the dog is not allowed to get up until you have placed it there. After several days your dog may well learn that the soft toy is the key to being allowed on your lap, so now try putting the soft toy *near* your lap and refuse permission for your dog to get up. Most will learn to pick up the toy and put it on your lap to be granted permission. If they do not work it out for themselves, you can teach your dog to pick it up and jump up with it. (See the section on how to get your dog to play, page 111.)

SOCIALISATION

One of the disadvantages of attempting any formal socialisation, such as attending a dog-training class, is that the young puppy will be exposed to other much larger dogs. This often results in the small dogs being constantly picked up to sit on their owner's laps. Even out for a walk in public, a young toy dog is likely to be picked up to greet people or when other dogs approach. The problem here is that the developing young dog is never allowed to make the decision whether to approach or withdraw from an approaching person or other dog. So from the safety and security of their owner's arms they start to throw out challenges to anyone approaching or trying to touch them. Similarly they never learn how to communicate effectively with other, larger dogs and become fearful.

The first thing to be learned from this is to resist the temptation to constantly pick up your puppy and allow him to stand on his own four feet. If he is sitting on your lap and growls at anyone approaching, all you need to do is make him get off your lap! For the first year of his life with you, try to treat him as though he is a bigger, stronger dog with the same capacity to learn. In my experience, toy dogs are not retarded and certainly do not seem to have any kind of learning difficulties. In fact, despite their smaller skull size, many seem to be quicker to learn than their larger counterparts. So you cannot use size as an excuse for your dog's behaviour.

PROBLEMS

The main issues with toy breeds are lack of self-confidence, unless they are cradled in their owner's arms, and over-attachment, which often results in separation anxiety.

Most breeds of toy dogs were developed to form strong attachments and become household companions, so it is not surprising that some by nature and some by nurture develop forms of separation anxiety. When you get your toy puppy, start the way you mean to go on and do not let it follow you from room to room. Make sure you close doors behind you as you move around the house and, particularly when the puppy is tired, teach him to spend some time each day by himself.

OTHER BREEDS

Examples: Alaskan Husky, Brussels Griffon, Manchester Terrier, Labradoodle, etc.

Unfortunately the majority of books addressing the training and raising of individual breeds of dogs are written by breed enthusiasts rather than dog trainers, so the information is sometimes of very limited benefit. What is important is that you take your dog's breed into consideration in terms of how you are going to train it, but perhaps more important is how you are going to socialise it and turn it into a loved and respected member of your family and community.

Always take the time and trouble to find an accredited trainer who has knowledge of your breed before enrolling in a course of lessons. This is even more important if you are experiencing problems with your dog's behaviour, as when you seek help you need to remember that your dog is not just the result of behaviour learned in the environment where it was raised but also behaviour that is driven genetically. Without appropriate breed knowledge it is difficult to understand how a trainer or behaviourist can be in a position to advise an owner on how best to cure a problem effectively. Breed societies sometimes have their own training or behavioural experts and it is often beneficial to contact these societies via a national kennel to get more information on your chosen breed, its training, socialisation and any problem behaviour you want help with.

But what about 'designer' dogs, mixed breeds like the Labradoodle, for example? Or how about a rescue dog, where the parentage is uncertain? What you should look for are dominant traits. Does the puppy or adult dog show terrier-like or hound-like characteristics? Or maybe herding or guarding characteristics? The more experience your trainer, behaviourist or shelter have in working with many different breed groups, the better they will be able to advise you.

One of the big problems in getting a breed that is rare or obscure is that there is usually a reason that the breed is rare. Often it is that there is no longer a job of work for that breed, so it has outlived its usefulness. The Brussels Griffon is a good example, as its original purpose was to keep down the number of rats at stables where horses and carriages were kept. With the decline in horse-drawn vehicles, came the decline of the breed as a working dog, so it had to adapt to life as a companion dog. Unfortunately, due to the small genetic pool, the high mortality rate in litters and other health concerns, it seems this is a breed that has had its time and is destined for extinction.

Manchester Terrier: A changing breed

It is also possible that your chosen breed has evolved into something quite removed from its original purpose, or that it was never really any good at its task in the first place! Take the Manchester Terrier. This breed nearly became extinct in England after the Second World War. Originally developed from dogs that were required to find and eradicate rats and vermin in cities in the North West of England, the breed was popular but obviously not greatly successful – there are still rats in Manchester! It was then crossed with other breeds to try and make it a dog that would also catch rabbits but again this proved to be not as successful as the breed enthusiasts wanted, so they again modified it to take part in rat-pit killing as a sport. At last the breed had a purpose in which it excelled but as the rat-pit sport declined, the breed declined with it. Then another group of enthusiasts got together to resurrect the breed, which was then almost exclusively developed for the show ring – a far cry from its original predecessors.

10

Socialisation and What It Means

It is a common mistake to think that by merely taking your puppy to lots of places where there are people and other dogs it will grow up to be well socialised. Socialisation means learning how to behave in a socially acceptable manner with other people and animals. Strange as it may seem, the puppy's mother begins the socialisation process by slowly rejecting her puppies, forcing them to seek social relationships elsewhere. If a mother is too protective and constantly gives in to her puppies' demands for affection and attention, she does immeasurable harm to their proper social development.

Good social skills have to be learned. Socialisation does not mean making your dog so friendly towards people that it becomes a nuisance. Your puppy has to learn to largely ignore people it meets simply because not everyone wants to be its best friend. Take a look at a guide dog and you will understand what we are trying to achieve. When was the last time you saw a guide dog jumping up to greet someone in the street, or backing off and barking at someone approaching them? There are minimum standards of social behaviour that we need to teach our dogs and that is achieved by a careful programme. Aggression is the biggest anti-social behaviour and will get owners and breeds banned from public places quicker than any other form of bad behaviour.

Again we have to look at life from a puppy's point of view. Yes, you can go to a puppy socialisation class but from my experience most are a waste of time and effort. Dogs only learn from their own personal experience, so when a puppy arrives at a training facility, is that where the puppy thinks people in the class live? In a facility? The puppy knows it lives in a house and that is completely different to the facility where the socialisation class is being run. Surely the only way a dog can learn about people is by teaching it that every person is the same as its owner, even though they look different, sound different and smell different.

Here is my socialisation programme. Meet at my house with your puppy – don't bring any food or toys as I need to supply them. I want your puppy to realise I am the same as you. I live in a similar house, I have dog treats in my cupboards, I have interesting toys, and I can turn on a tap and fill a water bowl. Tomorrow night we will take the puppies in the class to someone else's house and apply the same rules. The next evening it will be another house until we have done this for around a week to ten days. This process does much to remove fear of the unknown and gives the puppies information about people being the same as its owners.

What about the puppy that is a little shy of strangers? Simple. Give your puppy the option to stay away from anyone it is uncomfortable about and it will never become aggressive towards strangers. It may remain fearful for the rest of its life but it will always choose to stay away from strangers. Similarly, I am sometimes asked what an owner should do when they have visitors, because the puppy will run into a bedroom and hide under the bed. My answer is to let it do that and no one will ever get bitten when they visit your house! Anything such as giving a stranger food to tempt the puppy carries a real danger that you will turn fear into aggression (see the chapter on nervous aggression, page 260).

As for socialisation with other dogs, all you need to do is find a friend with a mature, sensible adult dog and allow your puppy contact with it a couple of times each week under close supervision. Remember you should not allow your puppy to do anything to the adult in play that will get him into trouble if he tries it with other dogs when he gets older. It is your role to teach him what acceptable and unacceptable play behaviour is. A sensible, mature dog will have a great influence on your pup's developing play behaviour around other dogs as well. If you are your puppy's best friend then you should experience few problems, and with a little care and understanding he should grow into a much-loved and admired family pet.

11

Teaching Verbal Language: Name and Recall

The first word that you are going to teach your puppy is its name, and this name should be its own unique identity. It is also likely that the name that you choose will tell me a lot about you, your dog and the relationship that you have with it. Names do not just drop randomly out of the sky.

There are basically three ways you may have chosen your dog's name. One is by doing some research on the breed and picking a name that is traditional for that breed, such as Khan for an Afghan Hound, Harris for an English Pointer or Fly for a Border Collie. If the name is traditional for the breed then I know that at least you did your homework before you acquired your puppy. The second way is as an extension of an interest or your own personality, or maybe as an indication of what you want the dog to turn into. So if you acquired your puppy as your next agility dog, naming it Turbo would tell me what you wanted it to turn into.

The other way people name their dog is to get it first and then choose a name that fits its character. So what does the name Panic or Rip tell you? When I deal with 'problem' dogs I often suggest renaming the dog as part of the recovery process in which the dog gets a new identity and learns a new set of more acceptable behaviours.

Choose a name that you, your friends and family are comfortable with and that is easy to say. Write this name on pieces of paper and stick them on every door of your house. Tell everyone that this is your new puppy's name and that it is the only name they are to use when they communicate with it. Otherwise there can be problems. Unfortunately most dogs do not have a single name – they have three different ones. There is the name you tell me that you call your dog, such as Barney. Then there is usually an extended or shortened version, such as or Barnabas or Barnes. Thirdly, there is the silly name you use that bears little or no resemblance to the chosen name, such as Whiskers! This has to be hugely confusing for a dog, so keep things simple and pick one name that will become your dog's identity.

You teach your dog to recognise its name by using that name to gain its attention. When you say your dog's name, it means, 'Pay attention to me. I am talking to you.' It does not mean, 'Come here'! Whenever you give your dog's name, you have just two seconds to get a response. You could plan giving it at a time when you can guarantee you will be able to get its attention, such as when you start to mix up its food at meal times. You could give your dog's name and clap your hands to get attention. You can also touch your dog to get its attention when you give its name. You could even offer a tasty morsel of food to get it to listen for its name. The whole idea is to oblige your dog to pay attention when it hears its name. Don't fall into the trap of simply repeating the name over and over without any consequence, as this will quickly teach your puppy that its name is of little or no consequence and it will start ignoring you. You must insist that it pays attention and then reward it for doing so – usually a smile, touch or the words 'good dog' will do.

Only when your dog has learned its unique identity can you think about teaching it another important lesson: to come to you when called. The reason this is a vital lesson is because if you have lots of control over your dog, it can be allowed more freedom, and more freedom generally means less frustration. Less frustration, in turn, means fewer problems.

Recall training is best started at a few weeks old, as soon as your puppy has settled into your environment and you have built up a good relationship with it. It is a big mistake to wait until the puppy is a few months old as by then he will want to explore further afield, which makes training him to come to you much more difficult.

Now this is where an understanding of canine psychology comes in, because training a young dog to come when called does not have to be approached as an obedience exercise trained on a specific command. It is more about the relationship that you have with your dog! (See the chapter on name and recall, page 64.) When you teach your puppy to come when called, you should be the reward. That way you will not be burdened with huge amounts of food or bags of expensive toys to bribe your dog to return to you.

So, you have had your puppy for a week or so and you are its principal caregiver. It can't really survive at this age without you. It needs you. Put your puppy into your car and drive away from home for about an hour. Then find a big open space, park your car and take your puppy out for a walk. Your puppy will want to explore this new area but should do so cautiously, using you as a base for its exploration of the area. Don't say a word – just go for a walk. After 20 minutes head back to your car and when you get there call your puppy. It should come to you immediately. Why? Because you are the ride back home. If your puppy does not come right away, just get into your car, close the door and duck down out of sight. That should do the trick. When your puppy arrives at the car, open the door, lift it in and really praise it well. No need for food – you are the reward. So the puppy has learned in one lesson to come when called. This is then used as a foundation to go on and teach a better and faster recall. Remember that a recall is not negotiable – your dog *will* come when called and that is how you are going to train it.

It will also help your dog to further understand your recall command if you do the following in the house. Begin by calling his name and using the command 'come'. Offer him a food treat, smile and appear inviting. There is no need to bellow the command, just an ordinary spoken voice will do. When your puppy arrives expecting the food treat, stroke him first, give him a big beaming smile, tell him what a good puppy he is and give him one small treat. Now wait three seconds and repeat the sequence of stroke, smile, speak and treat at least seven more times. The sequence or rhythm of rewards is crucial to teaching a good recall. Remember that you do not simply want your puppy to come to you, grab the food and wander away again; you want him to come and remain with you in the expectation that there are more rewards to come. So use small pieces of his ordinary dog food as the treat and do not be tempted to use anything extra tasty. Special treats are reserved for when you go outside, where there may be many distractions for him to cope with.

As soon as he is reliable in coming whenever you call him in the house, it is time to start taking him outside. The sooner you do this the better, as his instinct to explore will not be very well developed and he will usually not wander too far away. It is best to use a fully enclosed area away from roads for the first lessons. Repeat the training but the trick now is to keep him guessing what reward he will get when he returns. If you already have your puppy playing retrieving games with a toy, use this most of the time rather than food. Why? Because the biggest reason that a dog does not come to its owner is because it is enjoying playing a game. So it follows that if you can get your dog to play with you with a toy, it will be easier to get it to come for a toy than food. And what happens if your dog is not hungry when you call it?

When you have repeated this lesson a few times and taught your puppy the rewards that he gets for coming to you, then you are ready to put Thorndyke's Law – that behaviour changes because of consequences – into effect. For this last stage in your training you are going to teach a consequence to the behaviour of coming when called and a consequence of disobeying the command to return.

You will need a 15-foot length of very fine cord attached to your puppy's collar and an assistant who is known to him. Let your puppy off the lead but allow it to trail the line behind. When your puppy is preoccupied in sniffing or exploring, call him back to you. If he comes to you, explode with excitement and give several rewards. If he does not come immediately, then have your assistant stand on the end of the line to restrict his movements. Walk up to your puppy and show him all the rewards that you had for him. You can tease him with them but do not let him have anything. Then calmly walk away and ignore him, get into your car and drive off!

Ask your assistant to now fasten the line to a fence, tree or similar and walk a short distance away but stay in sight. After around two minutes you should return and your assistant should release the line from its point of restraint. You will now probably find that your puppy will run to you. Be a little cool and rejecting, and do not offer any rewards! Your puppy should wonder why you are not giving him anything and will probably try to attract your attention, but just go on ignoring him. When he does wander away, call him to you and when he comes running, you should shower him with rewards. It usually only takes a few sessions for the puppy to realise the consequences of his actions and you should then get a good, fast recall each and every time you call him.

Remember that if you have good control over your dog, then he will enjoy more freedom than a dog that is out of its owner's control.

12

Leaving the House

The next important behaviour to teach is walking on a leash so that your arm is not pulled out of its socket. Most owners introduce their puppy to a collar and lead by attaching a soft collar for a few minutes each day until the puppy accepts it. They then attach a lead and let the puppy drag the lead around to get it used to that too. Is it then a surprise to see owners being dragged around when they are at the end of this lead?

The question I pose to people with dogs that pull on the lead is, how is it possible for a six-year-old girl to lead a pony that is 12 hands high on a slack lead when the horse is infinitely stronger than she and could easily have led her if it had wanted to? It always makes me smile when I see a man who weighs over 200lb being dragged along the road by his 15lb dog!

So what is the answer to the problem? Clearly the owner of the pony, knowing that as a foal it was going to grow up to be so much bigger and stronger than the rider, really paid attention to teaching the correct set of desirable behaviours. This took place when it was young enough for her to be able to influence its behaviour so that the lessons were learned for life. The man walking his dog (or should that be the dog walking his man!) would not have paid attention to teaching correct behaviours because he would never have considered it important early in his dog's life. So we end up with the dog being able to do what the girl is doing: controlling and leading an animal much bigger and stronger than itself!

It is interesting that many dog groomers can tell within minutes how hard a dog pulls on its lead without ever having seen the owner walking it. This is because if the dog pulls and struggles against being restrained when they fasten it on a lead for clipping, it follows that the dog will do the same when it is being walked. If, when this dog was still a puppy, the owner had taken the time and trouble to attach a soft collar and lead fastened to a fixed object and handled and groomed the pup, ignoring any struggling and only releasing it when it was calm and accepting of the restraint, then pulling on the lead would never have arisen.

This is due to a process called 'premature conceptual learning' – a fancy term meaning simply that when an animal is still very young, we can imprint on it with lots of information about the world in which it lives before it has had the chance to explore these boundaries for itself. Thus if we teach a puppy to accept that when fastened on a collar and lead to an immovable object, its world extends only to the extremity of the lead and that struggling, biting at the lead or pulling has no effect on the restraint, then it will usually accept this for life.

Car travel usually presents few problems as long as the puppy is given

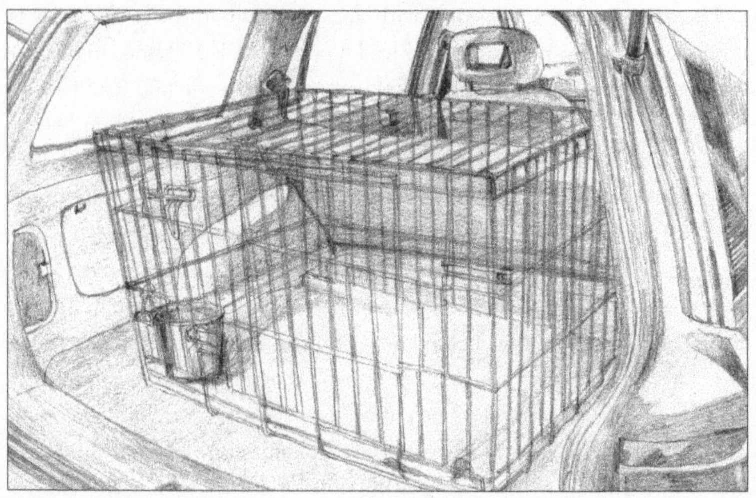

A purpose-made dog cage in a car

many opportunities to associate going in the car with pleasant experiences. For many puppies, the first car journey is very traumatic: it is when they leave their mother and siblings for the first time and the car takes them to a new and strange place. Often the second journey in the car is to the vet and that again is not a pleasant experience. So you can see that the reason some puppies fear the car is because they believe it will transport them to somewhere they may not want to go!

The best and safest place for a puppy in your car is behind a sturdy dog-guard or, better still, a purpose-made dog cage that can be removed and taken into the house. Start in the house by getting your puppy used to spending short amounts of time in the travelling cage. If you also let your puppy rest in the cage when he becomes tired, so much the better. This will habituate him to it and decrease any suspicion he may hold towards it. The next step is to put the cage in the car and allow the pup to spend time in it with you sitting in the driver's seat. A few food treats usually help it to settle. There is no need to go anywhere or start the engine; just sit and let the puppy realise that nothing unpleasant is going to happen. When your puppy is relaxed and confident then you can get him out and either take him for a walk or play with him, so he comes to associate going in the car with a very pleasant outcome. When he eagerly tries to jump in by himself, take him on as many short journeys as possible, making sure he has something in the cage to occupy his mind.

It is usually not necessary to sedate a young dog that is a bad traveller and indeed this can often make matters worse. Just use the above advice and your dog will look forward to trips out in the family car.

13

Housetraining

Housetraining is one of the simpler tasks to teach a young dog, because most arrive trained, courtesy of their mother! What the pup's mother will have taught her litter is to move away from their sleeping area and seek an alternative surface to eliminate on. To continue this training, simply provide access to a surface or surfaces for your puppy to eliminate on that are different to those it rests or sleeps on.

First keep a diary of your puppy's eating times, resting times and elimination times for around three days. You should notice a pattern emerging where the puppy wants to sleep at certain times, is hungry at certain times and wants to go to the toilet at certain times, and on certain surfaces. Armed with this knowledge, all you need to do is predict when the danger times when he wants to go are likely to be, then give him access to *your* preferred toileting surface while denying him access to anything other than his preferred sleeping surface. Simple!

The only problem is that the surface that you choose may not be as attractive as the one he chooses. To encourage him to use the surface you decide he should use, all you need to do is transfer the smell of his urine and faeces to it via a pair of rubber gloves, then take him there at the appropriate times and allow him to sniff. A little trick here is to scatter small food treats in a large circle around this area, which will encourage him to sniff the ground and circle, and then nature will do the rest.

Now for some dos and don'ts:

- Don't use ammonia-based cleaning agents to clean up afterwards as the smell often encourages the dog to use these areas again.
- Don't scold your dog physically or try to rub its nose in the mess. This will only make your dog hide from you when he wants to go to the toilet, thus making housetraining much more difficult to accomplish.
- Only scold your dog verbally if you catch him in the act.
- Do keep a daily diary of elimination times, exercise times, your dog's preferred toileting surfaces etc. This makes it easy for a behavioural specialist to provide you with a programme that will cure even the most difficult housetraining problems.
- Do always inform your vet if you notice any sudden change in your dog's toileting behaviour.
- Do be patient and try not to clear up any mess with your dog in attendance, as this may have the effect of teaching him to mess on the floor to gain attention.

It is a sad fact that some breeders make the job of housetraining much more difficult for owners by keeping their puppies on just one type of surface. Without at least two surfaces available, it is impossible for the mother to teach her puppies how to move to an alternative one when they want to go to the toilet. So remember that when you go to get your puppy, ask to see where the litter is being kept and then ask to see where they go to the toilet!

There you have it: some examples of how you can very simply and quickly train your puppy using a system that satisfies all the rules by which the dog learns. Of course if you do not take the time and trouble to teach your dog these things, the environment will do it for you by rewarding actions that you will then find unacceptable. But you cannot blame your dog for that: it is down to you to either formally educate your puppy or leave him to educate himself.

14

When Things Go Wrong

The art of raising a young puppy presupposes that not only are you available, knowledgeable and willing to take responsibility for your dog's education, but your dog will fall into the normal pattern of developmental behaviour for its breed. If you run into difficulties then you should seek help earlier rather than later.

Some behaviour problems in a young puppy, such as chewing and destruction, are only temporary and many will grow out of them as they begin to mature. On the other hand, some problems may look almost insignificant with a young puppy but develop into serious problems with maturity. Take a puppy that starts to wriggle around and turns attempts to groom it by the owner into a big game. If this strategy proves successful in avoiding the owner restraining and touching the dog, then the behaviour invariably gets worse as the dog gets older and more confident. It can even lead to episodes of aggression whenever the owner tries to touch, examine or groom the dog.

Now the problem is who do you contact if you are having problems? Some behaviour problems can be traced back to health issues, so a visit to your veterinarian would do no harm. Some trainers/behaviourists will not see you unless the dog has been given a clean bill of health by a vet. If you obtained your puppy from an experienced breeder (and you should have done), then contacting them might also be beneficial. It would also be a matter of courtesy to let them know you are having problems, because there is always the possibility that the problems are genetically driven.

Whatever your first point of contact is, you will probably end up seeking advice from a trainer. But how can you be sure that the trainer you contact is any good? One way is to look at the qualifications that your trainer possesses. This is where you need to do your homework. One of the best ways to pick out a good trainer is to make an appointment to meet them somewhere in public with their own dog(s). Go for a walk and observe how well their dog(s) are behaved. If what you see is good, go ahead and ask for advice on the problems you are having. If what you see is a dog or dogs that are badly behaved, it would probably be best not to involve them in helping you.

Also, it is important to make sure you choose the right trainer for your needs. If you are experiencing problems with a puppy then you would be best advised to go to a puppy-training specialist rather than a top competition trainer!

Section 2
Training and Behaviour Theory

'The noblest pleasure is the joy of understanding.'
– LEONARDO DA VINCI'

15

How Does My Dog Learn?

This is a section on theory, so please feel free to move on Section Three on page 97 if you start getting restless.

All learning involves building a set of associations in the dog's mind. These associations are the key to understanding how your dog 'thinks' and reacts. There are basically two ways that an association can be learned and these are known as classical and operant conditioning. The first of these is achieved by pairing a naturally occurring reflex action with a signal (stimulus, command). This is known as classical or Pavlovian conditioning (or in technical jargon, the 'pairing of an unconditional stimulus to a particular response').

One of the best examples of this classical conditioning was brought to my attention when a client, whose dog I was treating for barking at visitors, called me to give a weekly progress report. Dusty, a two-year-old Labrador, had always displayed annoying barking behaviour when anyone other than his owners arrived at the house. Dusty really liked his food, so I advised a four-week preliminary programme to change his response. By the third week the owner phoned to say that Dusty's previous display of barking had almost disappeared, but now he had become accustomed to being fed whenever anyone outside the immediate family entered the house. Dusty now began to drool profusely whenever the front doorbell rang!

Note that no new behaviours have been learned (salivation is a naturally occurring function). All that has happened is that Dusty has learned to pair the previously different functional signal (stimulus) of the doorbell to the production of food.

Now take a look at the section on fear aggression (page 260) and you will see why it is not a very bright idea to get people that your dog is frightened of to offer it food!

OPERANT CONDITIONING

The word 'operant' simply means 'producing effects'. In operant conditioning, or stimulus-response training, the dog learns to make an association between a signal or stimulus (in this context the command), a response to the signal and the consequences of that response. Put simply, it means that the dog learns what effects are usually associated with which particular behaviours, and which behaviours to link to which commands or cues.

The speed at which a dog learns to make these associations will depend on many factors but top of the list comes the skill of the trainer. Probably one of the biggest differences between classical conditioning and operant conditioning is one of choice. In classical conditioning the dog cannot choose to respond to a signal; it does so automatically. In raising a dog, training it or trying to modify its behaviour we aim to teach the dog that when a choice is presented, the consequences of its action will bring about a satisfactory or unsatisfactory state of affairs. When we teach a dog to jump over a hurdle we are presenting it with several choices – to jump, run around the hurdle or refuse to move – but through good timing and with a skilful trainer the dog will quickly learn the action that is required.

Operant conditioning principles emphasise the consequences that are associated with a behaviour. The dog is therefore asked to make an informed judgement on how best to control the outcome of an event or series of events. Nearly all the training that we see taking place in dog-training classes relies on operant conditioning. As stated earlier, the success of the dog in training is almost entirely dependent on the skill of the trainer in building up the correct associations so that the dog may make the desired choice correctly and consistently. A badly timed reward or bad experience will easily elicit an increase in the undesired response as indicated in the following example.

The dog is enjoying exercising off the lead and is playing with another dog when the owner calls his dog back. When the dog arrives he jumps up at his owner, putting wet and muddy paws all over his best white jacket. The owner becomes angry and chastises the dog both physically and verbally. On the next occasion that the dog is exercised off-lead and is given a command to return, because of the consequences of his actions the previous time, he makes an informed decision to avoid getting close to the owner. After very few repetitions the dog may well become operantly conditioned to stay at a safe distance from its handler on the command to 'come', i.e., it is the most favourable outcome from all the available choices when the dog is given the command to return.

Here are several types of 'learning' to illustrate the whole process:

TRIAL AND ERROR LEARNING

This is where the dog has a fairly high desire for something and this desire motivates the dog to experiment using different strategies to try and find a successful outcome. Unfortunately, most companion dogs learn most of their life lessons by trial and error and not by any kind of structured learning programme.

For example, a young dog is placed in a room of the house by itself and the door is closed. From the dog's perspective there is an access route back into the room where the owner now sits watching television but it is blocked by a big piece of wood. Dogs are social animals, so if it has a high desire to be with its owner then clearly it has to get the big block of wood (i.e., the door) out of the way. So the dog starts going through some behaviours that are designed to get the door open.

Let's imagine the first thing the dog tries is barking at the door. The dog will stand very close to the door and bark at it using a particular sequence or pattern of barks. Perhaps the pattern is five barks in quick succession, a slight pause and then a further three barks, followed by silence for a few seconds, and then the pattern of five, pause, three is repeated over and over. If the owner can ignore this barking and the dog gets no useful result from this behaviour then the barking will eventually stop.

But if the desire is very high then the dog will try something else. How about jumping at the door? The owner hears the dog bouncing off the door and again decides to ignore it. After a while the dog will discard jumping at the door as it did not produce the result of the door opening. But again, if the desire is still high enough then the dog will try something else. Now it starts to scratch at the door and immediately the owner throws the door open and yells at his dog. This fixes the idea in the young dog's mind that scratching at the door gets it to come open!

The dog has found the formula by trial and error. Barking got no result, jumping at the door got no result but scratching did get a result: the door that was preventing the dog's access to its owner opened. The owner's yelling will have little or no effect because it happened *after* the door opened. What the dog may well learn is to scratch at the door to get it to open and then run for cover when the owner comes in yelling and shouting.

If the owner had gritted his teeth and ignored the scratching and the dog's desire to get the door to come open was still very high, it would have kept trying different ways to get the result it wanted. While jumping up and scratching at the door, it discovers there is a part of the door that smells strongly of the owner – the handle. Eureka! That is now the area on which the dog is likely to concentrate its attention and lo and behold, it hits the handle with its paw or teeth and the door pops open. The dog has now trained itself by trial and error to open the door by using the handle. The more opportunities it has to practise opening doors, the better it will get at the behaviour.

Now look at the section on bad behaviour (page 191) and see how much learning by trial and error plays a part in shaping your dog's behaviour.

This brings us to:

LATENT LEARNING

This can be a very confusing concept even for a dog enthusiast, but if you understand it, then it will help you when we get to the section on modifying bad behaviour. Imagine you are on a five-day seminar and take lots of notes. There are lectures each day: some on aggression, some on training, some on separation problems and some on learning theory. Each evening you sit down and try to put your notes into some kind of order so that you can easily access them later. Now imagine your dog's mind during a similar education session. The dog receives lots of sensory input covering many topics and, when its mind is relaxed, it has to put things in order. Much information can be discarded as being of no particular use but it files away the important stuff so it can be recalled when it is needed. We use latent learning when training a dog, especially a very young dog, by letting it have frequent time-outs to relax and assimilate the information from each lesson.

The number of repetitions of an exercise and the time allowed between training sessions will be entirely dependent on the breed being trained.

OBSERVATIONAL LEARNING

This is the mechanism by which a dog learns by observing and participating in the behaviour of a strong role model. The two most likely behaviours for a dog to learn observationally are anything to do with excitement and anything to do with stress or fear. If you take your young puppy to the vet and other older dogs in the waiting room are showing signs of fear, your puppy will quickly pick up on the fact there is something not good about this environment. Similarly, if you take your dog somewhere where there is a really exciting activity going on, your dog will quickly become excited.

This is something that we can use in training our dogs to play with toys or to enjoy a particular activity. If you are a strong role model for your dog's behaviour then if you get really excited so will your dog. If you become really stressed then it is likely that your dog will become stressed as well. Observational learning can be used to a trainer's advantage when running classes or correcting severe behaviour problems. It is just a matter of learning how to manipulate the behaviour that you want.

AVOIDANCE LEARNING

This is where a dog learns to avoid an action because that action is linked to a disagreeable experience. Unfortunately the idea of avoidance learning has been used extensively in the recent past and has spawned a whole industry that seems to be devoted to finding more and more ways to train dogs that way. Like any other form of training or learning, there are degrees of avoidance from mild behaviour to absolute panic and flight.

The problem with using a system of avoidance learning is (as with rewards) you cannot guarantee what association the dog is going to make in its mind. At least if you get it wrong while using rewards, it will not damage your relationship with your dog. But with avoidance learning techniques – particularly those that involve the *owner* administering punishment – a dog can quickly build up distrust in the very person it needs to have a close relationship with. So putting a shock collar on a dog to teach it not to run off may well work but it will not make the dog want to return to its owner. If the dog realises it is the owner who has pushed the button, then bad timing can easily teach the dog to run away on the signal to return.

To understand this, you have to understand what the dog hears at a distance. Radio waves travel faster than sound. The dog is three hundred yards away. The owner calls his dog and then immediately presses the button to give the dog a shock. He thinks his timing is perfect as the dog receives the shock a fraction of a second after hearing the command. In reality the dog got shocked first and then immediately heard his handler call, probably making an association between the handler's voice and the shock! So my advice is that you should *never* use this kind of man-made electric shock equipment if you want to retain your dog's trust in you.

GUIDED LEARNING

The origin of the term is believed to originate from the training carried out by Guide Dogs for the Blind in England. In this type of learning the dog is physically shown how to perform the required actions rather than trying to get it to work things out for itself. For example, it is sometimes easier to put a dog on a lead and physically show it how to position itself on a walk along a pavement and thus avoid obstacles, than to let the dog learn this by trial and error.

There is no doubt that a dog can eventually learn all the manoeuvres required of a guide dog purely by trial and error but there are two fundamental problems with this approach. The first is that the dog would probably be retired long before it qualified as a Guide Dog. The second is that a lot of promising young dogs would be lost during the trial and error approach to stopping at the kerb when traffic is coming!

Some agility trainers find it easier and quicker to teach the dog to weave in and out of a set of poles on an agility course by putting it on a lead and repeatedly guiding it through, rather than to use one of the many alternative approaches.

The whole secret of using this approach is having a dog that does not object to being physically helped and guided into the required behaviour.

INSIGHT LEARNING

The best way to illustrate insight learning is to imagine a chimpanzee in a room with a bunch of bananas hanging out of reach from a high ceiling and a number of randomly placed boxes on the floor. The chimp will look at the problem and be able to solve it by stacking the boxes under the bananas and climbing up to get them!

In general terms it is better to believe that dogs are not capable of this level of insight so it is better to take the responsibility to solve your dog's problems yourself. We are good problem solvers. Dogs are not as most of what they learn is by trial and error. There can be no doubt that on very rare occasions individual dogs might be capable of insight learning, but in most cases other factors are responsible for the dog's success in solving a problem, so it would be unwise to consider insight learning as a way to train a dog.

We now come to two systems of training that make use of more than one type of learning. These systems are known as shaping and chaining.

SHAPING

Defined as successive approximations towards an end goal, shaping is the process more commonly known as clicker training, whereby the dog is rewarded for any behaviour that loosely approximates the desired behaviour. When this behaviour becomes fixed, the trainer goes on to ask for the next step or approximation of behaviour until the dog finally completes the task. In shaping, the behaviours are built from start to finish, unlike chaining where the behaviours are built from finish to start.

You can only shape behaviours that the dog offers. For shaping to work there must be a high desire on the dog's part to offer different behaviours by trial and error to get the desired result. The desire in this type of training is usually provided by high-value food treats given by the trainer and is often carried out without any display of emotion on the trainer's part. Food is usually then the only reason that the dog will learn to get creative and keep offering different behaviours.

One of the saddest days of my life was when I watched a group of young children training a group of dogs at a shelter. They were taking part in this programme to teach them basic communication skills because they were having difficulty in school and most had been excluded for bad behaviour. They were all using food treats and clickers. The idea of a clicker is to teach the dog that the sound of the click marks the exact moment in time where the dog carried out the correct behaviour, for which it then gets a food treat. The training session lasted for over an hour and the dogs were learning different tricks like begging, playing dead, turning in a circle and other cute things. The children were showing the dog a very tasty food treat followed by a signal for it to obey and then giving a click and food for each completed behaviour. Not once in the hour-long session did I see a child stroke the dog, smile at it or even tell the dog that it was great. It was all done without showing the dogs any emotion at all. The children were seen by the dogs as mere food containers.

It does not have to be carried out this way, of course. Even using a clicker and food it is still possible to stroke, smile and talk to your dog before you give it the treat.

CHAINING (SOMETIMES KNOWN AS REVERSE CHAINING)

This is a process by which a whole string of desired behaviours are chained together, with each response in the chain triggering the next one. It is termed *reverse* chaining because the end point of the exercise is trained first, then the behaviour that precedes it, and so on until the starting point is reached.

Reverse chaining is a particularly effective and efficient way to train complex exercises that require many separate elements to be mastered and decisions to be made. The success of chaining depends on the dog having a sound understanding of all the separate elements or links that make up the whole exercise; a chain is only as good as its weakest link.

The following sequence indicates how reverse chaining can be applied to an exercise such as retrieve, which is made up of many elements:

Elements of Retrieve

From beginning to end point:

1. Sit
2. Stay (while retrieve article is thrown)
3. Outrun to article
4. Pickup
5. Hold and return
6. Straight present in front
7. Sit (holding article)
8. Release article when required
9. Remain sitting in front
10. Move to heel position
11. Sit straight at heel until released.

Each element is trained separately to begin with, sometimes using a shaping or guided learning process. The chaining process does not begin until the dog has mastered each behaviour to the satisfaction of the trainer. For example, if the dog has no understanding of the command or signal 'sit' then the chain will break down if the exercise as a whole is attempted. Once the dog has mastered all the individual elements that make up the exercise, it is then chained in reverse, commencing with element 11 and slowly working back to element 1 as the dog's understanding of the chain that leads to the endpoint and subsequent reward improves.

This should by no means imply that the only reward should occur at the completion of the exercise, as verbal rewards and encouragement serve to increase the probability of success. One feature of chaining is that it can become unnecessary to reinforce each individual chain response, as each successful response cues the next in sequence until the end point is reached. This means the dog can eventually be trained to carry out a complex exercise without any extra commands or encouragement, other than a reward at the end. In practice it is good training policy occasionally to reinforce each separate link of the chain.

The only problem that reverse chaining presents is that there is potential for a great deal of confusion when an unskilled trainer attempts this procedure, because it demands that the dog makes a correct series of responses in the correct order.

16

Positive & Negative Reinforcement

A great deal of confusion seems to have arisen in recent years between academics, dog trainers and behaviourists regarding the use and misuse of the terms positive and negative reinforcement.

Basically, positive reinforcement is a mathematical term used to predict the anticipated frequency of a behaviour occurring. For our purpose it can be described as anything that, when given to the dog during the occurrence of a behaviour, will increase the likelihood of that behaviour being offered again. Negative reinforcement is defined as anything that, when *removed* from a behaviour, will increase the likelihood of that behaviour being offered again! Confused? Well, don't worry as I still have to find a dog who fully understands the terminology.

REWARDS

This system also utilises Thorndyke's Law of Effect. The consequence of carrying out the requested behaviour is that a reward is given, while the consequence of failing to respond results in the reward being withheld. For this to work effectively, the handler not only has to have a great many rewards but also good control over the way they are given.

Rewards do not always increase the probability of a dog adopting a desirable behaviour. Take a dog that shows a great desire to chase after rabbits, for instance.

The handler takes the dog out on a long line to where there are rabbits. The dog spots a rabbit and tries to chase it but is stopped from doing so because it reaches the extremity of the line. The handler then hauls the dog back in and tries to reward it by giving a food treat, which the dog eats but is all the time straining to get back to the rabbits. The same procedure is then repeated several times but the dog shows no increase in desire to return to the handler for food.

That evening the handler is sitting watching TV and eating a sandwich. The dog is called and it moves slowly towards the handler, sits and is given a food treat. Later that evening the dog is called

Bribing a dog to sit

again, but this time it runs straight towards the handler and is given a food treat.

Even though the dog was given the same food treat on each occasion, it could only be described as increasing the probability of a desired behaviour on one occasion. The next time the dog is chasing rabbits, it will still not return when called, will it? It would be acceptable therefore to describe a reward in the context of training or behaviour as a valued item that the trainer presents and which increases the likelihood of the dog striving to achieve it, even if there is a behavioural cost attached.

Traditionally, rewards are given for the satisfactory completion of a specific task but they can work as effectively if they are sometimes given during the task.

The more consistent you are in applying rewards to behaviours when you first teach the behaviours, the quicker the dog will learn, but with a trained dog, strangely, the more inconsistent you are in applying rewards, the better the behaviours will be maintained.

PUNISHMENT

The dictionary definition of punishment is 'penalty for a crime', so by definition it occurs *after* the event. Because a dog is not able to alter its behaviour retrospectively, it is extremely unlikely that training can be achieved or behaviour modified by the use of punishment more than a few seconds after an event has occurred.

Furthermore, if the level of punishment exceeds a given threshold (variable for each individual dog) it is probable that the dog, instead of modifying its behaviour, will become fearful of the handler or the environment in which the punishment occurs. Punishment is *not* the same as negative reinforcement. Negative reinforcement gives the dog the ability to switch off the disagreeable experience *at the time it is happening* by adopting a desired behaviour. Punishment does not. For the dog to switch off this disagreeable experience, it has to know what behaviour is desired, and this desired behaviour must be available.

VARIABLE REWARDS AND EXTINCTION

When a reward is removed from a learned behaviour, we might expect that behaviour will slowly reduce in frequency to the point of extinction. Although this is true, we have also found that in practice there is a sudden *increase* in the behaviour as soon as the reward is removed before it begins to reduce in frequency. This is called an 'extinction burst', and attention-seeking behaviours are prime examples.

To reduce the amount of attention-seeking barking when a dog is left fastened up on a lead at the dog-training hall, we tell the handler to ignore the dog when it is making a noise. If the dog had previously learnt to bark to get the handler's attention and the behaviour is now ignored it will, for a while, bark longer and louder in a desperate attempt to get the owner to give it attention. After some time the barking will decrease, and if only the quiet behaviour is given attention, the barking behaviour will become extinct. If, however, the barking is given attention during the time the 'extinction burst' reaches a peak, the behaviour will increase still further and may now prove extremely resilient to modification.

The main problem about removing a reward to decrease a behaviour is that most owners will give up when they see an *increase* in the undesirable behaviour, believing that the technique does not work. Also, there are many behaviours that cannot be safely ignored when exhibited by a dog within a family environment.

17

Learned Helplessness

Learned helplessness can easily occur when an overly aggressive or bad-tempered handler uses inappropriate punishment when the dog's control over its ability to avoid the punishment is removed or not understood. A dog can learn to accept that punishment is the result of being in a particular set of circumstances that are beyond its control.

Place a dog in any situation where punishment is inescapable – such as on a check chain and lead – then keep on shouting commands and applying sharp 'corrections' and each time the dog will learn something. Some will learn to modify their behaviour in order to switch off the punisher; others will learn that attempts to do this are ineffective and will learn to accept it. It takes a very skilful trainer indeed to monitor the effect that a punisher is having on a dog's behaviour and to make the decision to increase, decrease or remove the punishment accordingly.

The competition retrieve on a dumbbell is a really good example of how a dog can easily be forced into learned helplessness by use of corrections when it makes a mistake. The exercise consists of several elements in sequence. These start out with the dog sitting while the dumbbell is thrown and then the retrieve sequence starts when the handler gives the dog the command 'fetch'.

1. On the command 'fetch' the dog should run out to the dumbbell.
2. On arrival at the dumbbell the dog should pick it up.
3. The dog should now turn to locate the handler.
4. The dog should return to the handler.
5. On arrival in front of the handler the dog should sit straight in front.
6. The dog should remain in a sit position, still concentrating on holding the dumbbell.
7. The dog should release the dumbbell allowing the handler to take it.

The sequence below shows just how much confusion can be caused by a poor trainer if the dog makes a correct response but out of sequence.

1. On the command 'fetch' the dog runs out to the dumbbell.
   Consequence – no reward
2. On arrival at the dumbbell the dog picks it up.
   Consequence – no reward
3. The dog now turns to locate the handler.
   Consequence – no reward
4. The dog returns to the handler.
   Consequence – no reward
5. On arrival in front of the handler the dog releases the dumbbell as it sits.
   Consequence – 'bad dog!'

So, wanting to correct the problem, the handler repeats the exercise and this time:

1. On the command fetch the dog runs out to the dumbbell.
   Consequence – no reward
2. On arrival at the dumbbell the dog picks it up.

Consequence – no reward

3. The dog now turns to locate the handler.
   Consequence – no reward
4. The dog returns to the handler.
   Consequence – no reward
5. On arrival in front of the handler the dog holds the dumbbell but does not sit.
   Consequence – 'bad dog!'
6. The dog then drops the dumbbell to sit.
   Consequence – 'bad dog!'

The dog did not initially make a mistake as such – it had simply got a behaviour out of sequence (it carried out 7 before completing 5 and 6 in the list of elements). The resulting punishment could teach the dog to predict that the probable outcome of a series of behaviours is going to result in unpleasantness.

From the dog's perspective changing its behaviour to try and avoid the punisher still results in being punished. The dog assumed it was being told 'bad dog' for dropping the dumbbell and for sitting, so it changed its behaviour the second time in an attempt to avoid being punished. The change was to concentrate on holding the dumbbell and not sitting, but when it tried this, punishment still resulted. So after a few repetitions what the dog will probably learn is that no matter what it does, when it gets back to the handler with a dumbbell in its mouth, it is going to be punished. The result is that it starts to accept the punishment and gives up trying to change its behaviour. The trainer then describes the dog as inconsistent – sometimes he will drop the dumbbell and sit, sometimes he will hold it and stand and sometimes he will actually hold it and sit for a few seconds.

The other exercise that commonly causes the same type of confusion if punishers are used in training is the sit stay. Why? You'll find out when you read the section on stay training on page 149.

To understand the concept of learned helplessness just remember the expressions 'out of the frying pan into the fire' or 'can't do right for doing wrong'. Apply it to your training and you will be getting closer to understanding the code.

Section 3
Training an Adult Dog

'Nothing can be loved or hated unless it is first known.'
– Leonardo da Vinci

18

Putting Theory into Practice

Before we look at the physical process by which we train a dog, it is a good idea to consider some of the principles involved in training.

First, think about the words of command you are going to use. Each command should sound different from any other commands so that your dog can easily distinguish between them. Try to limit the commands you are going to train to fewer than five – even the real experts struggle to train more commands than this. To be an effective dog trainer you do not need to be able to shout louder than anyone else. It is the various tones in your voice that your dog can be trained to respond to, not the volume at which they are given. What you are going to do is create an association between your command, the response you want your dog to give and the reward that results from the correct behaviour.

This is how it works in practice. You give your dog either a verbal command, a signal or, more commonly, a combination of command and signal. From the moment you give your command you have precisely two seconds to get your dog to show a response. If you take any longer than that, your dog will not learn to associate the command and response as being linked. You could adopt the guided learning approach and physically show your dog what you expect him to do in response to your command. You could also use a lure, bribe or shape the behaviour (see the section on learning theory on page 77), but the fact remains that you only have two seconds to get the correct response. If your dog does not offer it and you do not show him what the correct response should have been, he will learn to ignore the command. If you do not get a response and then repeat the command, this is known as actively teaching disobedience!

Now let's suppose you have given your command and your dog has shown the correct response. Now again you have just two seconds to show him the result of his response. At this point this means give him a reward, but it could also mean, later in training, applying a penalty for an incorrect response.

The total association time from the command to the reward for the dog showing the correct response has to be less than two seconds. Now go and watch some of the great trainers in your area and you will find what makes them great is that they have their total association times down to less than two seconds.

Now let's look at how a trainer uses body language as well as commands. First, how not to do it. A really bad trainer teaching a dog to stay gives the dog the command to stay, then walks away a few paces and turns to face it. The dog looks at the handler, who is now looking very tense. He is standing upright with very stiff shoulders and there is not even the faintest glimmer of a smile on his face. Not a word is spoken. The dog moves out of the stay position and the handler immediately exhales, gives a wry smile, relaxes his body and walks towards the dog to replace it in the stay position. As he gets to the dog he gently holds it by the collar, strokes it and says 'good dog' before replacing it in the stay position.

So if you were the dog, what has your handler trained you to do? Well, if you love your handler then you would hate to see him so tense and not smiling when you are holding the stay position. Obviously, the desired behaviour is to break the stay position that you were left in and move towards your handler, because he immediately relaxes and smiles, greets you, strokes you and tells you 'good dog' when you move!

A really good trainer teaching the same exercise gives the dog the command to stay, then walks away a few paces and turns to face it. As soon as he turns around to look at the dog there is a relaxed smile on his face and his whole body posture is relaxed. He is breathing normally and speaking very gently to his dog to reassure it that all is well. The dog then breaks the stay position and instantly the trainer stands very stiff and upright, stops smiling, stops speaking to the dog and does not make eye contact. Then he gently gets hold of the dog's collar and without saying a word, replaces the dog in the position it was originally left in, giving it the command to stay as he does so. As soon as the dog is in this position, he immediately relaxes and continues as before.

If you loved your handler and observed these two almost extremes of behaviour in him, you would very quickly learn that staying where you were and relaxing is the required behaviour, and moving from this position is not a desired behaviour. So it is no good just being able to give a food treat at the right time – training your dog is all about how you are able to control your emotions to give your dog almost constant feedback all the time you are training him.

The easiest way to understand how rewards and punishers are designed to work is like this. Every dog has desires it wants to satisfy. The basic desires are for food, water, rest and reproduction. But there are other daily desires as well, such as companionship and going out and experiencing freedom. On top of this, all dogs have dreams, just as we do. Maybe the dream is of chasing and catching a squirrel or finding out where the scent of a rabbit leads. Most dreams in dogs seem to be a function of instinct relative to the breed of dog. Dogs also have their own personal list of penalties to avoid, such as their owner deserting them, being socially excluded, being exposed to something frightening, not being allowed to play with a favourite toy or having to watch their favourite food being emptied into the mouth of another dog!

The trick when you start training your dog is to ensure that you first negotiate the starting wage your dog is to receive for the task you are going to ask him to carry out. For example, it is no use going out for a day's training with two pounds of cooked liver pieces to reward the dog at the completion of every exercise. After a period of time, which varies from dog to dog, the reward becomes not worth the effort of working towards, and the reward that worked earlier in the session becomes less rewarding as it progresses and the dog becomes less hungry. In other words, the overuse of rewards during a training association will lessen the dog's responses and desires.

How do you keep your dog motivated to learn and ensure that the training that you are about to embark on continues to maintain your dog's enthusiasm? Remember that some behaviours are self-rewarding and therefore self-sustaining. Agility and tracking are good examples. Although many people use food or toys to start training their dogs to run an agility course or to follow a person's track across fields, in a short space of time the activity itself becomes the reward for many of these dogs. Some love to do agility and would happily leave a full bowl of food just for the pleasure of running a course. Similarly, many dogs that have been trained in how to track will get really excited when they see their tracking harness and line in their owner's hands out in open fields. It is then not uncommon to see a dog happily following a track and completely ignoring the food that has been left on it as a reward. The dog is self-rewarding on its natural behaviour.

Unfortunately for us not all behaviours are self-rewarding. Behaviours like giving up freedom and returning when called or doing unnatural competition-style heelwork are not naturally rewarding for most dogs, so we have to invent a reason or a desire to get our dog to carry them out. Also some behaviours that are naturally rewarding for some breeds are not so for others. Many Golden Retrievers are happy to return to their handlers with a thrown dumbbell but to get the same behaviour from a Wire-Haired Fox Terrier you have to think of a suitable reward for your dog to engage in this task.

How do you decide which rewards you are going to use in training your dog? The golden rule is always start with the lowest reward that your dog will carry out the behaviour for. If you start your first training session with rewards that are too high your dog will retire in a few short months. Here is the explanation.

It is easy to suppose that in order to increase production in a factory, all one needs to do is make the financial rewards higher for the employees. For example, a man working as a bench fitter for 40 hours per week might be taking home £300 per week. If we asked him to increase his work load and rewarded him by paying him £600 per week, he would certainly work harder due to the added incentive we have offered him. Let us now reward him even more by paying him £1,000 per week. Will he work harder still? At first, there is the possibility that he might, but after a while he starts to realise he can afford to have time off work and has more money to spend on alternatives to work – his leisure activities therefore increase. In time he may have saved enough to retire early, start up his own business or buy a share in someone else's. So far from making the worker more productive and conscientious, we have actively encouraged him to be less so by over-rewarding him. If you are using food to train your dog, take a look at its waist line!

A *dog going over a scale jump*

Now let us translate the story to a dog-training exercise. In working trial competitions, dogs have to negotiate a six-foot high wooden wall. As in all training, the extent that we can get our dog to carry out a command is directly proportional to its desire to get a reward or avoid a penalty. We start by having the owner stand on one side of the jump while I take their dog to the opposite side (it is usually easier to get the dog to jump towards the owner) and put up the barrier. The jump height is set at six inches and, holding the dog on its lead, I ask the owner to call their dog.

Holding the lead tight, I check to see how much the dog wants to get to its owner and then slacken the lead to allow the dog to negotiate the jump in front of it. At this stage I really don't care if the dog runs around this six-inch high jump. What I want the dog to understand is that it is possible, from one side of the barrier, to successfully return to its owner. If I try to make the dog jump over the barrier and it refuses, then I might put the idea in its head that crossing the barrier is either not possible or allowed. Remember that I am trying to make it really easy for the dog to learn what is required.

After three repetitions of this just for the reward of physical and verbal praise, I change the rules. This time I am not going allow the dog to run around the outside. Inspired by the knowledge that it can get to its owner, the dog always tries something else and quickly makes the decision to go over the six-inch high jump. At this stage the dog is not jumping at all but stepping over.

After one or two repetitions to fix this new pattern firmly in the dog's mind, we start to raise the height at each attempt by six inches at a time. After just a few minutes of training, the dog is now jumping over the obstacle set at a height of three feet. When we ask the dog to increase his effort to three feet six inches, he looks at the jump and decides that the reward of the owner being there to tell him 'good dog' and stroke him is not enough and he hesitates. Immediately I ask the owner to get out a tasty food treat and tease him with it. On seeing the higher-value reward on the other side of the obstacle, the dog immediately makes the decision to go over the jump.

We now continue up to a height of four feet six inches until once again the dog refuses to attempt that height. I now ask the owner to get out the dog's favourite toy and tease him with it. On seeing the toy the dog cannot contain itself and immediately makes the decision to jump. As soon as the dog lands on the other side the handler throws the toy for him to play with. We now continue up to a height of five feet six inches but when I put on the final six-inch board to make the jump six feet, the dog – a male German Shepherd obsessively bonded to his owner – has second thoughts about jumping it. I then ask the owner to get in their car, say goodbye to the dog and start the engine. Without any thought whatsoever the dog makes the decision to go over the jump and join their best friend in the car!

The point here is that if we had given the dog an outrageous game with a favourite toy for jumping six inches, then why would it ever need to jump three feet? There would be no incentive to put in more effort when the dog can get the same reward for much less effort.

So establishing a desire for the dog to carry out your training task is carefully negotiated before training commences. Always start with the lowest reward for the first step in your training programme, leaving room for bigger rewards as you ask more of your dog.

It has been suggested that once a behaviour has been learned, it gets stronger if it only gets rewarded now and again (random rewards). Put simply, there is no such system that has any practical application in dog-training! Stop rewarding your dog and it will stop carrying out the behaviour you want. It really is as simple as that. Don't believe me? Try this little experiment. For the next six months, every time that you take your dog out and let it off the lead, call it back to you ten times and when it returns do not even acknowledge it. In other words remove *all* rewards for returning when called and guess what will happen. You will lose your recall on command.

If you still think that the system of slowly removing the rewards does work, then look no further than your own behaviour. You are going to come and work for me for six hours each day and I will pay you a wage at the end of each day. This continues until you are very good at the job that I ask you to do. So now that you find the job easy, I am only going to pay you every other day – that is, you are now getting paid only half of what you were getting for the same work. A couple of weeks later I am going to pay you once every five days, then only once every ten days. Now you are only getting a tenth of what you were in the beginning. How long would you continue to work for me? Not for long, I would guess. You would soon start to look for work somewhere else, correct? Not quite, because if the work you are doing for me is really interesting, you might find the job is so self-rewarding that the payment is not the primary reason you continue to work for me.

The whole idea of random reinforcement came from experiments on rats in a laboratory. The rats learned how to operate a series of levers to win a pellet of food. Once the rats had been conditioned to operate the pedals, the experimenters started only offering rewards at a reduced ratio but to their astonishment found that the rats operated the pedals even more when they were only rewarded for around two in ten correct responses. The rats were now operating the pedals even though at times they were not eating the food rewards that were dropping. I think that what actually happened was that in that incredibly small and sensory deprived environment with nothing else to do, the rats had developed something called a 'stereotypic behaviour' – a repetitive and pointless habit.

The code says that if you remove the reward from the behaviour, then the dog will cease to carry out the behaviour. Some behaviours are naturally self-rewarding, such as coming back when called for a dog that suffers from separation anxiety. For all behaviours to be repeated there has to be a desire built into your dog's mind and it is better that you put it there or you buy a breed where the instinct is put there for you by selective breeding.

Once the dog has learned to obey a command using the smallest reward that will sustain the response, it must be offered every time the dog carries out the correct action. By using a variety of rewards training becomes more exciting for the dog, as he should not be able to anticipate what he is going to get, when he will get it or how much of it there will be. In other words, substitute the word 'surprise' for random rewards.

A group of students on a recent training course that I ran were given the following question to answer: 'Assuming that you have trained your dog to do a recall for food by giving one piece of baked liver every time it responds to a command to come [this is called fixed ratio reward training], describe how you would then switch to a system of random rewards.' Every single student then described a system of only rewarding one in three recalls, then one in five, then one in ten etc. This is not random reward training but reducing rewards, and it simply does not work in maintaining behaviours. So after spending weeks of training a recall for food, the handler simply throws all this good work away by withholding the very rewards that the dog is working for.

When we start to teach the dog a new behaviour, we must pick the lowest reward it will work for and be absolutely consistent with the type of reward that we give, when it is given and how much of it he gets (type, frequency and amount). The type of rewards available are physical praise, verbal praise, games with various toys and different types of food. The frequency refers to either a period of time or the number of times a behaviour is repeated. The amount is the value of the reward to the dog, and three pieces of liver are of more value than one piece.

When we start an exercise, we fix the type (lowest value), the frequency and the amount (smallest amount). As the dog becomes more skilled, the first thing we change is the type of reward that he is given. If we start off with the very best rewards for very simple behaviours then we have nothing better to give when the dog becomes more skilled at his job. It is also possible that if we use very high-value rewards for too long in the early stages, then when we try to change them the dog becomes frustrated and even aggressive. (This is referred to as 'fixed reinforcement aggression' but I think temper tantrum is far more descriptive and accurate!)

The next step is to try to change when the reward is given and at this time we also change the amount that is given. (Again, think of the word 'surprise' instead of random reinforcement and it is much easier to understand.) It then follows that the more rewards you have at your disposal, the easier it is going to be to train your dog. If your dog will only play with one tennis ball, does not care for being touched or stroked and is not a good eater, then you will have your work cut out trying to train using the reward system.

By now you will want to know how to apply all this information to train your dog to a standard that you could only have dreamed about before. So let's make things really easy, because making it easy will mean your dog learns things faster.

Dog-training has undergone many changes over the past 20 years as we slowly move away from the old system of confrontation to a new era of understanding. The training instructor's vocabulary has also changed and now includes new words and phrases that have become part of this new wave of scientifically based training. Sadly, we seem to have lost our way and many pet owners are being shown techniques that no longer require them to touch and talk to their pet dogs while training them.

No one would ever want to return to the old days of correction and reward, but what is of concern is that there are a growing number of instructors and behaviour consultants who are no longer dog trainers! Back in the 1960s, almost everyone involved in instructing in dog clubs and training classes was a trainer in their own right and therefore fully understood the principles of the exercises they taught. Today, it is becoming increasingly difficult to find a training instructor who fully understands how to apply the new reward-based system of training in practice.

How do you apply reward-based training in practical situations? There are five basic types of reward we are going to make use of in training:

- Physical praise
- Verbal praise
- Food
- Games with toys
- Freedom

Remember, in order to use these rewards in training you have to have complete control over how they are presented and removed. So, let's try a few simple tests and see if your dog is ready for reward training.

PHYSICAL PRAISE

Sit on the floor and touch your dog in the way that he prefers. After a couple of minutes, stop touching your dog and terminate the interaction by using a word or phrase such as 'that's enough' and turn away from your dog. Wait for a couple of minutes and then invite your dog back for more attention. Repeat three times in quick succession. If you can initiate and terminate a touching session at will then you can begin to use physical praise as part of your reward-training programme.

VERBAL PRAISE

Sit in front of your dog and use your voice to tell him how great he is. Do not simply use the words to express your emotion, use as much excitement as you can. You are not allowed to touch him but you can smile as much as you want. Keep this up for around ten seconds and you should see his tail wagging enthusiastically. Now suddenly stop verbally praising him but continue to look at him. You should see his tail slowly drop and stop wagging as enthusiastically as it was when you added your verbal praise. Having the ability to use the words 'good dog' as a reward will give you a huge advantage when training your dog when he is a distance away from you as it is the only reward that you can get to him quickly.

FOOD

Place several pieces of your dog's favourite food in your open hand and tell your dog not to touch them. You can use any tone of voice or facial expression as long as you do not touch your dog. Now, without moving your hand, give your permission for the food to be taken and eaten. Repeat three times in quick succession. If your dog makes no attempt to take the food until told to do so and then took the food happily and willingly, then you can start to use food as a reward in training.

GAMES WITH TOYS

Have a tugging game with a toy and then tell your dog to let go. Do not pull the toy away from the dog; your dog should release and stand back or sit. Again, you can use any tone of voice or facial expression but you may not touch the dog. Your dog should let go instantly and wait to be invited to join in the game again on your invitation. Repeat three more times in quick succession. If your dog takes hold of the toy and releases whenever you ask then you can use this toy in training.

If your dog prefers chasing a toy to tugging games, throw a toy and allow your dog to chase after it. Do not move from the position you were in when you threw the toy. Call your dog back to you and ask your dog to drop it in your hand. Repeat three times in quick succession. If your dog returns and delivers the toy to your hand each time then you can begin to use this toy in training your dog.

FREEDOM

Go to one of your dog's favourite places. Release your dog from the lead but indicate that you require it to stay next to you for several minutes before being allowed to run free. You are allowed to talk to your dog and give verbal instructions but do not touch the dog in any way. Now give your dog a 'release' word that gives your permission for it to run free. Wait exactly one minute then call your dog back and attach the lead. Walk a few paces and repeat this exercise three times in quick succession. If your dog waits with you until given permission to run free and then returns immediately when called then you can begin to use freedom as a reward in training your dog.

19

How to Get your Dog to Play

Before reading this chapter it would be helpful to re-read the paragraphs on the importance of play in chapter four (page 22).

First of all, there are probably as many ways to teach a dog to play as there are breeds of dog. Let's begin by recapping on the concept. Play is a way of:

- measuring or comparing yourself against others around you
- building or cementing a bond between two individuals
- releasing stress or unwinding and is sometimes an aid to relaxation
- stimulating body and mind
- removing inhibitions.

How – and probably more importantly why – we set up a play session can be critical in understanding the process of getting our dog to play. Just whom the dog plays with is also going to be important, as is what we are going to play with and when we are going to play.

All dogs have a need to play. If your dog's play requirement is one hour in every 24 and he satisfies that every day by playing with another canine playmate, you are going to find it really difficult to get him to play with you. If you pick a toy that does not fire off his natural predisposition to engage in genetically based behaviours – in other words, a toy he does not like – then play is going to be difficult. If you choose a person (i.e. yourself) who inhibits his desire to play – usually by having too much control over him in that environment – then play is going to be difficult. If there is little or no bond between the two of you then play is going to be more difficult. If the environment is more stimulating than the game on offer then play is going to be difficult. If a game was organised in the presence of a greater controlling authority (your other bossy dog, for example), then play would be difficult to achieve. If your dog is tired it is more difficult to get him to play. So getting a dog to play is not as easy as you might think.

First, select a suitable toy. The canine definition of a dog's toy is something that is fun, novel and good to interact with using a suitable playmate. A human definition of a dog's toy is something made of rubber that says 'dog toy' on the packaging and has to be purchased at a dog shop. If you can't tell the difference, I promise you that your dog can!

Sometimes the toilet roll from your bathroom would be seen as a suitable toy by your dog and the store-bought kong toy nothing more than a missile that you throw at him! Be creative and inventive. Don't go out and buy dog toys, but ask your dog what he wants to play with. Is there anything in your house you have difficulty keeping his teeth off? Anything that he would pay a penalty to get hold of? Can you safely use this as a toy? Some things that your dog might want to play with would be too dangerous to use, such as items that might be easily swallowed.

If you want to play retrieving games, the secret is in the choice of the toy. If it is not valuable enough the dog will not run out and pick it up; too valuable and the dog will run out and pick it up but will not want to bring it back and give it to you! If you want to fire up the dog's instincts and play games relative to his breeding, then taste, movement, visual appearance and sound become important. The obvious things here are the high-pitched squeaky toy for the terrier to shake and kill, the ball on a rope for the Border Collie to chase, or the tug toy for the Dobermann to grip and hang on to.

Now let's consider who the dog plays with. It may be that you are far too dominant – even if that word is out of favour at the moment – in your controlling influence over your dog, with the result that you inhibit his natural desire to play. Is there anyone who comes to your house who your dog is crazy about, gets silly around and behaves in a very immature, somewhat out-of-control way when they are present? That might be the best person to start the ball rolling, figuratively speaking.

The worst place to start trying to teach a dog to play is either where you do lots of obedience or control training or where the environment is more exciting than you or the toy on offer. That's why it is usually very easy to get a dog in a shelter kennel to play with you with a toy but difficult to get a pet dog to play with a toy during a walk in the woods! If you have another dog, do not try to teach your dog to play with you with this other dog in attendance. If your other dog is in the habit of taking the toy away or even competing aggressively for it in your presence, your dog's desire to play will be severely inhibited!

Next, pick the correct time of day. Choose a time when your dog is on an upward curve towards getting excited but not at the peak of excitement. As dogs are predators/scavengers, the time they are usually most mentally and physically active is around dawn and dusk. The idea is to utilise times of naturally building excitement to generate the desire to play a game. Don't wait until the food is mixed and the bowl is in your hand before getting your toy out for a game – do it 20 minutes before you usually start to mix up his food. Some dogs are morning dogs while others are night owls, so you will need to experiment.

How far have we got? You have chosen the correct time to start teaching your dog to play. You have chosen the correct location and eliminated any other controlling influence, including yourself in some instances. Your dog is getting excited.

The person playing with the dog should now lose all inhibitions and get silly. Don't expect that your dog will immediately start playing or wanting to join in the game. The game should only run for around five minutes and one of the most important things to remember is that the person doing the playing should not get frustrated at the lack of progress during the first three play sessions (ideally one session per day).

If you see no progress after three days, you should reduce your dog's access to any other dogs for three days before trying again. This means that if you own another dog, they are not allowed any unsupervised access to one another and should not be allowed to play together. They should also be exercised separately for three days prior to your play sessions and for three days after play sessions commence. The reason should be obvious: to reduce play contact between your two dogs to get one to play with a person instead.

With some breeds, Hounds for example, you will have to change the toy every two or three sessions so that it retains some novelty value. With some breeds, like the Border Collie, the same toy can be used extensively.

As the dog begins to enjoy the play sessions and to join in the game with your toy, you have to start thinking about explaining the rules of the game that you are playing. If this is carried out correctly, the game should become more exciting. If carried out incorrectly, the game ceases to be fun. For a dog that is reluctant to play, you will have to allow it to win most of the time until its confidence improves. If it compares itself against you in early games and realises that it has no chance of ever winning, he may retire early in his play career! On the other hand, if he never loses, he may throw a temper tantrum if it looks like he is losing and never let you play with it again! After the first session your dog should be eagerly anticipating the next one.

Still stuck? Don't despair – even the most difficult dog can learn how to play. This next section goes into the subject in more detail. Set up all the requirements I outlined in the last section, and you are ready to try any of the following play techniques.

PLAY RETRIEVE

The choice of toy is the most critical part. The secret here is to find a toy of just the right value – too valuable and your dog will not want to bring it back to you, not valuable enough and he will not want to go out and pick it up. For a puppy, a full explanation was given in the chapter on puppies (see page 40). If you have an adult dog that likes to play with a toy, you could use that system to get your dog to retrieve.

Teaching an older dog to retrieve when it has no inclination to play with a toy is just as easy. Providing your dog is of good temperament and not at all food aggressive, have a try at this. Get a small container that you can put some food treats in. It has to be small enough for the dog to pick up and carry around in his mouth but large enough so that he cannot swallow it. Now, attach a very light nylon cord to his collar and have a friend come and help you. It is better if your friend is known to your dog but this person cannot be anyone that the dog lives with and likes better than you!

Now sit on a chair in your house, call your dog over and encourage him to eat some treats out of the container. It also helps to talk to him in a really nice, relaxed tone – and don't forget to smile. You are the role model for his behaviour and you are not only giving him permission to eat the food treats but also helping him to get them out of the container.

Next have your friend pick up the line and, without saying a word, gently pull the dog away from you. As soon as your dog is held at a distance of around ten feet, encourage your dog to come back and continue eating his food treats. Have your friend restrain him for a few seconds and then slacken the line to allow him back. Immediately he reaches you, tell him what a great dog he is and allow him to start eating the treats. After a few seconds, throw the container into the middle of the floor and let him go to it. When he picks it up, don't do or say anything – simply sit there and observe his behaviour. In the unlikely event that he brings the container back to you, stroke him and tell him what a great dog he is and open it up for him to get the food treats.

If your dog does not bring the container back to you but either stays where he is or takes it somewhere else to try and get at the treats, have your friend pick up the line and restrain him. Now, they should, in the gentlest way possible, lead him to you so that you can open the container for him to eat the treats. It is very important that they keep a smile on their face to make the dog realise this is just a game. You are not trying to make your dog possessive and even possibly aggressive over food! After a few repeats your dog should get the message that you are the only person who can easily get the container open so that he can get to his food treats and he should willingly bring it to you without any help from your assistant. You can now dispense with your assistant and the line. You have now established that you are the best and safest place to bring the container of treats.

Can you see what we are teaching the dog? Actually, teaching any dog to retrieve is best approached by thinking of this not as an exercise but a concept – the concept of sharing something with you.

Next try putting a split tennis ball containing a few tasty treats into a sock before you throw it. Now when your dog returns with it, get excited and open the sock, take out the ball and open it to deliver the treats. It should not take too long before your dog will retrieve a ball.

What?! You still cannot get your dog to play? OK, when all else fails I use this one. Pick up an old newspaper, tear off a small piece and let your dog see you place a food treat on it before you crumple it up. Don't crumple it too tightly to begin with; the looser the better. Now drop this to the floor and let him sniff it. Drop to your hands and knees and behave in a really excited way. Holding the edge of the paper with one hand, start tearing the paper to pieces to finally reveal the treat. Let your dog eat it from the paper; do not pick the treat up to give to him. Repeat a few more times until he gets the hang of joining in the ripping part of the game by putting one foot on it and tearing it with his mouth to get the treat. Encourage him as much as you can. You are trying to get him to mimic what you are doing (i.e. to set up allelomimetic behaviour). This is the same as teaching him to dig by getting on your hands and knees and scrabbling at sand on the beach.

Now crumple the paper tighter and tighter to make him work harder to get the treat. The last bit is to have him on the lead and let him see you crumple the treat tightly in the paper before you finally throw it for him. When he runs out and tries to rip it apart, simply put some pressure on the lead and hey presto! He will pick it up and carry it. Only ask him to carry it for around three paces and then drop to your knees, praise him and help him to get the food treat out. When he will happily carry it for ten paces or so, you will need to get a friend, a fine length of cord etc., etc.

How can you get a dog to play a game of tugging with you? The easiest

A dog tugging a sock in a doorway

way is to hold of a piece of rope or fabric between two hands with the centre portion long enough for your dog to grip comfortably. Now get your dog into a high level of arousal by getting excited yourself. Smile, talk in an excited voice and run your hands all over your dog to excite him. You might try playfully pushing him away from you and then encouraging him to jump back. At the height of the excitement, produce your toy and stroke him all over the body, legs and feet. Keep the toy moving and with any luck he will grip it momentarily. As soon as he does, pull gently to free the toy. Then tease him and get him to grip it again. When the toy is in his mouth you should smile, stroke and talk in an excited voice. If he lets go then stop smiling, stroking and talking to him. By carrying out this procedure you should be able to slowly increase the amount of tugging that your dog does at each session.

No luck? Try this. Start with an old sock – the smellier the better! Now place some really tasty treats inside and tie a knot in the top. Attach a length of bungee cord to the top of the sock and suspend it in an open doorway of your house. The bottom of the sock should be around six inches from the top of your dog's nose when it is standing with all four paws on the ground. Now sit back and watch the dog's attempts to get the food from the sock, occasionally giving a few words of encouragement. As your dog tries to pull the treats from the sock it will keep bouncing away from him. When this happens he will learn to hold on and tug in order to pull a hole in the sock and release the treats. I did tell you to use an old sock, didn't I?

Repeat this three or four times each day and then one day when your dog is eagerly awaiting his opportunity to pull the treats from the sock, hold on to one end of the bungee cord instead of hanging it in the doorway. Hold it at the same height and in the same doorway as before and wait for the dog to start tugging against you. Verbally encourage him as you gently pull and release, pull and release, pull and release. Finally, stand still and allow him to make a hole in the sock and get his food treats. When you have reached this point you can occasionally let go of the bungee and allow your dog to take the sock away to a safe place to pull it apart for the treats. As your dog does this, go over and give him some assistance. Then continue as for the previous retrieve – get a friend, a fine length of nylon cord etc.

You have now trained your dog to bring a toy and play tugging games with you. This is merely a slightly different slant on the basic retrieve game – retrieving to play tug, as opposed to playing tug to win the game and take the toy away.

Still having problems? Then try this. Take a handful of small dog treats that are easily seen and conceal a small squeaky toy in the same hand. Stand in front of your dog and start throwing the treats for him to catch. (If you cannot get your dog to catch one, read the section on training, page 156.) Once he has started to catch them, set up a rhythm: throw, catch, three seconds, throw, catch, three seconds, throw, catch, three seconds and so on. After catch number ten, wait three seconds and throw the squeaky toy. If you got your rhythm right I bet he catches it and may even squeak it. Quick as a flash, go to him – he will have dropped it by now – and pretend to find an even better small treat inside the toy. Allow him to eat it and then continue your throw, catch, three seconds sequence. Surprise him with the toy at random, rewarding him with a better food treat when he catches it. Only reward him when he manages to squeak it and in no time at all he will enthusiastically grab and squeak the toy whenever it is thrown to him. If he grabs the toy and runs away squeaking it, make sure you don't get excited and chase around after him. You can now either leave this game as it is or get a friend, a length of fine nylon cord etc.

Still no luck? Then you'd better accept your dog is trying to tell you something. Maybe you are simply a boring handler, in which case lighten up and enjoy yourself. Drop the obedience in favour of just playing for the next few weeks. Ask your dog what game he wants to play, when he wants to play, where he wants to play and what toy he wants to play with, and listen to him.

20
Walking on a Leash

You are going to start training your dog to walk correctly on the lead. What could be easier? All you need is a soft nylon or leather lead around five feet in length and a normal flat collar of the same material.

Why is it important that your dog walks correctly on the lead? The first thing is that if your dog walks well on the lead, you will be inclined to take it out more often and you will stay out for longer periods of time. A dog in a high level of arousal that is dragging its owner along the road creates a bad impression because the dog looks – and is – out of control. Also, dogs that pull badly on the lead are more likely, because of their higher level of arousal, to be on the edge of being aggressive and often provoke aggression in other dogs that approach them.

Why would any dog want to pull on the lead? A dog cannot pull on the lead unless there is something to pull against and here lies the heart of the problem. If you keep the lead so tight that you keep a constant pressure on your dog's neck, you will teach it to brace itself against the pressure you are applying. Also a walk to a park where the dog is let off the lead to run around and have fun will have a great tendency to encourage the dog to pull all the time on the outbound part of the walk.

You should also examine how much attention your dog gets when he pulls on the lead. Many owners only talk to their dog or pay any attention to it when it pulls on the lead. Walking correctly on the lead without pulling rarely gets noticed, so if you were a dog and wanted your owner to pay some attention to you what would you do?

Now for the practical training side. If you get this right, it should take you all of ten minutes before you see a significant improvement in your dog's behaviour on the lead. If you go to a dog-training class they will probably want you to teach your dog the command of 'heel'. This is a throwback to the days when most classes used exercises required for competitive obedience, where the dog is required to walk to heel in a precise position for two minutes in front of a judge. Forget 'heel' – no words of command are needed. Even if you own a dog that has extreme learning difficulties, it should realise that when you attach a lead to its collar it restricts its movements to within five feet of you.

The next thing to understand is that you really do not need to use food! The walk is the reward. Surely the idea of taking a dog for a walk is that it can get some physical and sensory exercise. How would you feel if I took you out for a walk to a really interesting place but made you look at me all the time by holding some really tempting food in front of your nose? How can that make any sense at all? The idea of using food to train heelwork again goes back to competitions, where the dog is required to walk in a particular way, paying full attention to the hander. It is like dressage: stylised and over-controlled for a very short period of time. Also by using food you will keep your dog in a higher level of arousal when what you really want is a dog that is relaxed.

You also need to understand that going out for a walk is not obedience-driven behaviour and should benefit both dog and owner. So if you want to stop to look at a particular view for a minute or two, then I expect your dog will be patient and wait until you are ready to continue the walk. Similarly, if your dog finds an interesting smell then, providing he is not pulling you, you also have to be patient and wait for him to continue the walk.

If your dog pulls on the lead, there are many approaches that you can take to fix the problem. Providing your dog has a really good emotional bond to you, which might be doubtful if you own more than one dog, this first technique usually works really well in just a few minutes.

Hold the leash loosely in just one hand

Hold the lead loosely in just one hand. (If you want to know why, read the section on lead-walking behaviour problems, page 125). Now simply start walking and as soon as your dog puts enough pressure on the lead, all you need to do is trip and fall to the ground. Feign injury and your dog should show concern for your welfare. You can now see why there has to be a really good emotional bond between the two of you. Stay down for a while and have a pained expression on your face. Your dog should be blinking its eyes and licking your face, disturbed by your fall. When you get to your feet, make sure you do so slowly and gingerly and when you do start to walk forwards, you should really hobble for the first hundred yards or so. Two or three repetitions when your dog puts any pressure on the lead should be enough to do the trick, especially with a young dog.

The next two techniques work on the reversal principle, which means we reverse what is in the dog's mind.

Set off on a set circular walk that finishes at your front door. Have your dog positioned on your right hand side and your lead held loosely in your left hand and walk forwards. As soon as your dog puts enough pressure on the lead to start drawing it through your hand, immediately turn around

180 degrees to your right and drop your lead hand as low as you can. Now gently pull your dog forwards. (When your dog gets ahead of you and you turn on the spot, your dog will now be behind you.) The gentle pull forwards is really important as this is the opposite direction he expects you to put pressure on the lead. His immediate reaction will be to lean backwards against the pressure you are applying. Remember that the pull should come from under your dog's neck and not on top. This is why your hand had to be really low to get the maximum lean back from your dog. As soon as your dog is level with you then drop the lead as slack as you can and continue walking.

A demonstration of lead walking using the reverse principle.

It is important that you do not say a word at this time. Keep on repeating this and you should find that within a few minutes your dog will tend to stay fairly close to your leg and that the number of times you have to turn and pull starts to decrease. When the dog starts to walk correctly alongside you then you can smile gently and begin to talk to your dog in a calm voice. The idea is to keep it relaxed and not to excite it with lots of praise. All you are trying to do is assure your dog that you are pleased with the way he is walking.

Technique number two is very similar but this time as soon as your dog catches you up after you have turned around and given him a gentle pull forwards, immediately turn through 180 degrees and do the same again. This effectively doubles the effect on your dog. Because the penalty for getting in front of you and tightening the lead is that he finds himself constantly trying to catch you up, the pulling should self-correct within a few minutes.

Technique number three is used for really bad pullers, where the dog puts so much pressure on the lead that you really have to brace yourself or be pulled over. For this type of problem we have to change the whole association with pulling. So the first thing to do is to invest in a brand new lead, one that is different from your old lead. The idea is to teach your dog that when you attach this new lead pulling is no longer possible. Start in your own living room and regularly tether your dog on this new lead to something that cannot move. Now you can sit with him for ten minutes at a time and let him work out that trying to pull on this lead gets him precisely nowhere. If you cannot tether your dog without him trying to pull, you certainly are not going to find walking easy.

When your dog accepts the lead restraint it is time to go out for a walk. Just before you do this, try to get your dog to play with a toy in your back garden for around 20 minutes – if he is tired then he will learn not to pull on this new lead really easily. Again, go on a circular walk where you end up back at your own front door. As you walk forwards, hold the lead as loosely as you dare. As soon as your dog begins to advance ahead of you, take a couple of quick paces forwards and use the lead to pull your dog as far forwards as you can. You are trying to get your dog out as far in front of you as your lead will allow. When your dog is at the end of the lead, turn around smartly 180 degrees, switch hands behind your back and apply pressure in a forward direction until your dog has caught up with you. If your dog is walking on your left then you are going to turn to your left. This magnifies the effect that the pull forward has on your dog; it creates a huge penalty for pulling as you will be pulling him forward in front of you and then again pulling forward when he is behind you. The further in front of you that you can get your dog, the further behind you he will be when you turn, which gives you lots of opportunity to gently pull him forwards.

This is the most effective technique to stop a dog pulling and, carried out correctly, can easily result in your dog lagging slightly behind you when it walks. Remember to pay attention to your dog for the behaviour that you want when you are walking and remain silent and apply one of the above techniques if your dog starts to pull. Make sure that you and everyone else who walks your dog carries out the same strategy consistently and there should be no more pulling on the lead.

Now let's consider other lead-walking behaviour problems.

GRIPPING OR TUGGING AT THE LEAD

Why would a dog learn to grab the lead and tug on it when it is taken out for a walk? This is how it usually happens. When the dog is still very young, the owners start playing tugging games with a piece of soft rope or some kind of fabric tugging toy. When the game is played the dog gets excited. To keep hold of the toy the owner has to hold it in both hands as the dog is tugging. The owners encourage their dog to grip harder and very quickly this becomes the dog's favourite game. Now put this young dog into a high level of arousal because it's about to go out for a walk, take a piece of rope or fabric (the lead) and in your hands and what will your dog think? The problem then gets worse as the owner constantly tries to get the dog to let go of the lead, which adds to the competition, and so the dog becomes obsessed with this exciting game.

How do you stop it? Again common sense comes in. Attach two leads to your dog's collar and hold both leads in one hand. If your dog grabs one of the leads, simply let go of that lead and continue walking using the second lead. After several yards your dog should let go of the one he grabbed because there is no tugging game. He will then grab the one you are holding, so simply pick up the one he has dropped and let go of the one he was tugging at. He should soon tire of this as it is no longer a tugging game you are playing with him.

Some people try to get their dog to carry a toy so that it does not tug at the lead. This seldom works because when the dog does hold on to the toy the handler ignores it but when it grabs the lead it get immediate attention. So if you want to use this technique, you have to convince him you are competing for the toy throughout the walk. Try to visualise that the tug toy is something that you don't want your dog to tug on and you should end up with that being the only thing that he is interested in grabbing. Understanding this concept gets you closer to understanding the code of dog behaviour and training.

RELUCTANT TO GO OUT

This usually occurs because of some kind of fear problem. Almost all dogs like to go out for a walk just to exercise their senses in the changing world around them. If your dog starts to feel insecure about going out for a walk, you simply have to find a good reason for your dog to want to go out.

Sometimes you can make a start by driving your dog a short distance and then getting out and walking home. At least your dog now has a reason for walking with you. You could also start feeding your dog outside your house, starting just a few yards from your front door and slowly getting the food bowl further and further away. This would be the only food that your dog gets to eat; there would be no other food available for at least two weeks. If your dog is so frightened that he will not eat the food even just a few yards from your house, read the section on fears and phobias (page 232).

21

Coming When Called

Imagine two people being involved in a dog's education, one of them a trainer and the other a handler. If the trainer teaches the dog all the commands and behaviours necessary for its future job and then passes it over to the handler, what skills do you think the handler needs to possess to continue to be successful? Does a handler have to also be a trainer capable of teaching exercises? Or does the handler merely have to know how to maintain the behaviours instilled by the trainer?

Well, I know many people who could never even begin to train a dog but who have beautifully trained and well-behaved dogs. Their skill is in handling a trained dog. Don't believe me? Just go and have a look at some guide-dog owners, an army dog handler etc. Like many trainers I have allowed other people to work my dogs at the top level of competition. Some have been very successful, even though they could never train a dog to that standard themselves. These people take lessons from trainers who not only train the dog but show them how to handle it to maintain behaviours. In training the instant recall it is better to have both a trainer and a handler present for the first few sessions, only dispensing with the trainer when the dog fully understands what is required. From that point on it is up to the handler to maintain the recall.

If you have a problem with an exercise then it goes all the way back to your first training session on that exercise. That is where the first impression was formed. So if you have a problem getting your dog to stay down on command, go back to the first stay-training session you carried out with that dog – that is where it started to go wrong. The same applies to recall, retrieve, walking on a slack lead, tracking etc.

Occasionally I run five-day courses for training instructors at rescue centres where 16 prospective class instructors attend, each bringing their own dog. The first practical training session is in an open field for the recall exercise. My opening talk is usually tongue in cheek, as I tell them that I want all dogs off-lead by the third day. I also ask that if any dog chooses to run off, what does that tell the handler about the relationship between themselves and their dog? If the dog chose to run off then why condemn it to a lifetime with someone that it did not choose to be with? A recall is merely a test of your relationship with your dog!

I also point out that the shelter has lots of dogs that would be only too willing to build a relationship with any handler who had lost their own dog on the recall exercise! Of course I was only joking but it certainly made the audience pay attention. In fact we always manage to teach all the dogs off-lead recalls by the end of the third day!

Using the knowledge of how to use rewards in training, we can easily train a dog to return to its handler when called. But first here is a true story of how *not* to do it. The handler had let her dog off-lead reluctantly and immediately started to panic as the dog walked away from her. We were in a very large, fully fenced field so there was little danger of the dog getting lost. She called the dog when it was around 15 feet away; it turned its head and glanced at her before continuing to walk away. She then started to walk towards it, calling it by name and adding 'Look what I've got,' producing a ball and throwing it up in the air as she did so. The dog took no notice and continued to move away but now broke into a steady trot. The handler then took out a bag of liver food treats and continued to run towards the dog, calling it all the time. Eventually the dog stopped and allowed her to get within around 20 feet or so. She then dropped down on one knee and called the dog again, showing it the bag of liver. Then she turned and ran away, calling it all the time. The dog then ran past her and she stood still and coaxed it in. The handler then gave the dog a big hunk of cooked liver! I asked her why she had given the dog the liver and she replied, 'Well, he has to get a reward for coming to me when I call him, doesn't he?'

This was my response. Imagine your husband is going out tonight to play cards with his friends. You have to visit your friend later that evening to deliver something really important but you only have one car and your husband will be using it. So you ask him to be back by 10pm so you can use the car. By 10.30pm he still has not returned. Then 11pm arrives and still no husband. At 1.30am he finally arrives at the door. When you let him in, would you have a nice meal prepared for him and then throw your arms around him and give him a big kiss because he has decided to come home at last? Well, would you?

The handler replied that she would have thrown his dinner away or better still given it to the dog. When he finally got home she would have been in bed with her back to him and would have used body language to imply she was not amused. After refusing to speak to him the following morning, she would have made him work really hard to get back in her good books. She actually used the word grovel! She also agreed that if she had prepared a lovely meal and been really nice to him she would only be encouraging him to do the same again. When I asked her why the relationship with her dog was so different, she was at a loss to explain it.

Now I asked her to release her dog again and walk off in the opposite direction with me, paying no attention to the dog. After a short while I asked her to call the dog. The same thing happened: he totally ignored her. We carried on walking and the dog then stopped, looked at us walking away and stood still, seeming a little bemused. He finally decided to join us and as she was about to give him a food reward I quickly reminded her of her husband arriving home late. Instead I told her to show the dog the food he had missed by arriving late and then put it back into her pocket without giving him any. I also asked her to be really cool and rejecting in her body language. When the dog then jumped up at her, she turned away saying, 'If you think that you can get around me like that, you've got another think coming.' We walked away and the dog tried really hard to please her, refusing to leave her side. Her words were: 'I have never seen him try to suck up to me like this before.'

It was difficult to get him to leave her and go far enough to attempt a recall but finally he found a nice smell on the ground, which gave her the opportunity. When she called, he came running and I told her to pat him on the head and tell him how nice he was. The liver should be saved for the more difficult recalls that would inevitably follow over the next few days.

What had happened was that this dog had gained complete control over the handler, because rewards had been used for far too long to bribe it to come when called. The dog was making the handler increase the bribe until she had nothing better to offer. What I did was to show her how to teach her dog the consequences of his actions, knowing that this dog fully understood what was required of him. This system only works if the dog has a good understanding of what he is supposed to be doing, so you need to learn to manipulate the rewards to teach your dog how to come instantly when you call him. See if you can work out how this is going to be achieved; you already have lots of clues.

I am guessing that if most readers put on their dog-walking clothes, picked up the dog's lead, stood near the door and called the dog, it would come to them instantly. Actually, it probably would not need to be called as it would have read all the signals that meant it was time to go out for exercise. Now let's go out of the house and watch the dog carefully. When exercising off-lead the owner, still dressed in the same dog-walking clothes and with the same lead, calls the dog. This time we often see the reverse of what happened in the house: the dog deliberately avoids the owner. Why? Because the *consequences* of both recalls are very different, and it is the consequences of an action that maintain and strengthen that behaviour. We have already seen how the system of bribery, using rewards, was almost bound to fail because it gave all the control to the dog and left the owner with no control whatsoever.

As with all training, the basic idea of what you require your dog to do should be taught in an environment free of distractions. Your own house serves this purpose well as there are not likely to be many distractions you cannot control, unlike a public park where you have no control over events likely to take your dog's attention.

The first thing to establish is whether your dog understands how to come when called under almost ideal conditions. There are five tests for this and the rules are the same for each test. Have a clip from a lead (available from your pet shop) in your hand when you call your dog but not the lead itself. Otherwise, your dog may think it's time for a walk!

You are only allowed to give one command; if your dog does not respond then you are not allowed to repeat the command. You are not allowed to have any food or toys on show. When you call your dog, you are not allowed to move in any direction but must remain stationary. When you call your dog you may not use any verbal praise until your dog is actually moving towards you. The clip that you are holding must be attached to your dog's collar within ten seconds, after which you can give any low-value rewards that you have concealed on you.

Each test is to be repeated twice and your dog should respond within the rules above before you go on to the next test.

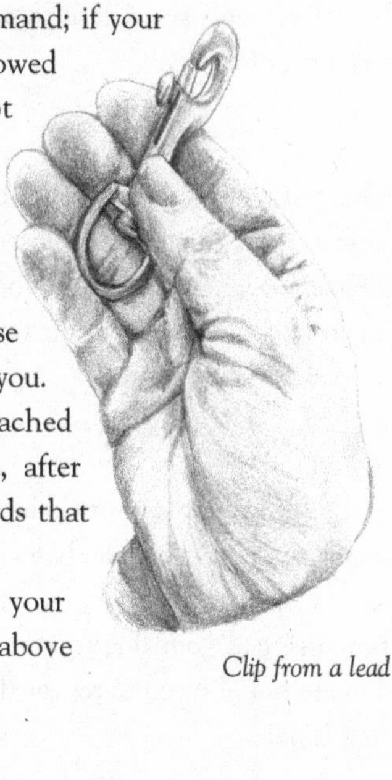

Clip from a lead

Test 1

With your dog in the same room but not paying any attention at all to you, give his name and your chosen command to come. He should come to you instantly and accept having the clip attached to his collar, after which he should be stroked, told how wonderful he is and maybe even given a small, low-value food treat or toy.

If he does not come instantly or you have to break one or more of the rules to get him to come to you and have the clip attached then you have failed the test!

Test 2

This is a repeat of test one but this time you must call your dog when he is out of your sight. You can either wait for your dog to wander out of the room you are in or leave the room yourself. Wait for a few minutes and then call your dog. Remember that you cannot give any verbal praise until your dog enters the room that you are in. Repeat this test twice and be honest with yourself as to whether your dog passes or fails under this strict set of rules.

Test 3

This test repeats test two but now your dog has to be out in the garden (as long as it is completely enclosed) while you remain in the house. Position yourself so you can see your dog but he cannot see you – peeking through a gap in the kitchen curtains will do. Call your dog using the same rules as for tests one and two.

Test 4

You are now going to introduce a controlled distraction. Assuming your dog is friendly to people, have a friend or relative walk into the room you are in and let your dog go and greet them. While the greeting is in progress, call your dog to you using your chosen command. Remember, you are not allowed to repeat the command if your dog does not obey the first time!

Test 5

Assuming your dog is friendly to other dogs, have a friend arrive in the room you are in with their dog on a lead. Allow your dog to go and say hello then call him back to you. The rules are the same as for the previous tests.

How did your dog fare? If it passed each one with flying colours then, and only then, can you think about training an off-lead recall outside your house. If you failed any of the tests, you must carefully retrain your dog to come when called in your home environment before commencing any training outside. It is a sad fact that many owners expect their dogs to return to them in the local park under all sorts of distractions when, in truth, they cannot get the dog to come when called in their own living room where there are no distractions! It is also very wrong to condemn a dog to a lifetime of being restricted on a lead when, by investing some time and effort, the recall exercise is so easy to achieve.

If your dog was one of the tens of thousands that fail one or more of these tests, don't give up. Try to think of a reason for your dog to want to come to you when you call him. Next you must think of the consequences of him refusing to come when called. Think of ways you can change the consequences to teach the behaviour you require. Providing the dog has had few opportunities to practise the bad behaviour, with a skilful trainer the dog can be trained to recall in a few minutes!

TRAINING THE INSTANT RECALL

With all the preparation and theory behind us, we can finally look at teaching a dog to return when called. I am going to divide this recall into three types. First, there's the training-class recall to be conducted by a training instructor in a class environment, hopefully outside. Second, there's the free-running recall, trained in the house to begin with and then progressing outside. Finally, there's is the chasing recall, to add to the basic recall for dogs that like to chase things they are not supposed to!

RECALL 1 - TRAINING CLASS

The first recall is the one that I use exclusively when teaching a class, because it very quickly establishes a pattern of behaviour in the dog's mind, making it very easy for him to learn what is required. I hate making my training complicated!

To teach your dog to come when called using the following technique you will need an assistant to help you. First, set up a chair in one corner of your training area. Alongside the chair have any raised surface such as a table or platform onto which you can put food treats. Now take your dog and sit on the chair. The instant you sit down, you should do four things in this order.

1. Talk to the dog in a reassuring way: 'good boy', 'clever girl' etc.
2. Stroke the dog
3. Smile
4. Only when the dog's tail starts to wag should you give the dog one small food treat from the table

After giving the treat you should wait for around three seconds (have your assistant count this for you) and then repeat the talk, stroke, smile and treat sequence. Wait for a further three seconds and then continue to repeat the procedure until ten food treats have been given. The main aim is to get the dog's tail to wag before giving the food treat. By pairing three secondary rewards (talk, stroke, smile) with a primary reward (food), it will probably enable you to just about dispense with the need to use food later in the programme. This means your dog will end up wanting to please you rather than just carrying out a behaviour for food. Don't confuse love with hunger!

As soon as the ten food treats have been given, you should stand up and walk away from the chair a distance of around 15 paces, taking your dog with you on the lead. It is important that when you stand up to walk away, *all rewards should stop*. That means you should not speak to, look at or touch the dog and you should also stop smiling. When you are standing 15 paces away stay there for around two minutes (this seems like an hour in practice). Then simply return to the chair and as soon as you sit down start the talk, stroke, smile, treat process all over again.

When ten pieces of food have been given you should stand up and walk away again, remaining there for two minutes before sitting down and repeating the talk, stroke, smile, ten treat process once more.

The third time you walk away (with some dogs it is the fourth), you should notice something happen. When you are standing and ignoring the dog, it should make an attempt to draw your attention to where it wants to go – back to the chair. Some dogs will merely look in the direction of the chair, some will whine, some will pull, some will look at the chair and then up at their owners. As soon as you see that happen ask your assistant to take the lead while you immediately go and sit in the chair. As soon as you sit down call your dog to come to you in the most exciting and inviting way you can.

It helps if this is the first time the dog has ever heard this particular word of command. Your assistant should find, if you have read the dog correctly, that they can now let go of the lead and the dog should immediately run to you. Remember that when your dog arrives, you should begin the talk, touch, smile, treat process all over again.

The reason that you should be using a command that is new to the dog is that we are trying to teach a very specific meaning to a command, and if the old (failed) recall command is used the dog may well go back to its old behaviour of not coming!

A handler sitting on a chair, calling her dog

Repeat the 'walk away and hand your assistant the lead' routine twice more and then end the session. When you finish the training session you should simply get up from the chair and walk away, taking the dog with you and leaving any food treats behind.

Some important points to note are:

- You should not ask the dog to sit. We are only teaching one behaviour – the recall. If the dog sits automatically then that is fine.
- After you have sat down you should not lift your bottom off the chair until your dog has returned to you. This prevents you trying to intercept the dog with a head-on tackle as it approaches.
- When your dog reaches you, make sure that you do not hold on to your dog at all, other than holding the extreme end of the lead. Holding on to the dog's collar is not permissible. You have only your voice, facial expression, hands to stroke the dog and a food treat to keep your dog with you. That is what I want you to work on.
- If the dog wanders away from you after is has arrived then your assistant should pick up the lead and restrain the dog or even guide it back to you.
- If your dog does not return to you within two seconds of you calling him then ask your assistant to show your dog how to obey the command by gently leading it to you. This procedure is referred to as guided learning and is designed to teach your dog to consistently make the correct choice when you call him. In other words, he cannot really get this wrong.

Be cautious about using food treats that are too valuable to the dog at this time. You will know if they are too valuable because when you try to stroke your dog, it will try and avoid your hand, almost as if it is irritating the dog in its quest to be given the food treat!

Your assistant is temporarily playing the part of a dog trainer and as such they are responsible for virtually guaranteeing your dog's response to your recall command.

By preparing the environment and setting yourself up for success, your dog's first introduction to your new recall command should result in the dog wanting to learn this new command very rapidly. But we now need to go further.

To extend the dog's perception of this new command we need to advance quite quickly but still only one step at a time. So for the next session sit on the chair and start using the talk, stroke, smile, treat routine as before but now, just as you are about to give treat number ten, ask your assistant to use the lead to take the dog away from you (rather than you walking away and handing the lead to your assistant). Ask them to walk your dog away for around 30 paces before calling your dog. You may actually find it difficult to get the dog 30 paces away because of its desire to get back for the rewards, in which case ask your assistant to just go as far as they can.

Now let us change your own behaviour a bit more. This time ask your assistant to take your dog away as before, only this time when you call your dog have a second lead in your hand. Put one arm behind your back as you call your dog. When your dog arrives in front, you should still repeat the talk, stroke, smile, treat routine but should then attach the dog's lead with one hand. Remember that one hand should remain behind your back all the time. Do you find this difficult? What would make this exercise easier for you? Try to work out a solution to the problem. I will give you mine at the end of this chapter.

Now let's strengthen the recall even more. When your assistant takes the dog away from you on its lead, ask another owner to position themselves with their dog between you and your dog. Now call your dog so that it now has to pass the other dog on its way back to you. If your dog is tempted by the presence of the other dog and prefers to say hello to it in preference to returning to you when called, quickly ask your assistant to pick up its lead, which is still attached to its collar.

Now ask the other dog's owner to let go of their dog's lead and call this dog to you while you are sat on the chair. Usually the sight of another dog being spoken to, stroked and given food treats is enough to turn any dog green with envy. Make sure that when you do this the 'visiting' dog is given some really good food treats and plenty of them. Your assistant's job is merely to hold on to the disobedient dog's lead and let it observe and learn from the situation that has developed in front of it.

Wait for at least two minutes before repeating the training. I would bet that when you repeat the lesson your dog ignores the other dog on its way back to you. When your dog arrives back in front of you then you should genuinely surprise it with the rewards that it gets. How about suddenly producing a whole roast chicken (bones removed) when the dog successfully carries out the recall? Each time the dog returns when called, it can now be given any number of rewards in any combination – all you need to do is keep your dog guessing!

When you are confident that your dog will obey your command to come you can dispense with the services of your assistant and finally remove the chair by sitting on the ground when you call your dog.

RECALL 2 - FREE RUNNING

For this recall to work you need to have the results of the five tests on pages 131-132 as we do not need to start from square one with each and every dog.

If your dog failed test one, do the following. Mix up your dog's food in the morning and put it into ten (20 would be better) containers and leave them dotted around your house. At any time, and without your dog's prior knowledge, pick up a container and call your dog to you. When he gets to you then talk, stroke, smile and treat as for the previous recall. If he does not come immediately (you set the rules) tease him with the food in the container but do not give him any – put the container away and wait for at least two minutes before trying again. Give your dog as many chances each day as it takes for him to learn to come when you call him. If you find that you can get six or seven recalls really easily but the last three or four are not good at all, you are feeding him too much each day! Repeat this for one week and then move on to stage two, which is also for dogs that failed test two.

Mix up his food as before and split it into your ten or 20 containers. Now recall him only the number of times each day that you have containers of food. If he satisfies your requirements for the recall then talk, stroke, smile and treat using that one portion of food. If he does not satisfy your recall requirements then use a very harsh facial expression, turn away from him in disgust and let him see you throw that container of food into your rubbish bin. That container is now gone forever and he now only has the remaining containers with which to work out Thorndyke's Law of Effect! Remember that this is the only food available each day – there is to be no other food. In the unlikely event that your dog goes for two days without getting any food then return to stage one of this programme!

After a few days move on to stage three, which is also for dogs that failed test three in the previous chapter.

For this stage, have eight containers of his normal food and two with something extra special inside. Now practise your recall in other areas of your house and garden, preferably when he is out of sight. For a successful recall, keep him guessing as to whether he will get a container of his usual food or an extra-special one. The whole of your attitude – that is the talk, stroke and smile – should almost allow him to predict that this is the special bonus container before it is opened. Of course if he fails a recall, then which container do you think he should be shown being thrown away? I would briefly show and tease him with it first while I was explaining that as he did not come immediately I called him I thought he must not want this container! Up to now we know that he must have a basic understanding of the command to come otherwise he would not have passed the first three tests, so we can use the consequence of *losing* a valuable reward if he chooses not to come when called.

Now move on to stage four, which is also for dogs that failed test four and/or five. Have a friend arrive, making sure your dog has a light length of cord attached to his collar beforehand. When your friend arrives allow your dog to run up and greet them and then, when the initial excitement has subsided, call your dog to you. If he comes straight away, keep him guessing as to how much of his daily food allowance he is going to get. It might be one tenth, one half, three quarters or all of it in one go. It might also be his normal food or a whole roast chicken! If he decides not to come when called, ask your friend to fasten the end of the cord to anything suitable and come and join you for a whole roast chicken, right in front of your dog's eyes.

Repeat this procedure if you failed test five from the previous chapter with other dogs that visit your house and garden.

Now that your dog has passed all five tests you can progress to the last part of your recall training.

All we now have to do is to transfer the two recalls that I have just described to six different environments outside and we are done. But what if the environment is more exciting than the food on offer? Then we have to think not only about the rewards we are going to use when the dog is successful, but also the penalties that he is going to incur if he makes the wrong choice and fails to return as soon as he is called.

To do this you need an assistant and a safe area to go to. You must drive at least one hour from where you live to a place your dog has never been before. Take your dog out of the car on a leash and walk for about ten minutes. Then attach a long light line to your dog's collar and remove the leash. Let go of the line and let your dog explore the area for around ten minutes, and have your assistant stay fairly close to your dog. Then walk back to your car. When you get to it, call your dog once. Make sure your dog has heard you (which is why your assistant should be reasonably close to your dog – if they heard you then you can assume your dog has also heard you calling).

If your dog returns to you immediately then reward it with lots of praise and perhaps a game with a toy or a tasty morsel of food. Now put your dog in the car, go for a short drive that takes you back to this area and repeat the training at least twice.

If your dog chooses not to return when you call, have your assistant pick up the end of the line and quickly fasten it to the nearest tree, fence post etc. Your assistant should do this without saying a word or showing any emotions. Now get into your car and drive out of sight.

It is vital that your dog is restrained by the line so he now has a real dilemma. Not coming when called has resulted in him being trapped and unable to escape in this unfamiliar area with no access to food, water or shelter. Worse than that he now sees his owner getting into the car and driving away!

Your assistant is on hand to monitor the situation in your absence. Stay in contact via a cell phone but do not return in the car until your assistant asks you to, normally within five minutes. Your assistant is looking for your dog showing signs of stress, usually indicated by barking, whining or repeatedly pulling in the direction in which he has seen the car disappear with you in it. If the dog starts showing signs of distress then you should return immediately. Likewise, if your dog becomes entangled in the line and panics, this should bring about your immediate return.

When you reappear, get your assistant to release your dog from his restraint by unfastening the line and allowing your dog to return to you. When your dog gets to you, reward him with lots of praise, put him in the car, go for a short drive that takes you back to this area and repeat one final time. Your dog does not need food or a game with a toy for this recall – you are the ultimate reward when the dog is under stress. You are his ride home, so if your dog has a good relationship with you this acts as both a reward for the correct behaviour and a penalty for the wrong behaviour.

RECALL 3 - CHASING

If you have a really good recall most of the time but just have problems when your dog begins to chase something, add this chasing recall to the basic exercise. As with all training, you will have to start in such a way that your dog quickly learns a basic behaviour and then has multiple opportunities to practise it.

Assuming your dog will chase after a toy (if not, read the section on how to get your dog to play, page 111), you need to understand the concept of category A and category B toys. If you gathered up ten different toys, teased your dog with them and then threw them all at once, which one would your dog choose to play with? If you threw all ten toys three times, is your dog's selection the same every time? In other words, is there one toy he prefers to all the others? This is known as an A-category toy. Now remove that toy and throw the nine remaining toys a further three times. Is there any one your dog shows a preference for? If there is, this is also known as an A-category toy. When these highly prized toys have been removed, are there any left that your dog simply will not play with? If there are, these toys are also removed. What is left are known as B-category toys. These are ones the dog will play with but not if the really good ones are available.

You will now need an assistant to help you and a large area, preferably with no distractions. Have an A-category toy concealed behind your back and with your dog off-lead and close to you, tease him with a B-category toy. Have your assistant positioned around 50 yards away and facing you. Throw your toy towards your assistant and let your dog chase it. When your dog is around half way to the toy, call him back using your recall command. If your dog does not return immediately on hearing your command, have your assistant either stand on the toy or pick it up. This makes it unavailable for your dog, who should now get to your assistant and then look puzzled as to why he cannot get the toy.

As soon as your dog looks in your direction (don't worry – he will eventually), call him as you show him the A-category toy you had concealed and then throw it in the opposite direction from where your assistant is. Chase after the toy yourself and make sure you manage to just pick it up before he gets to it. Tease him with it but do not let him have it. Repeat the exercise by recovering the B-toy from your assistant and starting all over again. Usually, within three or four throws your dog should break off his chase of the B-toy and return to chase the A-toy. When he returns immediately you call him, let him overtake you and get the A-toy for himself. Make this part of the game really exciting.

You should find that in a very short time your dog will anticipate the recall. When this happens and he slows down and turns without your command, switch to two identical A-toys. Now keep your dog guessing as to how the game will be played. Around 60 per cent of the time your dog should be allowed to get the first toy that has been thrown. Of the remaining 40 per cent you will sometimes need to call him back from the first toy and let him get the second one. Sometimes you will also call him back from the second toy as well and send him back for the first one. Sometimes let your dog get the second toy and also send him back to get the first one thrown. Sometimes surprise him with a whole roast chicken (bones removed) for returning when called. The more you practise this chasing recall, the luckier you will get when your dog decides to chase something he is not supposed to!

If you cannot get him back from a thrown toy, you are unlikely to be able to get him back when he is chasing another dog, bicycle etc. You cannot teach him to come back by taking him out and letting him chase other dogs or livestock! But you can teach him the essentials of the behaviour that you want on toys.

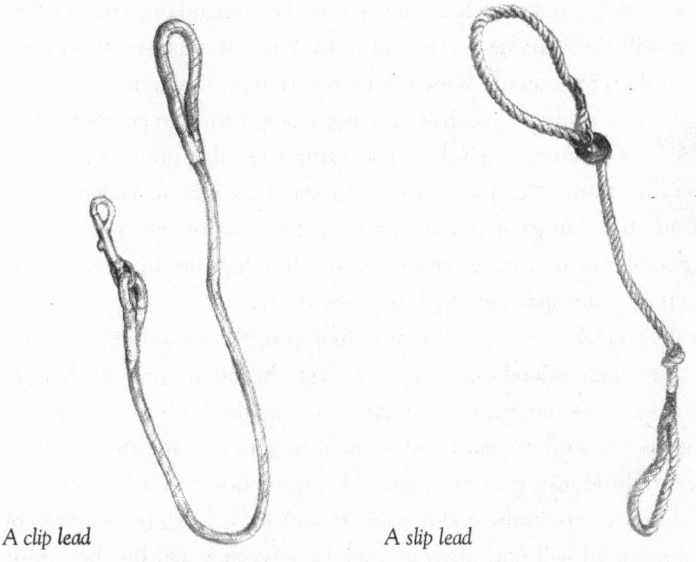

A clip lead *A slip lead*

In case you were wondering what my solution would have been to the problem I posed earlier on page 137, it would have been to make use of a slip lead rather than a regular walking lead.

22

The Running Wait

This is a very simple exercise to teach your dog. The idea is that when your dog is running free and you give a command or signal for it to stop, it will do so immediately and hold that stationary position for a short while. This exercise is used in preparation for stay training and has a multitude of other uses such as 'freezing' a dog at the exit contact points in agility or stopping a gundog or working trials dog prior to giving it further directions. It can also be used in search and rescue exercises and also water tests but its main use is probably for ensuring the safety of your dog. Sometimes it is easier and safer to tell a dog running free to stay where it is rather than getting it to come to you.

Ideally you will need an assistant to help you, plus something that your dog wants, such as food treats or a toy. Begin by having your dog held at a fixed distance – ten feet is quite sufficient – on the leash in front of you. Taking your reward in your hand, show it to your dog and then with an underarm throw, toss it to your dog. The reward should arc up into the air to land somewhere in the middle of your dog's back. With the majority of dogs the reward will not touch its back because they will lift their front feet off the ground to try and catch it. The idea is to make your dog think the reward is going to land behind him, so make sure you do not throw it so that your dog has to move forwards to get it. Also make sure your throw

Teaching your dog the running wait

is deliberate and exaggerated, with your hand starting and ending the movement from a vertical position.

Repeat this exact sequence six times to put a pattern in your dog's head. The pattern we are trying to establish is 'stand back, he is going to throw it, stand back, he is going to throw it, stand back, he is going to throw it' etc. When this is in place, move on to step two.

The only difference is that now you ask your assistant to slowly walk towards you with your dog still on the leash. You are also going to walk slowly backwards to maintain the same ten-foot distance between you and your dog. After walking backwards for a few steps, lower your hand and throw the reward in exactly the same way as you did in the first step. Repeat six times. This adds a new dimension to the exercise, where the dog is moving towards you under control, so he continues to learn that the same rules apply – 'stand back, he is going to throw it.'

The next step is to have your assistant holding your dog on the leash as before but now you encourage your dog to come towards you as your assistant drops the leash to the floor. When your dog is moving towards you and is approximately halfway to where you are standing, drop your hand and then throw the reward in exactly the same way you have done 12 times previously. The only difference is that you are not going to let go of the reward! I repeat, *Do not let go of the reward!*

Your arm should now be in a vertical position with the food treat or toy facing you and obscured from your dog's view. Your dog should have stopped in his tracks, expecting the reward to have been thrown as he does not see it in your hand any more. He may well glance around or even turn around expecting the reward to land, but he should then look at you. What he should see is a big smiling face and the reward still in your hand, now turned so he can see it is about to be thrown. Lean forwards, wait for just a second and then throw the reward. Now repeat six times, stopping your dog halfway four times before throwing the reward and twice throwing the reward without getting your dog to stop. At this stage we are allowing the dog to make its own decision as to the position it takes up. Most will stand but some will sit or even lie down. At this stage it is unimportant.

The next step is to increase the distance that your dog is held away from you and to make the distance that your dog stops from you variable – sometimes five feet away, sometimes ten feet. This distance is restricted only by how far you can throw your reward. To achieve really large distances you can use your assistant in a different way. Start by allowing your dog free range at a distance away from you. Have your assistant positioned around 50 yards away from you, between you and your dog. They should have a concealed reward in their hand that the dog has not seen. Now call your dog towards you to run past your assistant. When they have passed your assistant and this person is outside your dog's field of vision, give your signal to stop. When your dog stops, your assistant should wait a few seconds before throwing the toy to land behind or beside your dog. Your dog should have no problems hearing the toy land as he will be expecting it to arrive in this position because of the pattern you have built in his mind. If your timing is correct, your dog should be oblivious of your assistant's involvement and think you threw the reward that distance.

The last step is to change the stop behaviour from a signal, which only works if the dog is looking at you, to a command or whistle. To do this, select a word of command (or a whistle) and give it very quietly about half a second before giving your signal. The command 'wait' is the one most commonly used. Each time you repeat this exercise you will need to slightly emphasise your command or whistle prior to slowly reducing the arm signal.

Thus over six or so training sessions your command or whistle becomes a reliable indicator to your dog that your arm is about to move and the reward be thrown. Once you have the stop behaviour on command, you can then adapt it to suit any circumstance in training. If you want to get your dog to stop in a particular position (called 'drop on recall' in the USA), first teach the dog a reliable sit or down command or signal, then use it after the dog has stopped. If you then only reward your dog for adopting the desired position, your dog will anticipate the position and automatically take it up when you ask him to stop.

This exercise is foolproof if you understand all the basic concepts of training a dog. But a few problems may arise.

If the dog does not stop but continues to the trainer, the only reasons this could occur are because the reward has been too small for the dog to see – this very commonly happens with small breeds and minute food treats! – or the reward is too large, so the dog clearly sees it has not been thrown and remains in the trainer's hand. Try making the reward more visible, maybe by throwing a small container of food if your dog is having trouble seeing it, or try decreasing the size of the reward so it can be concealed more easily.

The only other problem is that sometimes the relationship between owner and dog is so good that the dog is more interested in getting to his owner than he is in the food or toy reward. If this happens, simply reverse the roles of the assistant and trainer so the owner is now holding the dog and the assistant (who should be known to the dog) is doing the throwing. Once the dog has learned the exercise then the roles can revert to the owner being the one who gets the dog to stop.

23

Stay

This is a useful exercise for all dogs as it teaches restraint and can also be used to get a dog to relax. It is also one of the most useful social exercises when visiting friends' houses or when friends visit you. An important point here is that whenever a dog is left in a stay position outside a shop or anywhere near a public highway, no matter how well-trained it is, the lead should be fastened to any convenient point to prevent the dog from wandering away. You may well be able to guarantee your dog's trained response to a command, but you cannot anticipate the behaviour of any dog that may come along and possibly intimidate him into moving onto the road. Even obedience champions sometimes make mistakes!

Let's look at the concept first. The question you need to ask is: How long does my dog actually do a stay during a normal 24-hour period? For most dogs the answer would be around six hours when we go to bed at night! So getting your dog to lie down and stay for 20 minutes or so cannot be much of a problem, can it?

Rest is a natural reward so one of the secrets of the code is to start teaching your dog how to stay by picking times when he is tired! It is also much easier to teach a down stay then either a sit or stand, as when he is resting at night he does not do so in a sit or stand position. So the concept is that you start with a dog that is physically and mentally tired. If it is past his bedtime, and he has just been given a drink of water and a full meal, you will be almost guaranteed success whichever method you choose.

The only problem you could face is that when told to stay, he gets up to come towards you. We already have that covered by making sure that for the first week of stay training he has a cord or light line fastened to his collar, the other end of which is fastened to something solid. Now you can introduce the idea of the command 'stay' with every confidence that he will eventually lie down, relax and stay where he is.

I always train the stay as a relaxed down position first, which should make perfect sense as the code relies on making things so simple your dog should understand them. If you decide to start your stay training by using a sit position, you have just broken this code by putting your dog in a very difficult position.

Why? Because once he has been told to sit and stay, and you move a few feet away from him, what do you do if he lies down? You are now caught between a rock and a hard place because whatever you do is likely to cause confusion in your dog's mind. If you tell him he was wrong to relax and lie down, then getting him to stay for any length of time is going to be difficult when we train stays of up to 20 minutes. If, on the other hand, you do nothing and allow him to disobey a command to sit, this is actively teaching disobedience! Much better therefore to just teach him to relax and stay where he is as a first step. Then, when he is confident you are going to return to release him in a short time, you can teach the sit and stand stays.

After having watched thousands of trainers around the world working with dogs, I noticed that the dogs who always carried out the stay exercise perfectly were the ones who were the most relaxed. Dogs left in a stay position under threat of death if they move are usually the ones who fidget, move and break the position they were left in.

The natural reward of rest is the preferred way in training but food can also be used as a reward. If this is going to be attempted then again the dog must be tethered in such a way that it cannot come towards you. Now place ten very small food treats on the floor about two feet in front of your dog. Sit on the floor within arm's length of your dog and point out the food treats. Any movement your dog makes towards the food – extending a paw, pulling against the restraint etc. – should result in you maintaining a blank facial expression and basically ignoring your dog. Any time he makes a movement that causes the restraining lead or line to go slack should result in you quickly smiling, picking up a food treat and giving it to him. It just requires a bit of patience on your part to teach him that by staying where he is and relaxing, you will produce the food treat that he cannot reach.

As he starts to understand what gets him the rewards, you should notice that he becomes more patient and relaxed. So, providing he remains stationary in whatever position he chooses, you can start rewarding him at a more fixed interval, which is every five seconds (fixed interval reinforcement training). Within a couple of training sessions he should be relaxed and holding the position, expecting the food treats every five seconds, so now you can think about adding a command of 'stay' as you place your food treats on the floor. You can also extend the total length of time your dog stays by increasing the number of food treats on the floor.

You will probably notice that as he gains experience, he is more likely to take a lying down position. If not, you can now begin getting him to lie down by using one of the following six methods, four using guided learning, all using rewards. If you believe that using your hands to guide your dog physically into the down position is incorrect (most dogs I have met actually like being touched) then try one of the final two of the six methods.

Method 1

Place the thumb and forefinger of your left hand over and across the dog's shoulders, just behind his shoulder blades. Give the name and command and *gently* press down and sideways, rolling the dog down onto one flank. Immediately reward him without letting him get up. He must associate the praise and possible food reward with staying down, never for getting up. Be sure to make sure your finger and thumb are positioned correctly:

too far forwards and the dog will merely brace itself against the downward pressure; too far back and you will hurt your dog.

A submissive dog will be the easiest to train the down on command. If you have had any past problems physically controlling your dog, it is better not to use this method in case he sees it as confrontation. If you try this method and meet with any resistance, do not continue but switch to method three, four, five or six.

Method 2

Kneel on the floor alongside your dog. Place your left-hand palm down on the dog's shoulders. Pass your right hand behind the dog's front leg nearest to you and lightly grip the far front leg just above its paw. Move the right arm forwards and press down with the left hand. This will sweep the dog's front legs forwards, putting him into the down. Again, this method presupposes that your dog will not be worried or frightened or see it as confrontational. If you meet with any resistance when trying this the first time then switch to method three, four or five.

Method 3

Put a tasty morsel in your right hand and place it palm downwards on the floor in front of the dog. Gently place your left hand on the dog's shoulders. Encourage him by showing him the food for a few seconds then covering it up. When he puts his nose down to investigate, use your left hand to gently assist him to lie down by stroking him. As soon as the dog is down, lift your right hand and let the dog eat the food. I recommend this method for a very strong or difficult dog as it avoids confrontation between dog and handler.

Method 4

This simply involves you sitting on the floor with one knee bent to form an arch. If you put your hand holding a food treat under this arch towards your dog's nose, and then use it to lure your dog through your arched leg, you should find he lies down under your leg. Great for small dogs but almost impossible for large ones.

Down on the table

Method 5

Still no luck? Then try using a table or other raised platform. Have your dog tethered so it cannot jump off the platform, then hold out a food treat lower than its level so that your dog follows your movement and goes into the down position of its own accord. No touching is necessary.

Method 6

If all else fails and your dog resists being guided into the down position, try this one. Note down the times of day that your dog likes to lie down and take a nap. You are looking for a consistent time of day for this to work. At the time he usually likes to lie down and rest take him out for a walk for an hour. When you get home try to get him to play with a toy for as long as you can. Now feed him a full meal and wait for ten minutes before taking him out for some more gentle exercise for half an hour. Now, when it is nearly two hours after his usual rest time, after exercise and on a full stomach he should want to lie down. Method three or four should now work.

Once you have your dog lying down and tethered, all that remains is to increase the distance you move away from your dog when he is told to stay. To do this, still using food treats in front of him, simply tell him to 'stay' and walk away for around ten to 15 paces. If he moves, stand there and ignore him by turning your head away. As soon as he relaxes and takes up the down position, smile and return to pick up one of the food treats to reward him. He should very quickly learn that relaxing and staying where he is gets you to return and reward him.

The last bit of magic to add is to *pretend* to put food treats in front of him before telling him to stay and then walking away. If he truly believes that there are food treats just in front of him, because of the pattern that you have planted in his mind, he should now have no desire to get up and come to you. He should wait for you to return to pick up the food treats he thinks you have placed on the floor. When you return, have some food treats concealed in your hand to *pretend* to find on the floor just in front of him. Only consider releasing him from the tether in training once you are sure he has a full understanding of what is required.

PROBLEMS IN TRAINING A DOG TO STAY

We have eliminated most common stay problems by using the code to make things easy for your dog to understand, but things do not always go according to plan. One of the most common problems is that the dog starts to bark or whine when tethered and asked to stay. This is usually because the reward the trainer is using is far too high in value, which then creates frustration when the dog cannot get to it. If this happens, switch to a lower-value reward and make sure you do not offer a reward if the dog is barking or whining. This means turning away and not looking at, touching or speaking to your dog when this is happening.

The only other problem is that sometimes the dog is so over-bonded to its owner that it becomes very stressed when the two are separated. In this case the section on separation anxiety should help.

If you want to add a sit position to the stay your dog has learned in the lying down position, all you need to do is teach your dog food refusal (covered in the puppy section on page 39) and then get your dog to sit. Place a food treat between his front feet and tell him to 'leave'. When you return, simply pick up the food treat and give it to him.

Another way of teaching your dog to sit and stay is tethering it in the early stages and using thrown food treats for him to catch. Get the throw right and your dog will maintain and hold the sit position. Throw the food treats at a fixed interval to start with and then, when your dog has the idea of what is required, you can switch to a more random time interval. Using this method, which is very similar to the running wait, you can get across the concept of being rewarded while you are still a short distance away. Most other methods of teaching a stay command result in the dog only being rewarded when the trainer goes back to it. It is not surprising that lots of dogs then learn to change or break the position they were left in just to get the trainer to return to them!

So having a dog that catches thrown food and toys is a distinct advantage when training it to carry out commands at a short distance from you, but what if your dog does not know how to catch? Let's teach him.

24

Catch

Start by using food treats that will be clearly visible to him as they are thrown. You will also need the help of a friend who is going to hold on to your dog's leash. Stand around five feet from your dog and have your assistant keep your dog at this fixed distance. Now throw a food treat underarm, aiming between your dog's eyes. Make the throw really deliberate and almost exaggerated. If your dog has no concept of catching then the treats will be bouncing off his nose and the top of his head and landing on the floor. Your assistant should allow him to pick them up and eat them as they land. Repeat your throw around 20 times and then make a subtle change.

Next when you throw the treats, your assistant should not allow your dog to pick them up from the floor but do so himself. Now your dog cannot get the food that is being thrown. This should result in him making some feeble attempts to catch them; at least he should be opening its mouth as you throw. Watch what happens to each food treat. If they hit your dog on the nose and bounce forwards, move a foot or two further away and try again. If the food treats hit the top of his nose and then bounce over his head behind him, move a foot or two closer and repeat. The idea is to time the arrival of the food treat to coincide with the exact moment your dog's mouth happens to be open. The ones he catches he gets to eat but from now on the ones he misses he does not get to eat.

If you are still having problems then try standing right in front of your dog and holding a food treat just and inch or two above his nose. Repeat as before but instead of throwing the food treats, you simply drop them, timing your release to coincide with your dog's mouth being open. When the dog is successfully catching the treats, you can start to increase the distance you move away from him.

25

Bark on Command

This exercise shows how you can take existing behaviours such as barking and put them under your control by teaching a command. This is a simple exercise to train, particularly if you have a dog that tends to be a bit noisy when he gets excited, when people come to the door, for example or when the lead is produced for a walk. If you know there is already a cue or signal that turns on your dog's bark then you can use it to good effect to transfer the environmental cue to a verbal command or signal.

Let's assume your dog barks when someone knocks at your front door. All you need to do is stand by the door with your dog and, half a second before you knock on it, give your dog the command to bark. Then knock on the door as you already know that this produces a barking response. Keep on repeating your command half a second before the knock and in a short space of time your dog should start to bark when you give your command without you needing to knock on the door. Simply reward your dog every time he responds to your command to bark and within a few sessions you should be able to start him barking at will. If your dog does not naturally bark when someone is at the door or when he gets excited, try the next method.

First, fasten the dog on a collar and lead, tying the end of the lead around a fence post or any convenient point. Stand immediately in front of and facing him. Tease him with a favourite toy or food and then start walking slowly backwards, calling him by name and trying to excite him with the reward. As soon as he makes any noise at all, even a whimper, quickly return and give the reward. Continue for a few sessions and then progressively alter the production of the reward so that he only gets it for barking and not for whining. At first a single bark will do, at which point you can introduce your command of 'speak' as you back away. When you have achieved a reasonable level of consistency you can reward for every second bark, then every third bark, until the dog barks continually on your command.

Now that you have your dog's bark under your control, it is time to think about teaching him the command to stop barking. How do you do that? Just as easily as you teach him to bark on command. For example, you can record the sound of someone knocking at the front door and let him bark three times. Then take your dog to the front door and open it to show there was no one there. Half a second before you open the door give your stop barking command (such as 'quiet!'). As you open the door and he sees there is no one there, the barking should stop immediately. Remember to reward him when he is quiet.

Now, for a week or so, you should tell him to bark when you know someone is about to knock at the door and reward him for barking. Then give your 'quiet' command just before you open the door to let him see the visitor. It is important to pair the recording with the actual sound as even the best recording will not exactly reproduce the sound of a visitor knocking at your door. Also several times each day play the recording; as he barks give your quiet command and reward him, and you should have better control over when and for how long he barks.

If you used the tether and frustration method to teach your dog to bark, command him to bark and try to anticipate when he will cease. Listen carefully to his pattern of barking and the number of barks before he stops naturally when you stop exciting him. When you anticipate he is going to finish barking, softly give your quiet command and immediately reward him verbally. Make sure that the barking has ceased for a few seconds before giving any higher rewards. Remember that your quiet command is designed to turn off the excitement.

26
Go to Bed and Stay

Now we come to a really interesting exercise that's great for teaching a dog good social behaviour, and one to which we can add our previously trained stay command. It can be used when visitors arrive at the house and you do not want your dog to bother them, when you are eating and do not want your dog to hang around the table, or generally when you do not want your dog under your feet. For this exercise we will assume your dog regularly uses a bed or blanket on which to rest and relax. If his idea of a bed is your couch then it makes the whole concept of lying in a plastic dog bed or new blanket somewhat more difficult.

As with all training or behaviour there is more than one way of achieving the result we are looking for. Let's start by looking at all the ways the exercise could be trained, in no particular order.

We could do it (though this definitely not recommended) by getting very cross and telling the dog to go and lie in its bed. Anywhere it goes other than its bed only means the owner will continue harassing it. When the dog eventually goes to its bed, the owner leaves it alone. This is a form of aversion training that removes the owner's bad temper when the dog carries out their wish and seeks the sanctuary of its bed. The big problem with this is that it often builds up an association between the bed and punishment. Ultimately this can lead to avoidance behaviours around the dog's bed or even the dog starting to throw out defensive challenges to anyone who goes near it when it's in this bed.

Another way is to 'condition' the dog to expect a reward such as food on a specific sound such as clicker, and then when it makes any movement in the direction of its bed, it hears the trainer's clicker and is rewarded with food. This is a slow but effective method of teaching the behaviour of going to the bed, but it is not good for getting the dog to *stay* in its bed. This type of training, technically known as 'successive approximations towards an end goal', relies on the dog being creative and offering behaviours, rather than holding the same behaviour for 20 minutes.

A third way of training the dog to go and lie in its bed is guided learning. It simply involves having the dog on a leash; on command, the dog is taken to its bed and, using one of the procedures for getting a dog to lie down, shown how to carry out the command. One advantage of using this system is that the dog cannot get it wrong. The downside is that people these days prefer to attempt only procedures that allow the dog to make up its own mind.

We could also try reverse chaining the behaviour, starting off with the dog in its bed and rewarding it when the command is given. The idea is to show the dog the finished picture of what the command 'bed' actually means. After a few repetitions it should start to associate the command with the action of lying in its bed and getting a reward. Now all that is required is for the trainer to slowly move the dog, step by step, away from its bed and at each step of the way rewarding the correct final behaviour.

It is also possible to train the dog to touch a 'target' such as a small card or piece of material. This is done by getting the dog to use either its paw or its nose to touch the target. Start out with a reward in your hand and clench your fist, holding it in front of your dog's nose or front paws. If the reward is high enough in value your dog should try to get it either by touching your hand with its paw or nose. Once this pattern has been established, it is simple to hold a 'target' in the hand that is also concealing the food and transfer the touching behaviour onto the target. Then you place the target further and further from your body, slowly teaching your dog that touching it gets the reward. Finally, the target is placed in the dog's bed and he is sent to touch it, then the running wait and stay are introduced to get the finished behaviour.

You want to know the fastest way? Providing you do not have any food-aggression problems with your dog, simply have a small box of large food treats in the location from where you send your dog to its bed.

Now simply take one of these large food treats and give it to your dog

A box of dog biscuits by the door

using the command 'bed'. Because the food treat is large, your dog will not be able to eat it standing up so it will have to take it somewhere to lie down and eat it. The chances are he will choose a resting area such as his bed! If he chooses anywhere else, go up to where he has taken it with a smile on your face and remove the food treat, pretending that you are going to eat it yourself. Now hand it back to him and repeat the 'bed' command. Very quickly he should take to his bed and when he does so simply smile, tell him 'good boy' and leave him to eat it.

Whichever way you train your dog to go and lie in his bed, it is useful to regularly place a food treat in his bed, thereby strengthening his desire to be sent there.

By reading these last two chapters you should realise that training your dog is more about understanding it on a more basic level, and that there is no such thing as the 'correct' way to train. Training is dependent on the breed and individual type of dog and on the temperament and emotions of the person doing the training. It is also about having knowledge of many different ways of training what appears to be the same basic exercise. It is also knowing that if you have a dog that is willing to learn but is not picking up the associations you want, there is no point sticking with that method. Knowing when to abandon something that is not working and having the knowledge to try something else will bring you closer to understanding the code.

Section 4
Rescue Dogs

'Time stays long enough for those who use it.'
– LEONARDO DA VINCI

27

The Rescue Dog: A Special Case

With overbreeding on a scale much larger than ever before and a huge number of puppies being advertised for sale, a greater burden is being put on dog rescue groups. Sometimes these are bursting at the seams with the number of dogs they are asked to find homes for. So if you don't want to encourage breeders bringing yet more puppies into a world where there are not enough permanent homes for them, it makes sense to find room in your heart for one of the many companion dogs at your local rescue. But before you decide, let's consider the advantages and disadvantages of taking on a rescue dog.

First of all, some of the disadvantages. At first glance getting a dog from a shelter may not seem like a very bright idea – these dogs are secondhand and already come from a failed relationship.

Your rescue dog may well have been given up for being difficult to manage, but most reputable dog re-homing centres carry out behaviour tests to ensure any problem behaviour is only very minor and usually easily corrected. Some notable rescue centres have members of staff dedicated to working with dogs with minor behavioural problems so that these are corrected before being offered for adoption.

You will also probably be getting a dog that is a little older and certainly past the puppy stage, which means some early socialisation skills may have been missed by the previous owner. With a little help from the organisation you get your new dog from this should not present a major problem.

You also have to remember that every dog in a rescue centre, for whatever reason, has had the experience of seeing the owner it was bonded to walk away and never return. Again, a small amount of care, love and understanding, your new dog should quickly gain the confidence it needs from knowing you will always return.

Now for some of the advantages.

A shelter dog is inexpensive and represents very good value for money. You should get a dog that has been health-checked, behaviour-tested – perhaps spayed or neutered – and matched to you, your family and your lifestyle – something many breeders simply do not have the experience to do when selling puppies.

What you see is what you get. If your new dog is around a year old then it will not grow much bigger and most of its behaviour patterns – such as housetraining – are already set. Although your first few weeks with your new dog will require some dedication on your part, some people want an older dog because they don't want the trouble of housetraining or going through the basic education processes, such as teething, isolation due to vaccination programmes, and chewing. These are people who often lead busy lives and cannot devote enough time to educating a puppy.

But the biggest advantage of getting a dog from a rescue is that not only will you be getting a dog that will want to live with you for the rest of its life, but you will also be helping to give a loving home to a previously unwanted and discarded companion. As a bonus you will also be helping your chosen rescue group to stamp out overbreeding by refusing to buy a puppy from a breeder.

If you think in any way that a rescue dog cannot be every bit as good as a puppy purchased from a breeder, take a look at some of the great hearing dogs, police dogs, military dogs, agility dogs, obedience dogs, working trials dogs, carriage dogs and so on that have been obtained from rescue organisations. There are many organisations such as Dogs for the Deaf in Oregon, USA who get *all* the dogs in their training programmes from shelters.

To understand more about rescue dogs, let's start by looking at the dogs that find themselves in a kennel looking for a new owner. There are two basic types.

The first type are dogs that are found as strays and handed in to the dog warden or animal control officer. These dogs will have no history of previous ownership and usually have not simply been wandering the streets for months but, more than likely, have been put out by irresponsible owners and picked up within a few hours of being abandoned.

The second type are hand-ins. These dogs are handed in to the rescue group by their previous owner, who is asked to fill in a questionnaire giving the basic details of the dog's background. Because there is more information on these dogs, it is easier for the rescue group to match them to suitable homes.

On arrival at the kennels, it is normal practice for the dogs to be placed in an isolation area pending a full veterinary check. It is also normal for there to be a full behavioural assessment prior to the dog being offered up for adoption. For dogs picked up as strays there is also a seven-day period during which the original owner can contact the rescue centre and reclaim their dog.

Once a dog is placed in a kennel for the general public to view, the sometimes long wait for the dog to find a suitable owner then begins, only ending when someone like you shows up looking for a companion.

With the trend towards owning a purebred pedigree animal increasing, you are more likely these days to find a recognisable breed in a rescue kennel than ever before. So don't be surprised if you see lots of purebred and sometimes exotic breeds being offered for adoption.

With a large number of rescue organisations and thousands of dogs looking for new homes – and believe me there are many great dogs sitting in rescue centres just waiting to be discovered – you are certain to find a dog of your dreams if you are prepared to look around. You should not expect to go to your local rescue and immediately find a dog that is suitable for you and your lifestyle.

Now we need to know what to look for when choosing a dog.

Well, you will already have had a family discussion on the type of dog that you want. Because spaying campaigns are rapidly removing the good old mongrel from the genetic pool in the UK, it is more likely you will see mainly recognisable breeds. Remember that dog breeds are often broken down into six or seven different types, depending on their original purposes so you may not get a purebred but one that has certain breed characteristics. The staff at the shelter should be able to guide you through the different types.

Next you should be given an extensive questionnaire from the shelter to find out what type of home you are offering one of their dogs. It is in the shelter's best interests to ensure that if you take one of their dogs it has a home for the rest of its life. Be wary of shelters that do not ask a lot of questions!

When you actually get to see the dogs, make sure that you pick one based on the behavioural characteristic that you like. Don't be fooled by how the dogs behave in their kennels – any dog you have taken a liking to must be taken out for a walk so you can get to see more of its normal behaviour. Any dog kept in a kennel, especially for more than five weeks, will have had its behaviour modified by its environment and by the behaviour of other dogs. Sometimes this behaviour, while it may seem unacceptable in the kennel, immediately changes when the dog is in a normal house and family situation.

Take housetraining, for instance. Perhaps in its previous home the dog was perfectly house-trained. In a kennel environment the dog cannot ask to be let out into the garden when it needs to go to the toilet, and even if it did there is no one around much of the time to listen to the dog anyway. So it learns, against its will, to go to the toilet where it lives in the kennel. So when you see a pile of fresh dog mess in the kennel it would be easy to imagine that this dog is not house-trained, yet as soon as they settle in to a new household their former housetraining ability returns.

28

How to Choose your Rescue Dog

A great deal of information may be obtained about an individual dog just by observing its behaviour within a kennel and its interactions with other dogs. It is more than possible to get an indication of a rescue dog's behaviour and trainability by carrying out some simple but carefully designed tests to highlight particularly strong characteristics. In 1990, I devised a series of tests to assess the behaviour of dogs in a kennel. They were created for organisations that regularly take dogs from shelters into their training programmes, and they have been adopted by the Universities Federation for Animal Welfare (UFAW) in the US in encouraging rescue centres to carry out behavioural assessments.

When a dog is sought from a rescue shelter with the sole purpose of using it in a service training programme, there are several traits that would be considered desirable or undesirable. If asked to list the undesirable characteristics that would make a dog unsuitable for a training programme, most organisations would come up with something like this:

1. Aggression towards people
2. Aggression towards other dogs
3. Too independent in nature
4. Over-dependent to the point of obsessively bonding to a particular person

5. Difficult to train, lack of concentration or motivation
6. Overprotective of owner.

A list of desirable characteristics would probably appear as follows:

1. Able to build a strong but not obsessive bond with a new owner or handler
2. Submissive enough to be led and directed by the new owner
3. Easily trained
4. Sensitive to both touch and voice
5. Easily motivated.

These tests can take place in the dog's kennel or in a communal run with or without other dogs present. Sometimes it is advisable to re-test by changing the environment and the other dogs present to obtain a more accurate assessment.

Test 1

Make the initial approach, which will bring you close to, and in contact with, the wire mesh. Do not make eye contact, speak or gesture, and observe how long it takes for the subject to come up to you and try to initiate contact. Also observe how active or passive the attempted contact is. Does the dog whine, bark or paw at the wire in order to gain your attention? After you have been in position for several minutes, has the dog has made any attempt even to come up and investigate you? Does the dog appear to really want to say hi but keeps looking at you, wagging its tail and then looking at the door?

This test highlights dogs who are very independent of people and therefore it is difficult to build up a bond sufficient to establish a working relationship with. Remember that failure to seek contact can be affected by the length of time it has been in a kennel and the attitude of visitors as they walk past.

Just imagine that you are in the same kennel. If your coat is more than one colour, fairly long and wavy or curly, and you are small to medium in build, you are very visually attractive. When visitors arrive they always look at you and smile, which you interpret as an invitation for good social contact, so you always go up and say hi. Now imagine your coat is a single colour (black, for instance) and very short, you are medium to large in size, your tail curls up over your back and you have ears that stand erect. In short, you are visually unattractive. When visitors come they glance at you and move on fairly quickly, which eventually tells you that no one ever wants to say hi, so you learn to ignore people that walk past! So if you visit a rescue centre where visually unattractive dogs are in brightly painted kennels that have humourous quotations and stories written on the walls, it is to get visitors to spend time there smiling so the dog gets frequent invitations for social interaction!

The test also reveals those dogs that are capable of building a rapid, almost obsessive relationship if allowed to. If you observe extremes of attention-seeking behaviour such as barking, spinning or repetitive jumping, this may indicate that the dog has expressed these behaviours in its previous home and you can expect the behaviours to continue when you take this dog home.

As for the dog that keeps looking at you and then the door, maybe it just sees you as a key to the door and has no actual interest in you at all. This could be confirmed if you opened the door: the dog would just run straight past you and have no further interest in you at all!

Test 2

Now talk to the dog. Gently speak to it and note its interest. Work through a list of common commands and phrases to find out if it is familiar with any of them. Continue talking for several minutes and note how easy or difficult it is to keep the dog's attention. Don't stare at the dog while you are talking but just hold a conversation for a few minutes. Does the dog try to listen to you? Does it look at your face to try and get some indications as to what you are saying? If it is more interested in looking at your hands and pockets, then someone has probably food-trained it! Maybe it only sees you as a food container?

Dogs that come from environments where they have been an only dog and have learned lots of human emotional language are usually the easiest ones to give a home to. Dogs that have been raised with another dog may not be able to understand much in the way of human language, so you will have your work cut out to teach your new dog this language. The easiest dogs to work with are those that show an interest in being spoken to and are able to maintain concentration and attention for several minutes. If you cannot hold a dog's interest and attention for more than a few seconds by talking to it, it shows a lack of communication skills on the dog's part.

Test 3

If it is allowed and safe to do so (if it isn't then don't take this dog home!), place your fingers through the wire and gently stroke and tickle the dog behind the ears and down onto his chest and shoulders. Continue for a minute or two and observe how much the dog enjoys physical contact.

For training purposes the best response is one where the dog leans into the fingers that are touching it. Disinterest would tend to signify a more independent nature and maybe a dog that has been raised with other dogs. A dog that growls or tries to bite when you try to touch it does not make a good family companion.

Test 4

While the dog is enjoying being stroked, withdraw your fingers and move them to a position two feet or so in front of him. Now observe how much the dog is prepared to maintain contact with your fingers by shifting its position.

This will give you some indication as to how much effort the dog is prepared to go to continue a pleasurable experience. A dog that remains idly in its original position and is unwilling to move a short distance – or, worse still, moves away – would be difficult to motivate by touch alone and therefore may be difficult to train unless food treats are used in the programme.

Test 5

Assuming the dog shows some desire to be spoken to and stroked, pick any naturally occurring behaviour that the dog exhibits, such as pawing at the door, and then stop speaking to, looking at and stroking him. As the dog goes through a range of behaviours to try and gain your attention, immediately reintroduce the three forms of attention (looking at, speaking to and touching the dog) as soon as he exhibits your chosen behaviour, in this case pawing at the door. Repeat several times for the same behaviour and you should get a measure of how quickly the dog learns to carry out a behaviour in order to obtain a reward. After several repetitions the dog should immediately adopt the behaviour when you withdraw the reward.

Test 6

Work out the total time that you have been interacting with the dog and now move away from the kennel or run so you are out of its sight. Check to see how long it takes for the dog to accept your absence and continue its normal routine.

As a guide, the dog should have settled in a time equal to, or less than, your total interaction time. If you continue to get attention-seeking behaviour (barking, howling, scratching or even chewing bedding) long after you have moved out of sight, this would indicate over-dependency and the likelihood of separation anxiety or extreme attention-seeking behaviour when the new owner leaves it by itself.

Test 7

Return and continue to interact with the dog by speaking to and touching. Then have someone else come up and give you a big hug.

It is normal for the dog under test to become excited but that excitement should be directed towards you and your interaction with this other person. Displays of aggression or extremes of frustration would tend to indicate that this dog is overprotective or jealous.

These tests were developed as a result of many hours of observation of dogs within a kennel environment and although they cannot be used as a definitive guide to predicting behaviour, they do nonetheless give a fairly accurate picture of behaviour and trainability.

Now let's say you have narrowed it down to a shortlist of three or four dogs that you like. What next? Staff at the shelter who look after the dogs on a day-to-day basis are known as principal caregivers. The dog you are interested in should have a deep trust of the staff who care for it. At this point one of the most revealing questions is to request that dog's principal caregiver grooms it in the following manner. They should stand the dog and restrain it on a plain lead and collar, then groom it at the rear of its front legs, lifting each one in turn as grooming proceeds. Next, gently taking an ear between finger and thumb, move it forwards and brush behind one and then the other. Now they should support the dog so that it cannot sit or lie down and brush in between its hind legs and from the base to the tip of its tail on the top and bottom. This grooming test needs to be carried out for around ten minutes in total.

Observe the dog carefully as the grooming proceeds and note any difficulty the staff member has in grooming any particular part. If there is only one area that the dog objects to having groomed, ask them to establish if there is any soreness or injury that is causing it any discomfort. Ask the staff member if the dog has an old injury or bad experience that might explain any resistance.

If the dog objects violently to being restrained and groomed or handled by its principal caregiver – particularly if there are bouts of aggression – then you must accept that it may be a liability to take the dog home. If the staff member who has been trained to carry out this procedure cannot handle the dog, it is unlikely that you, the new owner, would be any more successful. It also illustrates the dog's deep distrust towards the very person that cares for it. These are not nice dogs to have as a family companion as any relationship has to be built on mutual trust.

Ask for the dog to be taken out for a walk. Watch it being walked on

A dog being walked

the lead. How easy is it for the person walking the dog to control it? Does the dog pull like a train? Again, that member of staff should have been trained in how to walk a dog and if they struggle do you really think you will fare any better? How does the dog walk past other dogs and people? How relaxed and controlled is the walk? What you are seeing is a professional walking the dog so any problems that arise will probably be highlighted when you take the dog home.

The majority of dogs in rescue centres are around 18 months old, so the last step is to find out what behavioural assessments have been carried out, their extent and the results. If no assessments have been carried out, it really is pot luck as to whether the dog will turn out any good or not. Without any behaviour testing it is impossible to know anything about existing patterns of behaviour. Let's try a couple of basic tests.

How would you know if the dog has lived the early part of its life chained up in a garden or yard? Simple. Take a length of tether material such as a rope, attach it to the dog's collar and gently wrap it around one of the dog's hind legs. Hold on to the other end. If the dog flicks its hind leg out to remove the rope entangling it then it must have been tethered.

If it immediately sits and cries, panics or tries to chew through the rope then it has never been tethered.

What about car travel? I assume you are going to drive your new dog home in your car, so it should have been car-tested. Approach your car with a dog on a lead, open the door and invite the dog to get in. If it has travelled in a car regularly, the dog will tell you that. If it has a problem with motion sickness then you will know by the dog beginning to look 'green', and to drool and salivate, even before the car is started. If the dog has little or no experience of travelling in a car then it will be obvious from the dog's avoidance behaviours! So you need to ask for the results of the behaviour tests to see for yourself the form the tests have taken.

Now you have chosen the rescue dog of your dreams and you are about to take it home for the first time. What now? Few of the dogs that arrive at shelters come with detailed background information. Many have simply been abandoned because the original owner could not cope with the responsibilities of owning a dog. This means your dog will already have his own way of looking at the world and some of the habits that he may have learned from a previous home need to be understood.

29

Taking your Rescue Dog Home: The Honeymoon Period

It will help you to build a bond with your new dog if you also understand a little about dog behaviour. The way your dog sees you and other family members is very similar to the way he would see himself within a social group of dogs. One of the reasons dogs have remained in our homes as pets is because we too are social animals. All social animals have a structure that places the most important at the head of the group. This leader figure has the responsibility of setting all the rules and seeing that the group abides by them. The things that characterise a leader are not the ability to shout the loudest or having the means to terrorise other pack members but an outstanding ability to communicate with them. A leader is always fair and trustworthy.

First, it helps if you decide at the outset not to feed your dog from the table as this only encourages bad habits to develop.

Second, provide your dog with a safe haven such as a dog bed or blanket away from heavily trodden areas. Have your own resting area, such as a particular chair or your own bed, that your dog is not allowed to use at all, even when you are not present.

Third, encourage your dog to play with you with a set of toys. This helps to build a bond between you and your dog, but make sure you set all the rules of the games. Finally, groom and handle your dog every day for the first few weeks, even if he has a short coat that does not appear to require it. This will ensure that your dog learns fully to accept being handled and will make it easier for other people to touch and handle it. This may be very important if your dog ever requires veterinary attention. If the daily grooming session is carried out prior to feeding, playing with or exercising your dog, he will soon look forward to this activity.

TAKING YOUR DOG HOME

Don't be tempted to take your dog straight into your house. Begin by taking it either into your garden or the exercise area you intend to use. Encourage him to sniff the ground. He should soon feel the need to go to the toilet and you should praise him gently as he does so. Only now should you take him into your house, knowing that if he wants to go to the toilet again he might well try to reach the area outside where he went previously. It is now easy to watch for telltale signs, such as pacing up and down or standing by the door, which say he wants to go to the toilet. If you allow him straight into your house then he may be desperate to relieve himself and soil the carpet. He may then see this area as his toilet and continue to use it rather than your garden.

INTRODUCING YOUR DOG TO FAMILY AND FRIENDS

Always allow your new dog to approach people rather than allow other people to approach him. This gives him the opportunity to take things at his own pace and build up trust and confidence. It does nothing to build confidence in your new dog to have lots of people trying to force their attentions on it, and some dogs feel very intimidated by this approach. The best method is to give each person a toy or a treat and ask them to encourage your dog to approach. The more pleasant encounters your dog has, the better he will settle into your household.

INTRODUCING YOUR DOG TO OTHER PETS

It is always wise to try to introduce your new dog to existing pets by being as casual and off-hand as possible. Don't pick up the other pet and try to get your dog to say hello. This tends to overexcite a dog and places too much restraint on the other pet, making it likely to struggle in your hands and increasing the excitement still further. If you have another dog, this is best introduced away from your house on neutral territory. Before going back home with both dogs, pick up any dog toys that are already lying around and remove your other dog's blanket or bed. This will minimise any friction over possessions and sleeping areas. As your two dogs get to know one another you can put one or two toys down, saving favourite ones until last. Put back any bedding only when your dogs have been allowed several hours together.

LEAVING YOUR DOG BY ITSELF

Most dogs that are secondhand come 'primed' with the idea that at some point their owner walked away from them and never returned. This makes it reasonably likely that when they find themselves in a new home with a new owner they are likely to feel insecure for at least the first few months until they settle in and start to believe that this owner will always return.

Because of this early feeling of insecurity it is easy to end up with a dog that becomes so over-attached that it becomes difficult to leave it by itself even for a few minutes. The dog starts to suffer from separation anxiety, that is, it becomes over-stressed and anxious when it is separated from its attachment figure. (If you already have this problem, turn to the section on separation problems, page 222.)

It may seem strange but leaving your new dog in a room by itself for a few minutes several times a day for the first few weeks will ensure it gets used to spending some time alone. Dogs that are allowed to follow their owners from room to room can build up a bond so obsessive that the owner is condemned to a life as a prisoner in their own home with a dog that refuses to be left by itself, even for a few minutes.

The first two weeks that a dog spends in a new household is the honeymoon period. During this time it will learn about all the things in his new home that are similar to his previous home and all the things that are different. Some dogs end up in rescue kennels because their previous owners had problems with their behaviour that they were unable to resolve. This does not mean that you will have the same problems. In most cases all you need to do is show your dog there is a difference between the rules that existed in the last household and the rules in your house. It is also important to allow your dog time to settle into his new home and you can use this time to observe how he behaves with your family, friends and other dogs and pets.

30

Training your Rescue Dog

The good news is that if you have chosen your rescue dog wisely and given it a week or so to build up a relationship with you, basic training is going to be really easy. Never assume your new dog has had some previous formal education; treat it as though its mind is a blank sheet of paper on which you are going to write all the information required to turn it into a great companion.

We can utilise the fact that your dog has spent some time in a kennel where there has been a lack of good social interaction with people for long periods in each day. This usually means that if your dog previously enjoyed lots of time with its former owner, it is likely to bond very quickly with its new human partner when taken out of its lonely kennel existence. Every rescue dog has experienced being parted from a human companion it truly expected to see again and return it to the home it knew. Finding itself in a kennel with little freedom or control over its environment will have placed every rescue dog under varying degrees of stress.

Just imagine what it is like for a typical dog in a rescue centre after their owner walked away from them and never returned. At first it expects the owner to show up any day to return them to the home they knew, but day by day hope starts to fade and the dog becomes subdued – maybe even depressed. As each day passes the memory of what life used to be like also starts to fade but never completely dies away. New dogs in a rescue centre then get into a routine of being walked, fed and taken care of but most days are exactly the same: the same food, the same routine and the same peaks and troughs of excitement, with little to do but reflect and dream. The longer they remain in this situation the more this way of life becomes the norm. We can use this information to good advantage when we consider training our new rescue dog.

The first hurdle we have to overcome is any preconceived ideas the dog might have about walking on a lead, coming when called etc. Remember that a previous owner might have used the command 'come' and the dog's interpretation of the command is to try and keep at arms length to avoid being captured and taken back home. This is why it is usually better to start off with a brand new set of commands. Think of all the words you want to teach your dog, making sure that they differ from traditionally used words so as not to confuse it. Remember that you are going to train your dog to do what *you* require.

Let's start by teaching your dog to walk properly on the lead. No commands are used for this, just the expression 'good dog' when he is walking correctly. The best time for the first lesson is a couple of hours after a meal and when your dog is tired after a vigorous play session in your back garden.

Start by attaching your leash before opening the front door. Your dog will probably become excited and if you go through the door now your dog will more than likely start pulling. So don't open the door! Simply sit next to him and wait for the initial burst of excitement to stop. When your dog is calmer, open the door and again sit back down next to him and wait for the excitement to die down before commencing your walk. Go out for around 50 paces then turn around and go back to your front door. Sit down as before and wait for your dog to calm down before repeating, only this time extend the distance to around 70 paces. The idea is that the walk keeps ending up back at the start point and each time your dog is given some attention for the behaviour that you want – arriving back home.

The first time you do this you may only achieve a couple of hundred yards over around ten repetitions. For the rest of the first week try to extend the distance by walking a circular or square route around your neighbourhood, each time ending back at your front door. Now read the chapter on training your dog to walk on the leash and then start to apply the principles of rewards and penalties for this aspect of training (see page 120). It is vitally important that you do take the time and trouble to walk your new dog around your neighbourhood and return home multiple times on each walk, so that in the event he ever finds himself outside your house and alone, he will be able to find his own way back home with ease.

THE RECALL

Of all the commands to train a dog to carry out, the recall with a rescue dog has to be one of the easiest – if you understand the psychology of the exercise.

First think of the command you will use to teach your dog to come to you. This would usually consist of the dog's name followed a second or so later by the recall command. Again, try to use a unique command that your dog will not have had previous training in. The commands 'come' and 'here' are the most commonly used ones, so think of something different.

Dogs obtained from rescue have the highest probability of suffering from separation anxiety. This simply means that once your new dog has settled in and built a bond with you, if you take it somewhere it has never been before and let it off the lead and then disappear out of sight before calling it, the chances are it will very quickly come looking for you.

It is for this reason that with rescue dogs I always advise training the first off-leash recalls out of sight. First build up an association to a recall command using rewards (as in the chapters on variable rewards on page 101). When you get to the stage of letting the dog off its lead for the first time, ask an assistant to hold on to its collar while you run out of sight a short distance away. This could be behind a tree or bush or any visual barrier in the area; for safety this is best accomplished in a place that is fully fenced. As soon as you are out of sight, call the dog and providing it is showing signs of wanting to find you, your assistant should release it.

Usually the relief of finding their owner in this new area is reward enough but if this is accompanied by lots of praise and perhaps a game with a toy or a tasty treat, it should cement the importance of coming when called firmly in the dog's mind. All the other parts of the chapter on coming when called (page 127) can then be applied.

31

Problem Behaviour

CHEWING

There are many reasons a dog will chew when left alone. The most common reason is simply to get the owners to give it attention by speaking to it, looking at it and touching it.

Let's consider events from the point of view of the dog that is left by itself and wants its owner to come back and speak to it, look at it and touch it. After it has chewed several items of furniture, the owner finally comes home while it is chewing the carpet. The owner enters the house, speaks to the dog, looks at it and touches it by getting hold of the collar. The dog is then taken over to what it has chewed, which tells it precisely what has brought the owner back into the house. Any punishment that may follow cannot be related to chewing the carpet, which has been rewarded by the owner returning!

The following suggestions are made in order to minimise the likelihood of your dog chewing when left.

Leave a sterilised marrowbone to occupy your dog's attention when you go out. If you stuff the hollow centre of the bone with liver pâté or sausage then your dog will amuse itself for some time when left alone. Always remove this item when you are present and put it in your fridge. This will not only keep it fresh for next time but should ensure it retains some novelty value.

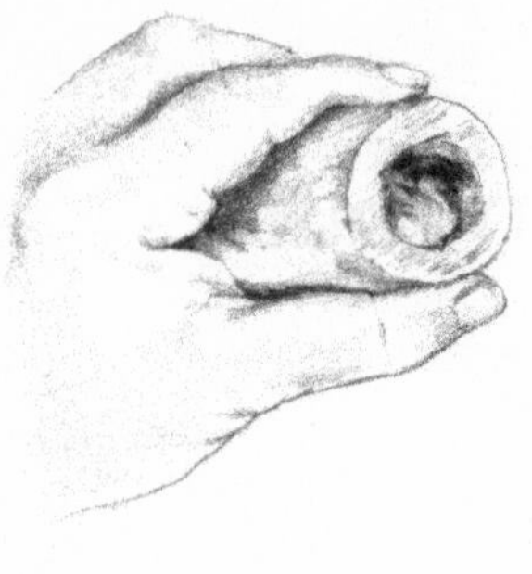

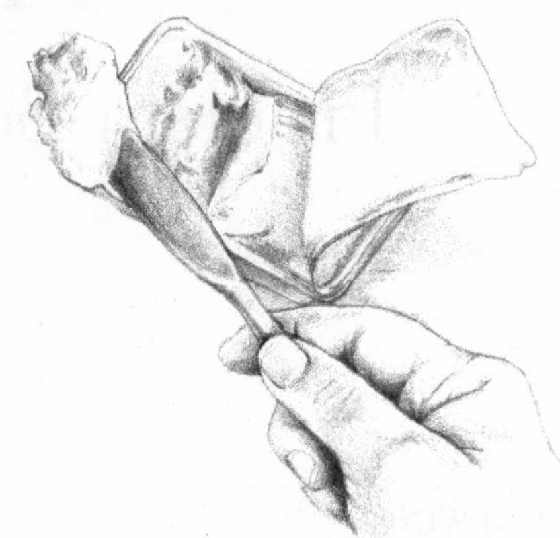

Stuffed marrowbone

Get your dog used to spending some time alone in a room while you are in the house to minimise the impact of your going out altogether. Give your dog plenty of energetic exercise an hour before you leave. For the 20 minutes before you go out, withdraw all attention. This minimises the contrast between you being there and being absent. Leave an item of recently worn clothing just outside the door of the room your dog is in. If it is placed at the foot of the door then your dog will sniff it and know you are not far away. Leaving a recording of a family conversation playing will also help to reassure your dog. Taste deterrents (available from a pet shop) can sometimes deter a dog from chewing.

PUNISHMENT

If a behaviour is rewarded it is likely to increase. The problem with trying to train a dog using punishment is that sometimes what the owner sees as punishment, the dog sees as a reward. Take jumping up for attention, for example. The dog jumps up on its owner to try and get him to give it some attention. The dog wants the owner to speak to it, look at it and touch it. The owner shouts 'No!' (speaking to it), looks the dog straight in the eye (looking at it) and pushes it down (touching it). The jumping behaviour then gets worse!

Remember that you should always reward behaviour that you want your dog to adopt, because if you reward this behaviour then it will increase. If you only give your dog attention when you want to and not when he demands it, you will find the whole process of settling your dog into your house much easier.

THE HOUSE LINE

If you experience any difficulty in controlling your dog for the first few days, try attaching a six-foot line to his collar and let him trail it around wherever he goes in the house. This is only to be put on when the dog is adequately supervised; it is used to gain control as necessary and avoids the need for the owner to grab the dog's collar or chase it around to catch it.

EXERCISE

It is important that your dog has at least two good exercise sessions each day when they can be allowed to let off steam. It is a good idea to take a favourite toy on exercise sessions so that your dog can chase around after it. If you teach your dog to play games with a toy it will decrease the possibility of him wandering away and trying to find his own amusements. Always exercise in enclosed, fenced areas until you are sure your dog will respond to your voice and return when called. If it is not possible to find a safe enclosed area, you could fasten a length of washing line to his collar while you are teaching him to come when called.

AND FINALLY...

Every shelter wants you, your family and friends to enjoy having a rescue dog as your faithful companion. With the right sort of understanding, owners who start off as they mean to go on can avoid problems. If you experience any difficulty with your new dog it is usually possible to sort things out with some timely words of advice.

Almost all problems are easier to solve if help is sought immediately. Although a few dogs have to be returned as unsuitable, the vast majority make loving family pets. They are just asking for a new start in life and soon learn to rebuild the trust they once had in their original owners prior to being given up or abandoned.

Section 5
Behaviour: Problems and Resolutions

'There are three classes of people: those who see, those who see when they are shown and those who do not see.'
– Leonardo da Vinci

32

Behaviour Counselling

To begin to understand the reasons behind the problems we appear to have with our pet dogs these days, let's have a careful look at the main reason that people decide to own a dog. Sometimes it is the reason that causes the problem.

In terms of numbers, companionship is the biggest single reason for anyone deciding to own a dog. A true companion dog fits into the family life, being able to both give and receive affection. Because of its average life expectancy, the companion dog is an invaluable aid in teaching children how to care for another living creature and how to accept the responsibility of raising a young animal that is totally dependent on its pack for survival. As time passes, the companion dog's last contribution to its family is to teach them how to come to terms with bereavement.

This means the initial selection of a puppy is critical if problems are to be avoided, so it pays dividends to be ultra cautious when deciding which breed will be suitable for the environment in which it is to be kept. Some breeds are totally unsuitable for first-time owners. Large guarding breeds may be attractive but they need more experienced handling and training. If only people would adopt a more sensible approach and accept such things, a lot of unpleasant first-time associations could be avoided.

If you own a well-behaved companion dog, the chances are that you will tend to get more exercise, you will be smiled at and engaged in conversation more when accompanied by your dog and you will meet more people with a common interest. Anyone living alone who is privileged enough to own a well-mannered dog will tell you there is no other animal that can compare for offering comfort, security, loyalty, affection and understanding. Our companion dog asks for only a small investment on the part of its owners but offers a huge reward in return for a bed to sleep on, food and water, a few games to play and a bit of love and affection.

Traditionally, small to medium breeds have been kept as companions, but lately the trend has moved towards much larger and physically stronger dogs. Also, due to the belief that working dogs are more intelligent and therefore easier to train, a growing number of owners are buying dogs with a predominantly working pedigree. It is a sad fact that there are many thousands of working dogs that are subjected to the most appalling mental cruelty as pets. They are kept in homes under conditions that do not provide an outlet for their natural instincts and abilities, and the owners then chastise them for the behaviour problems that arise as a result of denying the dog any forms of work or play that satisfy its desire to do what it was bred for.

Dogs are very simple animals. This, and the fact that almost all their behaviours are driven by self-interest (self-preservation), makes them really easy to work with. Every morning when you wake up, you have many different things on your mind and as you start your day, you know that you will have many complex decisions to make. Each and every day for your dog probably begins with just two thoughts: what do I want and how am I going to get it?

When I hear of people having difficulty controlling their dog, I always wonder if they have ever realised they always have the means at their disposal to get as much control as they wish. Sometimes by trying to see a problem from the dog's viewpoint will give you a totally different outlook and approach. Answer the following questions and you will look at control in a completely different way.

- Does your dog have any money of its own?

- Does it know where the shop that sells dog food is located?
- Is it able to open the front door and get to this shop?
- Is your dog able to turn on a water tap and fill its own water bowl?
- Does your dog know where toys are purchased?
- Does your dog know how to attach a lead and open the door to go for a walk?
- Can your dog let itself into the garden?
- Can your dog drive your car to the park, beach, field etc?

How much more control do you really want?

The whole idea behind a behaviour consultation is to try and get information from the owner. First of all, the basic information that I require is the breed of dog, so I have time to research characteristic behaviour before the dog arrives. The second thing I need to know is its age, and the third is how they came by the dog. Did they buy it as a puppy, or did they get it from a rescue centre? I also need to know when they first noticed they had a problem with the dog, when it was, what caused the concern and how the problem has been developing up to the present time.

I also need them to describe the worst memory of their dog's behaviour. This is usually a very recent incident. What I'm saying to the owner is, tell me the ingredients that you had to get the problem in the first place, and all the things you've done that have made the problem worse to the point where you've had to come and see me. Remember, you can't separate the dog's behaviour problems from the influences of the environment and from the owner. So the more I can get the owners to talk about their dog, the easier the consultation becomes.

How does the age of the dog affect its behaviour, and why is it so important in solving problems? What we look for is the age that the breed matures and the extent of the problem. Basically, if the dog is fully mature and the problem is severe, then we are most likely to offer a programme of management rather than trying to go for a full cure. A dog that has practised behaviour for most of its early life and is now fully mature is unlikely to respond to treatment easily. Let's take the case of a two-year-old Westie that became dog-aggressive when it was five months old, had been to training classes (more opportunities to practise the aggressive behaviour) and whose owners had tried everything. They described it as being untrustworthy when off-leash around other dogs and also leash-aggressive. Although it might be possible to reduce the aggression, it would be unlikely the dog would ever be a little angel around other dogs off-leash! We also have to consider the effect of hormones on behaviour, which is also related to the age of the dog.

Innate breed behaviours may conspire to add to existing behaviour problems or create new ones. Take the Rhodesian Ridgeback as an example. What advice would you give the owner of a three-year-old Ridgeback who complains that her next door neighbours have just acquired a cat and the dog now spends most of its time in the yard jumping up at the fence, obsessed with wanting to get at the cat!

A dog with a head collar

Sometimes it has to be recognised that instincts can be controlled by training or using mechanical aids, but they cannot be modified.

Everything I do in my work with dogs is relatively simple and straightforward and follows a very logical path. The response I get from most owners of 'problem' dogs is, 'It's all so logical now you have explained it to me.' There are no miracle cures, just plain common sense based on personal observations of dogs and owners in their natural habitat.

Remember that although our dogs may pose a lot of questions in terms of their behaviour, they also hold all the answers if we only take the trouble to talk to them on a level they can understand. Tens of thousands of dogs are given up, turned out or even put to sleep each year because they caused problems that their owners did not have the knowledge to put right. With the right advice, the vast majority of owners can turn what was a problem dog into a well-behaved family pet.

In its most simple form, behaviour modification involves no more than being able to understand two statements. If a behaviour is rewarded, it will tend to increase. If a behaviour is not rewarded, it will tend to decrease. So to remove a reward from an undesirable behaviour, we have to understand the behaviour from the dog's point of view.

Now for the big one: the relationship between the dog and its owner. No behaviour modification programme, however good it might be, will ever work unless the owner has the correct working relationship with the dog. Relationships are based on trust and understanding. That is why I often ask to see the owners groom their dog, restrain it and also play with it. There are lots of ways to assess an owner's relationship with their dog. Here are a couple of illustrative examples.

Have five food treats and give four of them to your dog, one at a time, in the following manner. Talk to the dog, smile and give one food treat. Now stop smiling for a few seconds. Then start smiling and talking to the dog and give the second treat. Repeat for treats numbers three and four. Now hold the fifth treat out exactly as before but remain silent and do not smile at all. The dog should try to get the treat for a second or two then look into your eyes for clues as to why it is not getting the food. When it looks at your face and sees that you are not smiling it should move away. (Most will now sit.) This tells us that the dog looks to you, its owner, for guidance when it faces a problem. Some dogs, however, will keep on trying to get the food treat and become more and more frustrated when they fail. We describe these dogs as self-interested.

Another test is to take your dog to somewhere it has never been before and let it off the leash. If it runs away and does not come back, and you have to go running off in search of it, then we can say that you do not have a close relationship. The dog is telling you it does not want to return to your home and live the rest of its life with you!

If the relationship between owner and dog is doubtful, this forms the first and most essential part of any behaviour-modification programme. This brings us to the problem caused if there is another dog or dogs in the household. Basically, there are very few programmes that will work when the 'problem' dog is spending 24 hours a day in the company of another dog or dogs. So an element of separation is vital if a good working relationship is to be built up between owner and their 'problem' dog. This is fully covered in the section on dog-to-dog aggression (see page 301).

Without establishing the reason for the behaviour problem, it is difficult if not impossible to work out a 'cure'.

What we are trying to work out is why the dog needs to carry out the behaviour in preference to other available behaviours. The majority of behaviour problems in dogs really are that simple to deal with providing you are prepared to sit and think about them and ask your dog a few simple questions.

33

Dogs Learn Only From Personal Experiences

Throughout a dog's life it is always much easier to prevent problems from arising than to correct them after they have been allowed to become established. The longer a problem is left and the more it is allowed to develop, the harder it will be to correct.

Dogs cannot learn, as you are by reading this book, from others' experiences. They learn exclusively by participating in life, by trial and error, and by following the behaviour of a strong role model. They do not have the capacity to think in quite the same way as we do. Let me give you an example.

Imagine that you walk the same path every evening on your way home from work, and on two consecutive Fridays you were harassed by a youth looking for trouble. First, you would know it was a Friday and you would have a week to plan a suitable strategy in advance of the following Friday. Perhaps you could hand the responsibility for your welfare over to someone else and report the incident to the police. Alternatively, you could choose to avoid this route next Friday. Or you could carry a baseball bat with you and intimidate your aggressor. Your dog can do none of these.

Your dog has little concept of time and cannot plan a strategy in advance. Your dog will simply react to the situation as it deems appropriate at the moment a decision is required. So if you put your dog in the same situation – another dog harassing it every Friday when it goes for a walk in the park – this is how it would work. Your dog would not know it was a Friday and with a history of harassment by a particular dog, it would have to make the decision on the spot about whether to run away from or bite the offending dog. It may well be that your dog would not like approaching the park now at all because of the bad experience he has had with another dog. Most dogs also quickly learn that they cannot hand the responsibility for their welfare to their owners and have little trust that the owners will protect them from harassment!

Bess & Mr McMurtrie

Dogs do not possess a great insight into their world. This story should serve to illustrate the point. Mr McMurtrie lived alone in a small apartment in London and had been in retirement for some years, so he decided to get a Labrador puppy as a companion. This was a great choice of breed as a companion as Mr McMurtrie was in need of exercise and getting a pet dog gave him a reason to go out for walks. So he got himself a puppy, but by the time she was eight months of age he had phoned the local dog shelter, wanting to give his dog away. The reason? She would not go out for a walk!

Mr McMurtrie told me he got Bess as a seven-week-old puppy. He did not drive so the breeder kindly delivered the puppy to his apartment. He was told that it should not be taken out until it had received a course of inoculations from a veterinarian, so Mr McMurtrie phoned his son, who had a car, and arranged for Bess to visit the local vet. Bess had her first injection and the vet advised Mr McMurtrie not to take her out until she was 16 weeks old because of the risk of infectious diseases. In the meantime she was to return for a second injection in a few weeks' time. Mr McMurtrie's son duly transported them both back to the vet for the second injection and Mr McMurtrie noted the date, a few weeks hence, when Bess would be fully protected and able to go out into the big world.

The big day arrived and Bess was put on a collar and lead for the first time in her life and taken out the front door. She panicked and reared up like a wild horse. Mr McMurtrie had to take her back inside to prevent the panic attack from getting worse. Maybe she is still a bit young, he thought, so he decided to wait for a week and try again. The result was the same – a panic attack. By the time Bess had reached eight months, Mr McMurtrie decided that he would have to part with his dog. Not only could he not take her out for a walk, but as she also did not like being left on her own when he wanted to go out, he was getting no exercise at all.

When I asked Mr McMurtrie where he would walk Bess if he could, he replied that there was a park just half a mile away. Does Bess know what a park is? I asked him. His reply? All dogs know what a park is! I then asked him if he had ever shown Bess a picture of a park or even pointed one out on the television. What was Bess's view or model of the world?

Everything that she knew she would have had to learn by personal experience. When she was taken away from her mother for the first time, she was put in a car and driven through the streets of London – past pavements, buildings, cars and traffic. When she was taken out for the second time in her life, she was again put in a car and driven through the streets of London – again past pavements, roads, and buildings – and a person stuck a needle in her neck. Her third experience of going out was the same – traffic buildings and another needle in her neck. Bess thought the whole world consisted of traffic, buildings and people that were scary. Would you ever want to go out into that world again if you were Bess?

As Mr McMurtrie had a paved rear yard, Bess had never seen a blade of grass so she had no concept of large green open spaces. So I put Bess on a lead and took her against her will to the park. I could see fear in the dog's eyes when we started Bess's incredible journey but it was amazing to see her eyes light up when she turned the last corner and we walked through the gates into the park. Like a child seeing the sea for the first time, she stood in total disbelief. We let her off the lead to run free and feel the wind in her hair. She took in all the smells and sights as though her senses were a huge sponge. Mr McMurtrie had no further trouble taking Bess out for a walk ever again.

So many people fail to realise they *expect* their dog to understand something that makes perfect sense to them, but fail to see things from their dog's perspective. So here are two more tales to illustrate the importance of learning from personal experiences and understanding your dog.

What about the dog that is fearful of people that it does not know? Why would a dog that is fine with you and your family be worried about me? After all, I am the same species as you. From the dog's perspective, it lives in a particular type of shelter that it shares with its human caregiver and family members. It has resources in that shelter such as a supply of food and water, plus enough resting sites for everyone in the family group. It is regularly taken out for a walk to places it likes to go. It is given lots of attention and affection by the unique group of people it shares its home with.

Now, after looking at life from your dog's perspective, answer the following questions about a dog that is fearful of people that it does not know.

When it was a puppy, how many other houses did your dog visit or is yours the only house it has had experience of? Where might it think that other people live? How many people have ever fed your dog in their own houses? Hmm. So your dog thinks that you are the only person who knows where to get dog food? What about water? Are you the only one who knows how to fill your dog's water bowl? How about toys? Are you the only person who plays with your dog with toys and knows where to get them? How about going out for a walk? Does anyone else ever take your dog out for a walk to those places it likes to go?

Ah, so your dog might think that you are the only human being on the planet that lives in a house, has access to a supply of food, knows how to turn a tap and fill a water bowl, knows how to play with a toy and where a supplier of new toys can be located, and has a lead and knows how to attach it, open the front door and go to places that are fun. So would you trust anyone other than your owner?

To decrease a dog's fear of people we have to teach them that people are basically all the same, live in the same type of house, have a plentiful supply of food and water, have toys to play exciting games, have leads and know how to open the door and get to places that dogs like to go. Again, it should be plain simple common sense.

The final example of learning how to deal with a problem by looking at it from the dog's point of view is a really interesting one.

Ben: A Difficult Case

Ben was a nine-year-old Border Collie, although his male owner did say that his age was uncertain as he had been acquired five years previously from a Border Collie rescue where they guessed his age to be around four. Ben was taken into his owner's place of work each day but was becoming increasingly aggressive when anyone entered the owner's office. Because of the aggression the owner was at the point where ending Ben's life had become a distinct probability.

When the owner arrived for a consultation he brought along his female friend who also had a dog. Her dog was around two years old and looked like a Wheaten terrier cross. When I asked a few questions to establish the reason for Ben's aggression, one thing became really obvious: Ben was older than nine years – more like 12.

When I see problem dogs I ask very few questions but I make lots of observations. This is what I asked the owner and his friend to do. I told them I was going to walk out of the room and return in a couple of minutes. Both were to keep their dogs on the lead and not let their dogs make contact with me but just to watch what I did and watch for their dog's response.

I entered the room and approached the Wheaten, smiling as I did so. I bent forwards, still at a distance, and then began to talk to the dog: 'Hello there, what's your name?' I also patted my leg with one hand. The dog immediately rose to its feet and pulled towards me, almost with a smile on its face and its tail wagging enthusiastically. I then asked if the terrier could talk, what would it be saying? They both agreed that on being invited to say hi, the terrier was smiling back at me and wanting his owner to let go of the lead so he could come over and be touched and stroked. The dog was asking for contact.

Then I repeated the test but this time with Ben. I entered the room exactly as I did on the previous occasion and approached Ben with a big smile on my face. Ben turned his head away, anxiously glancing back at his owner. I bent forwards, still at a distance, and then began to talk to Ben: 'Hello there, what's your name?' Ben licked his lips nervously. I then patted my leg with one hand and Ben rose to his feet and backed away, turning his head to one side and emitting a low growl. I then sat back down and asked what Ben had been trying to say. They both agreed that Ben had said he would rather not be bothered and just wanted to be left alone. He was saying he was comfortable where he was and was not enthusiastic about coming to me to be stroked.

All I had to say was, 'Why don't you listen to what your dog is telling you? He has given you the answer to the problems you have been having.' The owner confirmed he had been doing everything in his power to get the dog to interact with people who came into the office: by using food, by trying to get some of his employees to take Ben out for a walk, by getting them to come in and sit with Ben for short periods etc. All Ben wanted was to be left alone.

We talked about where the owner could position Ben's bed in his office so the dog would have some peace and quiet – presently it was in a position where people had to walk right past him. 'I have seen a number of behaviourists and trainers,' the owner told me, 'and they have all told me to try and associate people entering the office with rewards. I have even been teaching Ben some obedience commands. But you are the first person who has made me look at what the dog wants – I have been too focused on what I want.' Tears then welled up as he bent down and patted his dog. Ben lived for another two years, died a natural death and never bit anyone else.

The art of listening is not just confined to listening to the owners. You also have to develop techniques that will allow you to listen to what your dog is saying if you want to fully understand the code.

34
Behaviour Modelling

In order to solve a problem, gathering information is important but so is how we come by it. This is where the concept of behaviour modelling comes in.

Let's say the dog and its owner have arrived at my house and are sitting in my living room. How would we expect a family pet dog to behave in that situation? I measure every dog that comes in against a set of behaviours. I have a friend who owns a really nice pet dog, about two years old. My friend has never been to a dog-training class: he just happens to have a really nice, well-adjusted, well-socialised, well-mannered dog.

My friend comes to my house for the first time and brings his dog along. The first thing that happens is I ask him to take a seat, pointing to the seat I want him to take. As the dog is on the lead, it should follow alongside him. No command of heel should be required. Once my friend has sat down, he'll take a look around the room to gain some information. This is known as exploratory behaviour. He'll probably notice there are pictures of dogs. There's also a model airplane sitting on the bar at the far end of the room, and a big fireplace right in the centre. Looking down at his dog, I notice that not only is it looking around the room too, but he'll often sniff the air and cock his head to one side to listen to all the noises coming from around the house.

As we start our conversation, I notice my friend is sitting on the edge of the chair but when we start talking about airplanes a couple of minutes later, he visibly leans back and starts to relax, crossing one leg over the other. When where the dog notices this and realises that we're going to be in for a long conversation, it too visibly relaxes and lies down alongside its owner. No command to lie down was necessary. During our conversation I ask my friend what his dog's name is. 'Rocky,' he replies. As soon as he says 'Rocky', his dog looks around and then up at my friend's facial expression, then turns away again. I repeat the name: 'Rocky, that's a nice name.' Rocky immediately glances at me, giving a knowing little wag of his tail as I smile at him.

After a few minutes, I ask my friend to let Rocky off the lead. As soon as he does this and encourages him to explore, Rocky immediately leaves my friend's side and starts to investigate this new strange environment. As he walks around the room, he finds a box of dog toys in the corner. Seeing the toys, the dog stops to look around at his owner. As soon as the owner glances at the dog, the dog gives a wag of his tail and glances at the toys, as if he's asking permission to play with them.

My friend gives him permission, so the dog immediately picks one up and takes it over to him to invite him to play. Any time the dog approaches me, if I extend one hand and call it by its name, smiling at the same time, the dog comes over to see me, wagging its tail enthusiastically. I then extend my hand to stroke him and maybe have a quick game with the toy. The conversation about aircraft is really engaging, so after stroking Rocky for 30 seconds, I turn my attention back to my friend. As soon as I make it obvious to the dog that I no longer want to interact with it, it gives me one last little nudge underneath my arm and then leaves me alone. I never had to say a word to the dog to get him to leave me alone; my body language said it all.

At this point, my friend asks if he can use the bathroom. I explain how to get to it and as he is about to leave the room, the dog gets up and prepares to follow him. Without saying a word, just with a wave of his hand, he makes it clear to Rocky that he doesn't want him to follow him. My friend then goes through the door and closes it behind him. We now expect to see one of three distinct behaviours. The dog will either return to where he has been sitting and patiently wait for his owner's return, or it will hang around near the door the owner exited from and patiently wait for his return. The third possibility is that the dog will now sit next to me and patiently wait for his owner to return, which is what Rocky did in this instance.

When my friend comes back into the room, his dog greets him briefly then goes back to exploring the room. At any stage during the conversation, if I ask my friend to call the dog to him and put him on the lead, not only will the dog come immediately, but soon as the lead is clipped on, the dog then looks and heads toward the door.

Later I go out to make a cup of tea and when I bring it back in, the dog greets me enthusiastically. I offer my friend the cup of tea and a biscuit from a selection on a plate. My friend takes a biscuit, I take one, and the rest are put on a low coffee table. The dog sniffs the air near the coffee table, looks at my friend, looks at me, licks its lips and then turns away from the table, avoiding the biscuits.

That is my model of behaviour and I'm going to compare every dog that comes into the room to that model. Let's consider a few examples.

The first dog and handler come in. The dog is dragging its owner all the way into the room. I gesture to where I want the owner to sit but the handler take no notice of that, continually asking the dog where it wants to go as the dog pulls them all around the room. At one stage the dog jumps all over me, with the owner apologetically saying it just wants to say hello. I again beckon them to take a seat. As soon as the owner sits down, the dog wants to start his exploratory behaviour. He doesn't want to be on the lead, he wants to be anywhere but sitting near the owner. When it's obvious the owner isn't going to let go of the lead, the dog starts to act up, fighting against the lead, turning around and chewing the lead, laying on its back and wriggling, wrapping its legs in the lead – doing everything it can to get away from its owner.

When I give the owner permission to let the dog off the lead, it immediately goes careering around the room. It doesn't ask for permission to take a toy out of the box. It goes straight over and eats biscuits off the plate on the coffee table. Even asking the owner to call the dog back and put him on a lead has no effect whatsoever. In fact, most times when the owner talks to his dog, it doesn't even turn and look at him. The dog is constantly exploring. When it comes close to me, it doesn't need an invitation to come closer, but immediately jumps all over me in a really friendly outgoing way (good thing it doesn't have aggression problems).

The owner's feeble attempts to control the dog using voice commands fall on deaf ears. When the owner gets up to leave the room for a short period, the dog tries to barge past his legs and he has to physically hold it back. As soon as the owner leaves the room, the dog goes on a rampage through the room. When the owner re-enters, the dog rushes to the door – not to greet him but to try to get past him and through the door. It doesn't take an expert to realise this dog is in total control of the owner and the owner has no control over their dog. Remember control has very little to do with dog obedience classes and verbal commands. It has everything to do with the emotional relationship between the dog and its owner.

As soon as the second dog comes in, it's sniffing everywhere – obviously there have been dogs in the room. Its nose is like a vacuum cleaner, taking in every square inch of floor where the owner is sitting. When I ask what the dog's name is, the owner replies but the dog doesn't even look up. I repeat the name and the dog still doesn't look up. His head is constantly going from one side to the other, hoping to catch the faintest sound of any other dog in the vicinity. This is clearly a dog that's been raised around other dogs. He doesn't understand any human language whatsoever.

Dog number three comes in. The owner walks in ahead of it and when they take a seat, they're sitting on the edge of the chair. The dog sits almost pushing up against the owner. If the dog explores the room at all, it will do so using only its eyes, not even turning its head to the side. When I ask the owner what the dog's name is, as soon as the owner says it, the dog flicks his eyes up towards the owner's face. When I repeat the name, the dog then focuses its gaze on me. As it realises I'm looking at it, smiling and leaning forward, the dog pushes back, comes into close contact with the owner and then emits a low growl.

When I ask for the dog to be let off the lead, it is removed and the owner gestures for the dog to run free. But it doesn't want to leave its owner's side. It seems to have a giraffe syndrome where its neck wants to extend out as it tries to explore the different smells. Each time it will suddenly retract as the dog realises it is getting further away from its owner. Even if it does explore the room, it will do so reluctantly.

When we get to the stage where I ask the owner to leave the room, once again the dog tries to follow its owner through the gap. The dog is now frightened as it will be left alone in the room with a complete stranger. On the door you can see scratch marks that extend nearly up to seven feet where fearful dogs have been frantically scratching once the owner has walked through it.

We now have a picture, through behaviour modelling, of exactly what the relationship is between each dog and its owner. We can get a fairly accurate estimate of how much control the dog has over the owner, and vice versa. We can also usually find out if the dog has any understanding of human language or if it only understands dog language. So behaviour modelling is a really important part of a behaviour consultation.

35

Patterns of Behaviour

No dog I have ever come across just wakes up one morning at around 11 months of age and suddenly decides to attack another dog. Similarly, no dog ever suddenly decides to bite its owners just because it might be fun to try. Nor has any domestic breed of dog ever been developed with the sole requirement to tear a house to pieces when left by itself. This means all these behaviours have to have a pattern of learning.

You also cannot separate the behaviour of the dog from the behaviour of the owner they live with. Remember that I am looking at patterns of problem behaviour and trying to ascertain where the pattern starts. Usually it begins with a certain profile of owner. People can be divided up by their patterns of behaviour, so understanding people profiles is almost as important as understanding dog problems. In order for someone to have a dog that throws temper tantrums that person needs to fit a certain profile and the same is true for the owner of a dog that suffers from separation anxiety.

One such owner is the 'I Felt Sorry for Him' type. This type of owner tends to be very critical of themselves, and they have a strong need for other people to like and admire them. They also want to give lots of love and a big part of their lives to a dog that has not had the best start in life.

At times they do a lot of soul-searching as to whether they have done the right thing.

If you fit this profile and chose a dog from a rescue centre because you felt sorry for it, then you have the ingredients for certain types of behaviour problems. The most common would be difficulty in leaving your dog by itself, as sometimes these enforced absences leave the dog highly stressed or distressed (separation anxiety).

If, instead, you belong to the 'Permissive' type of owner, you will want to give your dog everything it ever wants or asks for. You are likely to allow your dog to do things that very few other owners would tolerate, just because it is your dog. Because of your permissive nature you are likely to end up with a dog that has temper tantrums and often takes advantage of you.

I could go on, but the many different people profiles would take a book in themselves. As I said earlier, you cannot separate the behaviour of a dog from the behaviour of its owner. There needs to be a set of ingredients for a problem to develop, and sometimes the main ingredient is the owner. So when we now take a brief look at some behaviour problems, the ingredients required to create them and the pattern the behaviour takes, it should be possible for you to start decoding your dog's behaviour.

36
Separation Problems

To understand why dogs chew when their owners go out and leave them on their own we need first to understand the mechanism by which they have learned – or rather been taught – how to do it. So if you have a desire to teach your dog how to tear the house to pieces when it's left alone for even a few minutes, read on!

The first thing to understand is that there are many different reasons why a dog will chew things up when left by itself, so making the correct diagnosis is the key to being able to solve destruction problems. The most common reasons are: attention seeking, insecurity, separation anxiety and boredom.

ATTENTION SEEKING

With a young puppy, the process is usually started by giving it a number of toys to play with and allowing them to be left lying around. The owners play with the new puppy frequently with these toys, particularly during the first month, so the pup learns that playing with toys, in itself a pleasant experience, is even better because it also gets the undivided attention of its owners during these games. After several weeks the pup will have started to use the toys to gain the attention of its owners, one of whom will always play when requested to do so by a little prompting with a toy.

The pup now starts to make more and more demands for attention by using its toys, and the owners rapidly reach a point where they tire of playing so many games on its insistence. They now start to reject the pup's constant demands to play so it goes from person to person, inviting them to play. No one is interested so it may try again with a different toy. Still no one is interested. The pup wanders off, still in a playful mood and wanting some attention. It then playfully puts its teeth on the leg of the coffee table or starts to pull a few strands of thread in the carpet. The owners quickly respond by telling it that it mustn't use its teeth on the furnishings but only on a toy, which they then give it and encourage it to play with.

Can you see what the pup is being taught? If no one will give it the attention it requires then playfully biting an item of furniture will prompt the owners to interact by offering it a toy. It will then alter its behaviour slightly to ensure the owner is taking notice. The very first time that biting the furniture produced the desired response it happened by accident rather than by design, the pup being unaware that the owner would respond by going over to it and giving it attention using a toy or sometimes a chew stick.

After two or three repetitions, when the pup wants to gain attention, it will deliberately go over to an item of furniture and turn round to watch for the owner's reaction as it starts to put its teeth on it. This is as if to say, 'Excuse me, but have you noticed that I want some attention'. The owner, of course, immediately complies with the pup's wishes even though, in human terms, the attention it starts to receive may involve a small measure of shouting or even attempts to smack it. These are usually only threats, but even if the owner actually smacks the dog this will happen so long after the event that it would be extremely doubtful if the dog could ever link the punishment with the crime it has committed.

We now have a situation where the pup has learnt to put its teeth on various items of furniture to gain attention. If the owners want to leave the pup in the house by itself they will normally gather up one or two toys for it to play with while they are out. The pup now gets excited at the prospect of playing a game and, lo and behold, it suddenly finds itself all alone with no one to play with. What do you have to do to get your owners to return and give you some attention? That's it – chew the leg of the coffee table. After five minutes of chewing, with its eyes fixed firmly on the door its owners went out of, it decides that chewing the coffee-table leg has not had the desired effect and so it turns its attentions to the carpet, which it understands usually works slightly better. When that, too, fails, it progresses to the cushions, understanding that it nearly always produces the desired reward of attention.

And so it continues to experiment, moving from one thing to another until, at last, the owner returns to give it some attention. And what is the first thing every owner does as soon as they walk through the door to find the pup has been chewing? They take the pup over to what it has chewed and advertise the fact that it was the chewing that has brought them back to the house!

This time any punishment that is meted out to the pup is certainly never going to be associated with the act of chewing. Most dogs simply learn that when the owner returns home and utter the words 'Who's done this?' it is about to be punished. Some clever dogs may learn to associate the owner's anger with the fact the cushions are off the three-piece suite, but would never realise that it was their act of pulling the cushions off some time earlier that caused the punishment.

So you can easily end up with a dog that looks guilty and runs away and hides when the owner comes in to find the cushions are on the floor, yet is happy to greet them when they come home and the cushions are not on the floor. How the cushions came to get on the floor would never be part of the association in the dog's mind.

Thus some owners know the dog has been chewing as soon as they walk in the door to find it hiding in the corner looking worried, whereas if they return home when nothing has been touched, the dog greets them happily. It's the same simple association of chewed carpet equals punishment, irrespective of who chewed the carpet. Remember that the pup, in its eyes, has never been punished for chewing the carpet; it has been punished for being in the same room as the chewed-up-carpet, and there is a world of difference between the two. With this type of chewing for attention, it nearly always has the desired effect of teaching its owners to leave it less and less and for shorter and shorter periods.

It is also never only one thing that has been chewed but lots of things, frequently mass destruction of every conceivable item. After an absence of only 30 minutes the owner can come home to find the carpet shredded, the vinyl floor ripped, the door frame chewed, the three-piece suite torn apart, the curtains down and the wallpaper removed from the wall.

The problem is made worse if the dog is allowed to have access to the owner 24 hours a day by allowing it to sleep in the bedroom. This means that although the dog may well separate itself from its owners for short periods each day to relax, the doors to each room are always left open to allow the dog to make contact whenever it wishes. In extreme cases the owner cannot even go the bathroom and close the door without the dog objecting and wanting to follow.

Most owners believe they have a problem only when they go out of the house. This is rarely the case because with most destructive dogs they would behave in the same way if the owner put them in another room to where they were, closed the door and ignored them for an hour. So the first part of the cure does not involve going out and leaving the dog – it involves teaching it to spend short periods by itself each day. Do not apply this to young puppies that are going through the teething process or to a dog that occasionally chews one or two carefully selected items.

Stage 1

For one week, wind down the attention you give your dog on his demands. If he comes over and puts his nose under your hand, tries to climb on your knee, makes whining noises or paws your leg to gain attention, turn away and ignore him. Ignoring means you must not look at the dog, touch him or speak to him if he is the one making the demands. This does not mean you have to ignore him all the time, only when he demands attention.

Stage 2

For a further seven days, teach your dog to spend five minutes by itself, confined to a room next to where you are. This should ideally be carried out three times each day in the following manner.

Place things that will make a noise if they are disturbed, such as aluminium cans with a marble inside, against or on top of anything that is likely to be touched. Put the dog in this room quietly without exciting it and close the door. Now sit close to the door and time two minutes on your watch. You will probably hear your dog sniffing at the bottom of the door, followed by whimpering, then usually followed by the dog disturbing one of your strategically placed audible chewing indicators (cans). As soon as you hear this noise, hit the door sharply with the flat of your hand. Do not shout or otherwise advertise your presence to the dog when you carry out this 'correction' as we do not want it to link its shock with you in any way.

Reset your watch again for two minutes and repeat, resetting the two minutes each time you have to bang the door. Do not enter the room until the dog has managed to remain in the room without disturbing anything for the whole duration of the time on your watch. When you achieve this first complete two minutes, go into the room and ignore your dog for a further two minutes. Repeat this process three times every day. It is always the first day that is the worst, so be patient if the first time you try it takes more than an hour to get the full two minutes.

In one week's time, or when you have reached the point where on three successive days you have achieved a full two minutes without having to correct your dog, you can move on.

Stage 3

Now start increasing the time the dog is left in the room by itself by five minutes every day until you reach a maximum of 30 minutes. You can now reduce the number of times you perform this each day to just once. When you manage three successive days without problems you can move on to Stage 4.

Stage 4

If your dog is used to sleeping in the bedroom, this is an excellent opportunity to move his bed outside the bedroom door. You should also repeat Stage 2, using a few different rooms if possible to accustom your dog to being by itself in any room you choose to put it into.

Stage 5

With the majority of dogs you can miss out this stage. It is necessary to implement it only if your dog is all right when you are in the next room, but is destructive when you actually leave the house. In other words, the dog differentiates between when the owners are in the house and when they have gone out.

First of all make a note of all the things you normally do before leaving the house. This would normally involve a set routine of brushing your hair, putting your keys in your pocket, putting on your coat, putting the dog in the kitchen and then going out. Now you perform the whole of your going-out routine before leaving your dog in one of the rooms you have trained it to stay in. Then open the front door and close it again but don't actually go out. Instead, creep back into the room alongside where your dog is, using the bang-on-the-door treatment if you hear any disturbance.

You are now teaching your dog to disregard all the signals you give when you are going out and putting yourself in the position where you are on hand to administer an environmental correction.

Stage 6

Now go out of the house for increasing periods of time starting at 15 minutes. Before going out place an isolation toy such as a cheese-stuffed kong somewhere you know your dog is likely to find it. When you close the door of the room in which you have left your dog, place a recently worn item of your clothing just outside the door, on the floor.

Leave the house and stay out for around 15 minutes. When you return and enter the house, do not greet your dog but simply look for the isolation toy. Pick it up and call the dog over using the words, 'Who's done this?' etc. Show the dog the toy and then immediately wrap it in cling film and place in the fridge. The idea is that you are going to continue to link the behaviour of your return to a chewed item, only this time it should be an item that you have dictated. Why wouldn't you praise the dog when you show him the chewed toy? Simple. The owner's existing behaviour is obviously sufficient to maintain the dog's behaviour of chewing lots of different items, so why change a winning formula?

Now your dog will:

- believe you are sitting just the other side of the door, because most dogs sniff the bottom of the door to establish if the owner is present. It will, of course, smell the item of clothing you have left
- have learned that by relaxing without disturbing anything but your chosen item you will return and pay attention to it
- understand that if it tries to chew or disturb anything, the door will get aggressive! The door, of course, will always be there.

Other things to help the dog to accept being by itself are:

1. Reduce the amount of contact you have with the dog for 30 minutes before you leave it, so that the difference between you being present and being absent is much less noticeable to the dog.
2. Make a particular effort to leave the dog by itself for several short periods at weekends, otherwise if it has a lot of attention on Saturday and Sunday it will object to being left by itself on Monday. The worst day of the week for problems of destruction is Monday in a normal week or Tuesday after a Bank Holiday. You should also get into the habit of closing doors behind you so that the dog is not allowed to follow you everywhere in the house.
3. Make sure your dog is tired before you leave it and give it a good meal. After strenuous exercise and a meal, all it should want to do is lie down and sleep!

DIGGING

Another form of attention-seeking destruction is when the dog digs up the lawn or flower beds and shrubs when left by itself in the garden. Again, we have to look at the clues that the dog gives us about its behaviour which, although unacceptable from the owner's point of view, is nonetheless rewarding from the dog's perspective. The dog is out in the enclosed garden all by itself for extended periods of time. On previous occasions, when accompanied, it may well have witnessed the owner (its main role model) pulling up plants and then discarding them. We call this weeding! Now, finding itself alone and wanting something to do, this dog starts to pull out plants but in a less discriminating manner than it has seen its owner doing.

The result is that the owner, on seeing their dog pulling out plants, immediately runs out to join the dog and engages in a game of chase. This eventually results in the owner removing the plant or shrub from the dog and replanting it in front of their dog. Before returning to the house and leaving the dog alone again they usually verbally threaten their dog if it touches the flowers or shrubs again. Isolated once more, the dog now has an easy solution to the problem of getting its owner to come out and play! So now it deliberately pulls out plants, frequently looking in the direction of the door to the house in the expectation of the owner coming out to join it.

Ah, I hear you say, but if the owner rushes out and punishes the dog, why does it still carry out the bad behaviour? To understand this you need to understand that many dogs, like many people, are very social animals. You also need to understand that to them, having the owner with them so they are not alone, even if the owner is being abusive, is preferable to being in isolation. This condition is usually referred to as the Stockholm Syndrome and often occurs most in abused children, partners, kidnapping victims and dogs. It is sometimes difficult to understand how a person or dog can seem to almost consent to abuse and even have fond feelings towards their torturer, but the Stockholm Syndrome also shows that even though an individual may have feelings such as compassion and even love in addition to fear, they are still very much a victim of abuse.

So the dog's punishment for digging up your flowerbeds and leaving holes in your lawn to relieve isolation will not only not work, but actually has the opposite effect to what you want. There are three possible solutions to the problem.

The first is to go out into the garden with your dog so he is never alone in that area. The second is to erect a strong, high fence so that when alone there he does not have access to the areas where he can get up to mischief. But the solution you would have worked out if you understand the code is this.

Construct a digging pit around six feet square and fill it with a mixture of half sand and half peat. Now let your dog see you bury some favourite toys, bones, hide chews and other dog treats. Go back into the house and watch out of the nearest widow and wait until you see your dog digging in the pit and uncovering one of these items. Immediately run out and chase your dog around the garden and pick up the item it has removed from the pit. Now, with a smile on your face, bury the item back in the digging pit and lightheartedly threaten your dog with death if he digs it up again! Your dog has now learned a new and more effective way of reducing his isolation by carrying out the same behaviour as he did on your plants and shrubs with exactly the same end result on his part.

If you do now see him digging up a plant or shrub after you have retrained him in the digging pit, you can either ignore this behaviour completely and sit down to watch TV or put up a temporary fence to remove the opportunity to practise this unwanted behaviour. This fence can usually be removed in less than two weeks once the dog has built a history of being rewarded by attention for digging in the pit.

Remember that if you simply provide a digging pit but fail to go out when he uses it to dig up a toy, then he will quickly revert back to the previously learned behaviour of digging up your shrubs to get you out there. Understand this simple concept and you are well on the way to understanding the code.

INSECURITY

Other reasons that dogs chew when they are left alone are much easier to deal with. Insecurity is characterised by the dog selectively chewing something that smells of the owner, such as a recently handled item or small piece of recently worn clothing. To counteract this you can either leave an old cardigan or pullover with the dog for it to lie on when you go out or allow it access to your bedroom, the area in the house smelling most strongly of you, and to your dog, the most secure. Also block off the dog door, which in your dog's mind not only allows it out into the outside world but when the dog is by itself, also allows the whole world into your house!

You should also leave a recently worn item of clothing that smells strongly of you just outside the door to the area where your dog is confined. Also leave a recorder running playing sounds of you being in the house, vacuuming the bedrooms, holding a telephone conversation with a friend etc. Basically you can convince any dog that you are always in the house even when you are out providing he is not allowed free run of the whole house but is restricted to just part of it! Dogs only have five senses and it is easy to fool every one of them if you think creatively.

SEPARATION ANXIETY

This is a more severe form of insecurity and the dog begins to become stressed when it cannot see or touch its owner. The treatment is to start by setting various times each day when your dog can be restrained at a short distance away from you for just ten minutes at a time. This can be achieved by sitting on your couch and using a short length of cord to tether your dog to the far end of this couch. This will put your dog under a small amount of stress because he cannot reach you and touch you. The distance only has to be a few inches for the stress to start but it should be low enough that, after several days of therapy, your dog should accept this lack of touch contact. When your dog is calm and confident when you do this, you can move to the second stage, which is to put up a visual barrier between you and your dog. This can simply be a curtain so that your dog now cannot reach you because of the restraint and also now cannot see you. This again will cause a small amount of stress but this should be minimal and after a few days your dog should be relaxed when you carry out this procedure. Now all you need to do is continue as for the treatment for insecurity above.

BOREDOM

Chewing out of boredom is usually an indication that the dog is not being given enough physical or mental exercise. Increasing the games you play and the amount of physical activity during the time you are available should improve things. Half an hour before going out, let your dog see you scatter all his meal for that period on to the garden. Then let him work to try to find and eat his meal. Even when he has eaten the last piece he will not be aware of this and continue to work. After half an hour of this physical and mental exercise he should be tired enough to be left by himself without boredom chewing.

Also, leaving a large chew for the dog to amuse itself with when left for short periods will give it something to occupy its mind. Make sure that the chew is taken away from it when you come home, otherwise your dog will chew it continuously and therefore be less likely to amuse itself with it when you go out.

37

Elimination Problems

Many people who experience a problem housetraining their dog fail to understand how easy it is to achieve, even with an older dog. With a housetraining problem we are sometimes faced with a real dilemma. We know the dog will only make an association between the owner getting really annoyed and the act of going to the toilet in the house, so what effectively happens when the owner punishes the dog is that it will refuse to go to the toilet in front of its owner, no matter where it is. If I ask if the dog ever goes to the toilet in the house right in front of you, the answer is invariably no. So the dog sneaks off somewhere when the owner's back is turned and goes to the toilet in secret. How do we fix the problem? Easy!

The first thing to do is establish that the problem is not a medical one, so a visit to your veterinarian is in order. Assuming your vet cannot find a medical reason for the behaviour and your dog does have control over bowel movements – we will deal with urination later – you can start your behaviour-modification programme.

Look at the diet you feed your dog. If your dog needs to go to the toilet more than three times a day then either the food you are feeding it is too low in digestibility or you are feeding your dog too much. Don't take too much notice of the quantities written on the bag of food. It is there as a guide and always advises feeding more than the dog actually needs – that way the company sells more dog food. It might be worth checking with someone who specialises in canine nutrition to find a diet that is over 85 per cent digestible. That figure will not be written on the bag so you have to do some homework. The digestibility figure means that if you feed your dog 100 grams of dry food and then weigh what comes out of its rear end, you will find out how much has been digested. If only 15 grams of faeces are produced, that means that 85 grams have been digested. So making the switch to a food that is over 85 per cent digestible and feeding that food in the correct quantity should result in your dog going to the toilet two to three times each day. At a stroke that makes it easier to apply a housetraining programme.

I have worked with dogs whose owners complained that their dog was going to the toilet more than ten times a day! For that to happen the food must have been either very indigestible or fed in huge quantities, or the dog was under huge amounts of stress. Stress has the effect of increasing the need for the dog to relieve itself.

When you have your dog down to going to the toilet just three times each day at the most, you now need to keep a diary of these elimination times. If you feed your dog at a consistent time and in a set routine, the elimination times should be fairly constant. Let's imagine that these elimination times are at 10am and 7pm. Next take a look where your dog is going to the toilet. Where and what is the surface that it goes on? As I said earlier, it is usually a secret area and the dog usually prefers a particular type of surface for toileting. This might be a mat near a door or an area of carpet. You will need to get a sample of this surface.

Now with this sort of predictability, it is simplicity itself to retrain your dog to go to the toilet anywhere you want. At 9am, one hour before your dog's predicted toileting time, make sure it is confined to a really small area, on a surface that he would not want to go to the toilet on. Sometimes this will be the dog's own bed. Sometimes you can use an indoor kennel or, if your dog usually sleeps on your bed, this is the best surface. You can increase the chances of your dog not wanting to soil this area by feeding it on that surface while it is restricted.

You also need to set up a screen in your back garden so your dog cannot be seen from all four directions. Remember that dogs in general prefer to go to the toilet away from the gaze of the world, so the screen is an important part of this programme. A simple screen could be a sheet of canvas stretched around three poles stuck into the ground. Inside this screened area, place a small square of your dog's preferred toileting surface that has been contaminated with the smell of his own faeces.

Now at 10am all you need to do is take your dog out into this screened toileting area that smells of his faeces and has the surface that he likes to go on. Hold on to your dog's collar and scatter a small handful of very small food treats in a big circle around the extremity of the surface that you have provided behind the screen. This will make your dog sniff and circle! After sniffing and circling at a time when he needs to go to the toilet in this prepared secret area, nature should take over. Leave your dog alone in this area for at least five minutes and then check that he has been before you allow him back into the house. He is then free until one hour before the next danger time.

You will need to keep this routine up for about three weeks, during which you should be using ordinary biological washing powder in solution to remove the smell of faeces from any contaminated areas in your house. Don't use proprietary solutions as they generally don't work! Also using anything other than what you wash your clothes in brings a new and novel scent into your house. If you use these purpose-made pet odour removal products, your dog will be attracted to the area to investigate the new and novel smell. This will cause him to sniff and circle…

After three weeks you can change the dog's preferred toileting surface to anything you want. You could slowly cover the surface in your secret area with gravel or paving slabs or grass – the choice is yours. After a further three weeks you should remove the old surface, leaving just the new one you have now trained your dog to use. If you want to take it one stage further, you can teach it on command. Just pair the sniffing and circling behaviour with a command such as 'be quick' and within a further week your dog should start to feel he needs to eliminate whenever he hears your command.

For urinating in the house you should start by reading the section on territorial marking, page 269, as this is often the reason that dogs leave wet patches on the floor and furniture. Again, a veterinary check-up is an important first step to remove the possibility of a medical cause.

Often excessive urination is down to excessive intake. With some dogs, particularly those that live in a house where there is another dog but just one water bowl, it is possible that competition over this resource is set up between the two, resulting in both drinking excessively. Strangely enough, providing multiple water bowls dramatically decreases this particular problem.

To prevent a single dog from excessive urination, some kind of restriction should be placed on its water intake but this is a very difficult thing to advise an owner to do because of welfare concerns. It is best achieved by giving your dog a frozen bowl of water or ice cubes so that water is actually available all the time but it reduces intake down to just what the dog actually needs for survival and stops the dog drinking excessive amounts. Talk to your vet before you do this.

FAECES EATING (COPRAPHAGIA)

Copraphagia means that the dog eats its own faeces and not that of other animals. Sometimes this occurs because the food that the dog is being fed is not very digestible, and when it emerges out of the dog's rear end it still contains food items. There are basically two approaches to fixing the problem.

The first is called management: if you were in attendance and cleaned up immediately after your dog then the problem could not occur. The lazier approach is to put pineapple juice in the dog's food. Grated courgette (zucchini) works as well, as does MSG (monosodium glutamate). When you add any one of these to your dog's food what comes out of the dog's rear end is generally unpalatable and the dog will avoid eating it. Ferrous sulphate tablets crushed into the dog's food also work really well, but it is vital that this is only carried out under veterinary supervision.

For a dog that eats the faeces of other animals, a good recall or a lead work well.

38

Barking Problems

The environmental nuisance created by dogs barking probably results in more complaints that any other associated with dog ownership. Let's start by examining one of the most common forms of barking and one of the easiest to cure – barking for attention when left alone.

For a dog to learn to bark for attention, the behaviour closely follows that of the pup that learns to chew to gain attention. Quite often on the first night it spends with its new owners, the pup barks and howls through the night and is immediately rewarded for his behaviour by the owner returning to him. Within a couple of nights the pup is either taken up to the bedroom or the owner sleeps downstairs with it. If it is then inadvertently shut in a room by itself the resulting barks will rapidly bring the owner along to open the offending door.

Barking that starts within five minutes of the owner going out is directed at the door through which they left, so it is possible to use exactly the same treatment as for chewing when left alone (page 213). Remember that you must not advertise that it is you who is applying the bang on the door; you want your dog to believe that it is the door that is doing it. The problem is that if you have neighbours who are complaining about noise then banging the door in addition to the dog barking might just push them over the edge.

The best solution for the attention-seeking barker left in a room by itself is to place an old sheet under the door so that most of it is in the room where the dog is to be left. Put your dog in this room and then close the door. Make sure you have a small area of sheet on your side of the door. Now every time you hear your dog bark, give the sheet a sharp tug. Your dog should now associate barking with earthquakes! Start off using a time of two minutes in the same way as for attention-seeking chewing when left alone.

BARKING OUT OF EXCITEMENT

This type of barking generally precedes a really exciting event such as going out for a walk, being let off the lead to exercise or getting in or out of the car. It is much higher in tone and continuous, subsiding only when the initial burst has died away.

A regime of subjecting the dog to frequent exposure to all the preliminary events leading up to the anticipated reward is usually effective. It works like this. The owner puts on his coat and picks up the dog's lead. The dog, recognising that this means it is going out for a walk, starts to charge towards the door barking hysterically in anticipation of the exercise session. Once the dog has been placed on the lead and is outside the house the excitement starts to subside.

So to eliminate the problem simply go through the normal going-out ritual of putting on your coat, walking to the door etc., then pause and count to ten. Now turn away from the door, take off your coat, hang the dog's lead back up and sit back down again. If you repeat this routine as often as you can but going out for a walk only about once in ten visits to the door, and even then only when all barking or excitement has ceased, you will with patience and perseverance cure the problem.

When applying this technique it is important you remain calm and quiet throughout. Shouting will result only in the dog barking louder to make itself heard over the top of your voice. If you think about it, if you get excited and start shouting, then your dog will not see your behaviour as being any different from its own.

TERRITORIAL BARKING

This is the type of barking where the dog hears a noise and starts barking to alert the family and to warn off the prospective intruder. This is welcomed by the majority of dog owners but can easily become a problem when the dog becomes over-enthusiastic and continues to bark, even when the person walking by has long since passed and the owner continually shouts at the dog to be quiet.

Most dogs, on hearing someone approach with whom they are not familiar, will bark a number of times then stop to listen to establish whether the person is still approaching or retreating. If the person is getting closer, the barks, although around the same in number, will get louder. If, on the other hand, the person is now moving away from the house, the barks continuously diminish in both number and volume. This sequence of barks is followed by two to three seconds of silence, after which the barking will either recommence with the same sequence, getting louder, or will start to decline with longer gaps between barks.

To enable the owner to control the number of times the dog barks to warn of impending danger, we must teach the dog to understand and obey the command of 'quiet' at the time when the dog is most receptive to actually hearing it. You can learn your dog's barking sequence by counting the number of barks, so you can anticipate when the barking is on the decline. The last bark in the territorial sequence is usually a half-hearted woof.

While you are training your dog, you will need the service of a friend to walk past the house two or three times each day for two to four days. They should be instructed to walk past until they hear the dog start to bark, whereupon they should stand still for a minute of so before continuing on their way, standing still again if the dog begins barking again. You should also arm yourself with the dog's favourite toy or food treat and wait until the barking starts.

Count the number of barks and anticipate when the dog will pause. If you then immediately give your command of 'quiet' in a gentle and half-hearted manner, and reinforce it with either a game with the toy or offering the food while continuing with a lot of verbal and physical praise, the barking should cease for a minute or so because the person outside is stationary and the dog is being distracted by your reward. The barking may start again when your assistant outside moves off, but simply keep repeating your sequence of silence, command, reward as much as is necessary.

After several repetitions over two days you should now give your command of 'quiet' at the first or second bark and start to delay the reward, so the dog has to remain silent for two seconds before the reward is offered, then three, then four, then six and so on. If the dog barks, simply repeat the command and make it wait a few seconds more before rewarding it. When you can successfully give the command 'quiet' and reward the dog some 20 seconds or so later, you can dispense with the services of your friend and use this technique each time the dog barks when it hears something. Vary the point at which the reward is offered between three and 30 seconds, making it more unpredictable and thereby maintaining the dog's attention.

This technique relies on rewarding the periods of silence rather than punishing the barking and is extremely effective in putting the owner in complete control while not diminishing the dog's desire to give warning of an intruder. Verbal punishment for barking usually serves only to compound the problem, as the dog will frequently believe that its owner is in fact barking at the threat in competition with it!

39

Fears and Phobias

Exposure to an event that may cause harm is called *fear* as long as the dog makes a decision based on all the options available to it. In other words, the dog is in control of its fear. A *phobia*, on the other hand, is when the dog is exposed to a fearful encounter and does not make a decision based on all the available options. In other words, it is not in control of its fear.

WHAT IS A FEAR RESPONSE?

Your dog takes in information about the world around him using the five senses that nature has given him: touch, taste, smell, sight and hearing. How well each sense operate depends on several factors, such as its breed, the abilities of its parents, the dog's early exposure to certain types of stimulatory experiences and the opportunities that he may have had to practise and develop his senses. If a dog shows a fear response then there are several physiological changes that occur naturally to prepare the dog for either a flight (run away) or a fight (aggressive) response.

In an emergency, the dog's body is primed in an instant for either attack or defence.

1. The senses become super alert. Touch, sight and hearing are all increased.
2. Blood is diverted away from the skin and non-essential areas (pupils become dilated) and channelled to vital organs and muscles.

3. The liver releases its store of blood sugars to send to muscles for quick energy. Red blood cells are rushed into the bloodstream from reserves in the spleen.
4. Breathing becomes faster and deeper as the need to take in more oxygen increases. There is a widening of the bronchioles of the lung to achieve this. Oxygen is needed by the muscles to help transform sugar into energy. Faster breathing also helps to remove excess carbon dioxide.
5. The heart beats faster with larger beats to transform the oxygen carrying the blood to the organs and muscles that need it. As a result, blood pressure rises.
6. To conserve energy there is a shut down of non-essential operations such as digestion. Bodily secretions also stop, which results in the mouth feeling dry.
7. Sweating increases from the pads to cool down the skin, which becomes hot due to the body's exertions.
8. The bladder and bowel may evacuate any excess loads they are carrying.
9. The muscles of the limbs become more tensely contracted and less liable of fatigue. Tense muscles give off lactic acid into the bloodstream, which has the effect of increasing anxiety.
10. More insulin is produced to break up the body's sugars for instant energy.
11. Painkilling endorphins are released to suppress pain responses.

These physiological changes prepare the body for the physical exertions necessary for either fight or flight. If the level of anxious arousal is low, the dog can review options and, if appropriate, learning can take place.

Although the sudden release of a strong surge of adrenaline prepares the body for the instant action necessary for real fight or flight situations, this intense process can interfere with new learning and/or choice of the correct and safe options. It is important to understand this process so the fearful dog is never put into a situation where he experiences more fear than he can cope with. It also shows how the process of desensitisation works, as the dog should only ever be subjected to the lowest dosage of fear he can cope with so that very little adrenaline is produced.

Fear can enhance the ability to learn. If a dog encounters something that may easily kill or injure it, it's vital that the dog learns to avoid it as quickly as possible. If it takes several repetitions before life or death lessons are learned then the chances of survival decrease dramatically.

If a dog is exposed to excessive amounts of fear then, rather than enhancing the ability to learn, the dog can easily have its learning ability interrupted or extinguished. A *fear* response is where the dog's actions are calculated to avoid and suppress the source of its fear and reduce danger. A *phobic* response is one that is irrational and not calculating, and sometimes places the dog in greater danger.

A dog that is not in control of its fear response is vulnerable to other cues not initially connected to the original fear. Thus a dog that has become phobic about gunfire may begin to respond in a similar fashion to other noises that previously did not produce a fear response at all. Once a dog is in a phobic state it is possible to trigger fresh fears, so expert handling is all important if this is to be avoided.

Strategies for treatment of a phobia are much more complex and the prospects for a complete cure are not quite as high.

The tests

To be able to select an appropriate programme for your dog's needs, you first have to assess your dog's level of fear when exposed to certain types of sound. To do this simply answer each of the following questions.

1. When your dog becomes frightened, for how long does he remain afraid?
   a. just a few minutes
   b. more than five minutes
   c. more than ten minutes

2. Can you identify the sounds that cause your dog to become frightened? Is it:
   a. one specific type of sound only

b. more than one sound of a certain type
c. many different sounds

3. When your dog is frightened, does he:
   a. run to you for comfort
   b. stay where he is and tremble
   c. run away from you or run around in blind panic

4. When your dog is showing you he is frightened, if you called his name and tell him to sit, lie down or carry out a command he usually obeys, does he:
   a. still carry it out but reluctantly
   b. find it difficult to concentrate on what you are telling him to do
   c. act as though he cannot hear or comprehend what you are saying

5. Over the past few weeks, have you noticed that your dog's fear:
   a. has remained about the same
   b. is slowly getting worse
   c. is very rapidly getting worse

Now add up your five responses to the questions. If you scored

- three, four or five As, use the habituation programme.
- three, four or five Bs, use the desensitisation programme.
- three, four or five Cs, use the counter-conditioning programme.
- two As with two Bs or Cs, then start with a desensitisation programme using the specific sounds your dog is frightened of, then a habituation programme using all the other sounds on the recording.
- two Cs with two or three Bs, use the desensitisation programme for all sounds on the recording and then the counter-conditioning programme for the specific sounds your dog is frightened of.

The three different programmes are designed to reduce your dog's sensitivity to noises. Each one uses the same recording, but the procedures are different.

THE HABITUATION PROGRAMME

This simply means letting the dog get used to the sounds that he is worried about by repeated exposures until they are of no consequence to him. Select an environment where your dog feels comfortable, such as its favourite room in your house. Also, select a time of day when you are going to be present for at least four hours. Then select the sound or sounds on the recording that most closely match those your dog is worried about. Finally, select a volume that is close to that at which he will normally hear this sound.

Now switch on your player and ignore your dog completely. Do not make a fuss of him or give any rewards while the recording is playing. Simply go about your normal daily routine as though nothing special is happening. If your dog seems worried about the sound you should not give any indication that you are acknowledging his behaviour. Instead treat him and the sounds as if they are no big deal. Once started, the sound recording should be used as continuously as possible: 24 hours a day for several days would be ideal. It is important that the tape is not switched off for at least four hours on the first exposure so your dog has the chance to treat it as background in nature. Each additional exposure to the recording should last for at least two hours.

Once your dog is taking no notice of the sounds on the recording, the trick is to move the recording to other locations such as your garden, a friend's house, dog club, during car travel etc., so your dog gets used to the sounds and will be unlikely to react to them in any given situation.

Use this programme to get your dog used to the sounds he will encounter at a training class or where dogs are competing by using the sound of dogs barking or the sound of a dog show. You can also use it to get your dog used to the sound of a new baby in your home or the sound of visiting children playing. It is also useful as an aid to socialisation for a young puppy prior to the age of nine weeks to accustom it to the sound of the big outside world into which he will be taken. It would be unwise to take a five-week-old puppy out into the outside world, but using this recording you can take a bit of the big wide world to where the puppy is!

THE DESENSITISATION PROGRAMME

This means very slowly letting the dog get used to the sounds he is worried by very small repeated exposures until they are of no consequence to him. Again, select an environment where your dog feels comfortable, such as its favourite room in your house, and a time of day when you are going to be present for at least four hours. Then select the sound or sounds on the recording that most closely match those your dog is worried about.

Now switch the volume on your player down to its very lowest setting – there should be no sound coming out of the speakers as the volume is switched all the way off! Sit down and relax before playing the recording. Now put one hand on the volume control and watch your dog closely. *Slowly* raise the volume until you get the faintest recognition from your dog. This usually takes the form of the dog tilting its head on one side or pricking up one or both ears. When you get this indication your dog has heard the sound, leave the volume at this level for at least three days. Leave the tape playing for as long as possible: 24 hours would be ideal but if this is not possible then the time must be in excess of four hours at the first exposure. The more the tape is played over the first three days the better it works.

When after three or more days you reach the point that your dog is no longer taking any notice of the sounds, slowly start to raise the volume on a daily basis until you reach the volume closely resembling the level your dog would normally hear them in the environment.

When your dog seems fine in the house and gives no fear response when the recording is played, it is time to change the programme slightly. Put the player upstairs, speakers down, in the room above where the dog is, so that the sounds now come from the fabric of the house instead of the speakers that the dog can see. When you do this you might have to drop the sound level for a day or two. The final step is to put the player or speakers just outside the window, so that your dog hears the sounds coming from the outside environment. Once again you may have to drop the sound level when you first do this.

The final stage is to take the recording to lots of different locations to expose your dog to the sounds in more natural environments. You will notice that no rewards have been offered at all during the programme because you are trying to remove your dog's fear response completely so he does not react to these sounds at all.

It is important for the duration of the programme that you do not react if your dog shows any signs of fear to these or similar noises. If you start to comfort and reassure your dog when it shows signs of fear, you will simply strengthen his fear response as showing fear now becomes rewarding. Treat the sounds as if you are not in any way concerned and your dog should quickly mimic your behaviour during this programme.

Use this programme to remove a dog's fear of such sounds as gunfire, fireworks, helicopters, other dogs, vacuum cleaners, road traffic, aircraft etc. Also use it to remove triggers that spark off behaviours such as dog-on-dog aggression, car chasing, excessive barking etc. By repeatedly exposing a dog to increasing levels of any sound that causes it to react by barking, chasing, aggressive or anxious arousal, you will remove these sounds as triggers for the associated behaviour.

For example, if your dog barks whenever it hears someone knocking on your door, the trick is to repeatedly expose your dog to the sound of someone knocking on your front door, starting at a low level and gradually increasing. This sound then becomes totally unreliable as an indicator to your dog that there is a visitor present and so his barking response will eventually become virtually non-existent. You will usually need to desensitise your dog to other triggers such as sight and smell associations. For example, if you have a dog that suffers from brontophobia (fear of thunderstorms), you may also need to play a strobe light outside your window blinds on a dark evening to simulate the lightning flashes and an air ioniser to simulate the change in positive and negative charged particles in the air. This is incorporated into your programme as soon as the sound part of the programme is completed.

THE COUNTER-CONDITIONING PROGRAMME

This means changing the way the dog responds to a particular trigger (stimulus). For this programme you need to have several rewards available in order of how much your dog values each one.

In the case of a dog under stress, water can be added to this list of rewards. Remember that physiological signs of fear include bodily secretions stopping, which results in the mouth feeling dry, and an increase in sweating to cool down the skin, which becomes hot due to the body's exertions. In this case, water will sometimes work better than food treats for the fearful dog.

Using your graduated rewards system (see page 37), you are ready to begin your programme. As before, select an environment where your dog feels comfortable, such as your dog's favourite room in your house, and a time of day when you are going to be present for at least four hours. Then select the sound or sounds on the recording that most closely match those your dog is worried about.

Next follow the desensitisation programme to the point where you have the volume closely resembling the level that your dog would normally hear it in the environment.

The idea now is to pair the sounds on the tape with some of the rewards you have listed in order of your dog's preference. Start off by *only* playing the tape in conjunction with an exciting activity such as feeding or playing with a toy. Make sure you start off with rewards that are fairly low in value – save the better rewards for later in the programme. Continue to play the recording all the time the rewards are being given and stop it immediately after the rewards stop.

Within a few days of pairing the rewards with the sounds you should begin to see the dog pleasantly anticipating the reward whenever he hears the sound on the recording. Now begin to take your dog out to various locations and expose him to the sounds on the recording, slowly increasing the value of the rewards you offer. The counter-conditioning programme would be useful for a gun-shy working dog as it teaches the dog to *pay attention* to sounds that previously bothered it by linking them to rewards.

40
Attention-Seeking Behaviours

In this chapter we look at behaviour problems caused mainly by owners who fail to understand the concept of rewarding certain behaviours.

Dogs are social animals and benefit from being singled out for special attention much in the same way as we do. Attention means speaking to, looking at, touching or simply being present. So if your dog stands in front of you when you are on the telephone and barks for attention, every time you look at him, touch him or shout at him to be quiet, it achieves the goal that he set – to decrease the time you give attention to the telephone and increase the time you give your attention to him. (Cats too are masters at manipulating their owners into stroking them when they are speaking on the telephone!)

To understand the strategies used to decrease undesirable attention-seeking behaviour, you have to understand the concept of disassociation time. As its name suggests, this is used to disassociate behaviour from a perceived reward. The time we use is usually two minutes. Here is an example.

An owner has a Dobermann that whines for attention. We know this is attention-seeking behaviour because of a particular rhythm or pattern of whines. All attention-seeking behaviour is characterised by this pattern or rhythm. Four whines short gap, three whines slightly longer gap, four whines short gap, two whines slightly longer gap, five whines short gap, three whines etc etc. Listen to the rhythm and watch what the dog does during the gaps. This pattern will typically repeat itself for around five minutes when there will be a long gap as the dog sees what effect its behaviour is gaining. This usually means a glance towards the owner.

If the owner is told to give the dog attention only when it is quiet, the problem will never go away. That is because there has to be a disassociation time of two minutes before the dog is given any attention. If the owner rewards the dog as soon as it is quiet, it is probable that the dog is preparing for the next sequence of whines and will then associate the attention received with the behaviour of whining. (It becomes even more critical to understand this disassociation time when dealing with aggression!)

So if you are sitting in a room and your dog stands in front of the TV and barks for attention whenever you try to watch a particular programme, then shouting, looking at or even chasing the dog and trying to smack it will all achieve the dog's desired result – to get your attention away from the TV and on to him. So if each time your dog barked in front of the TV you stood up and stormed out of the room, slamming the door and leaving him on his own for at least two minutes, I would bet that he would no longer bark for your attention when you watch TV. Why? Because it now achieves the exact opposite of what the barking was designed to achieve – social attention.

The big problem is that the owner is unlikely to give the dog the attention it craves for lying quietly when they are watching the television! For this and all other basic behaviour programmes to work, you must remember to give the dog what it wants (in this case social attention) when it is doing what you want. This means that for the above programme to be effective, the owner must be instructed that when their dog is behaving in an acceptable manner they should get up, switch off the TV and pay attention to their dog!

Look again at the chapter on the dog that is destructive when left alone (see page 213). In particular look at the example of the dog that digs up the garden and flowerbeds!

Most of what we describe as manipulative behaviour is simply the owner rewarding the dog by giving it social attention at inappropriate times. If you ask an owner of a problem dog to keep a record of how much attention – in the form of speaking to, looking at, touching or simply being physically present – he gave to the dog each day, and then work out how much of that attention was given on the owner's terms and how much on the dog's terms, you will see that the problem exists because the dog holds the keys to getting attention and not the owner.

41

Food Stealing

By itself, food stealing is not a serious problem and can be avoided by ensuring that all food is kept out of reach of the dog. Some dogs, however, are particularly adept at finding ways of opening cupboard doors, climbing on to work surfaces etc., making the elimination of the problem necessary because the relationship between dog and owner will start to deteriorate.

The more serious problem of aggression over food is made considerably worse if the dog takes to stealing food belonging to its owner and subsequently guarding it. As with all other behaviour problems it is essential to establish that the problem does not have its cause in the dog's overall health. A check-up by your vet will eliminate obvious physical reasons for the dog's desire to steal food and should always be the first course of action in dealing with the problem.

If the problem relates to a puppy or to a dog that is not fully mature, then a strip of double-sided sticky tape strategically placed on the edge of the surfaces where food is usually available will be enough to prevent the problem developing any further.

Most dogs learn that if they attempt to steal food when the owner is present, the owner becomes aggressive. For an adult dog that has learnt to steal food when the owner is not in attendance, a system has to be used whereby the dog learns that the act of stealing produces a disagreeable experience which is not connected in any way with the owner (environmental correction). For this to work effectively it relies on a strong role model to cement the idea firmly into the dog's head. It works like this.

Stick a small device known as a detonator, which is available from joke shops, on a surface where food is kept such as a table or counter. Set the detonator by loading it with a percussive cap. Then place a small piece of food on the device. Don't worry, there is nothing on the device that will physically hurt your dog – it just makes a loud bang. Now sit a short distance from where the device is set.

When your dog tries to get the food and sets off the explosive device, how *you* behave is really important. Make sure you jump back and act as though you are disturbed by the sound. Now, with your dog present, approach the detonator and food with a great deal of apprehension. Approach from different angles and when you get close, suddenly retreat with a worried look on your face. When you do finally make contact with the food and detonator, do so really cautiously. In short, if you let your dog know you are also worried about approaching after the bang, it will reinforce the idea in your dog's mind that trying to touch food on that surface is not a good idea.

Unfortunately I know people who, when the dog has discharged the detonator, have immediately and confidently gone up to the detonator and pointed at it while smiling at the impact it has had on the dog, who now is standing at a distance. The effect this often has is to give the dog the much-needed confidence to approach and try again!

Section 6
Aggression Towards People

'Just as courage imperils life; fear protects it.'
– Leonardo da Vinci

42

Understanding Aggression

In this section we look at dogs that become aggressive to humans. Some of the basic concepts will be just as true for dogs that become aggressive towards other dogs, which is covered more specifically in the next section.

First, a few words of caution. My definition of aggression is the intention to do harm. If you own a dog that intends to harm people or other dogs, then whatever the reason behind this behaviour, the only way of ensuring your dog does not actually bite is to see that it always wears a correctly fitting basket muzzle when out in public. Remember, too, that a dog with a muzzle on should not be allowed off the leash. A dog carrying out a muzzled attack on another dog or person is a truly terrifying and traumatic experience for the victim. Likewise, the only way you can ensure that your dog never harms anyone who enters your property is by having a secure area into which your dog is placed and the visitor never allowed to venture.

Any other strategy to try and 'correct' your dog's problems will involve a certain amount of risk. If *you* are prepared to take that risk then read on, but remember that no one ever has to take risks with a dog that intends members of its community harm.

Again – and especially with aggression – the very first thing to establish is that there is no underlying medical problem at the root of the dog's aggressive outbursts, so a visit to your veterinarian is in order to eliminate that as a cause.

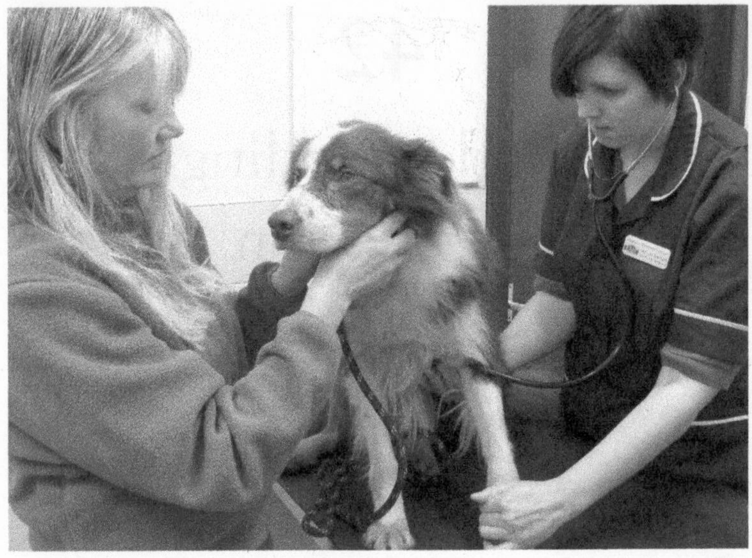

A veterinary examination

There are only two possible reasons behind the learnt components of aggression and they are known as the two F words: Fear and Frustration. The military and the police know there is no other way to train a dog to bite (I know because I do it as a consultant for the military and the police) and whether you do it deliberately or accidentally, the same two words keep on cropping up. Put even the most placid dog in a position where it is terrified and believe me it will bite you. Get any dog (or person) really frustrated and they too will bite you. Ever heard of road rage?

Let's examine two different scenarios. The light is fading when you are walking home. It is cold and you are wearing a dark hooded jacket that partially obscures your face. The path that you are walking on is narrow and walking in the opposite direction is a young guy walking a 14-month-old German Shepherd. Realising that the path is narrow, the owner of the dog tightens up his lead to manoeuvre his dog out of your way. Meanwhile you move to the edge of the path to try and put some distance between yourself and the dog, which is straining at the lead. As you are about to pass, you glance at the dog and then say 'Hi' to the owner. Quick as a flash the dog lunges forward and grabs your sleeve, tearing it as you pull away. The dog is instantly dragged away by its owner as it rears up barking explosively. You now shout abuse at the owner who is yelling at his dog. As soon as you are a distance away, the dog finally stops barking and straining towards you, and dog and handler go on their way.

The following night you happen to be walking along the same path. This time a young lady with a 14-month-old German Shepherd is walking towards you. As you approach she tightens up her lead and as you are about to pass she says something to her dog. Quick as a flash the dog lunges forward and bites your jacket.

The first dog was a pet dog owned by a pet owner. The second was a trained police dog! One dog was reacting to the situation and something called an external cue, outside of the control of the handler. The police dog was reacting to the cue given by its trainer. Strangely enough, both dogs have been trained the same way. The only difference is who is in control of the signal that starts the aggressive outburst. The police trainer can flick the switch on and off at will, but the pet owner cannot.

So if there are only two ways – fear and frustration – that you can teach a dog to bite, then it becomes obvious that if you remove frustration from your dog's life you will also reduce aggression. Equally, if you always give your dog an escape route and teach it to use it, then you will also reduce aggression.

Now let's look at how a dog can be deliberately trained to bite. I am not including this to encourage you to train your dog to bite but as a way of helping you to understand how and why aggression occurs. It needs a set of ingredients, remember?

The old-fashioned way of training a dog to bite was by having it held on a lead, cornered and intimidated by an agitator with a cane until the dog literally snapped. At this moment, the agitator would drop the stick and retreat. So the dog learned that the best form of defence was to attack and this was encouraged by the dog's handler, whose job was then to give the dog confidence to apply this type of aggression in lots of other situations. The reason that this type of training has been largely superseded (by the play and frustration method) is that using fear to induce aggression required an extensive confidence-building programme after aggression had been learned. It was also not as reliable a method of training as the more modern play and frustration.

Play and frustration-biting on a sleeve can be learned in one session; by starting with a game on a protective sleeve and then inducing frustration (teasing it), we have got a dog to bite a sleeve. Don't worry – it is still not aggression. This is how most of the people who train dogs for competitions like schutzhund, ringsport or working trials do it and, I would have to add, the dogs love it. To the dog it is and should always remain just an exciting game of biting a protective sleeve – they are strictly controlled by their handlers and the dog does not learn to be aggressive to people.

For example, with one of these trained bitework dogs, if you ran away wearing a protective sleeve and as the dog grabbed it you let go, would the dog then bite you? No, of course not. It would stand there with the sleeve in its mouth and invite you to get hold to play tugging. Alternatively, it would simply run back to its handler with the sleeve in its mouth. That would be great for an army dog, wouldn't it? Sent to apprehend a terrorist, it grabs their sleeve, tears a piece off and then returns to its handler wagging its tail!

Police and military dogs are trained to be 'arm true' (as opposed to dog sports 'sleeve happy' dogs). It would be inappropriate for this book to explain how it is done, but what we end up with is a dog that is no longer playing a game with a sleeve – it is biting a person for real. Unlike the sports-trained dog, the military or police dog intends to do as much or as little harm as is necessary to control their suspect.

If your dog shows aggression (intention to do harm) there has to be a process by which it has learned the behaviour. This means there must also be a process by which it can 'unlearn' the behaviour. The harsh reality is that it is often unwise to even try to fix problems of aggression unless it is a very young dog and the history of aggression is very short. Remember that to correct the problems of a dog that is people-aggressive, you cannot show your dog pictures of people and teach it to be nice to them. You have to expose your dog to people. Any strategy that exposes people to dogs with aggressive tendencies involves a risk. If you want to change your dog's behaviour then it is you, the owner, who has to bear the responsibility for taking that risk.

If your dog has never bitten but has only threatened to by giving an aggressive display, the risks of running a programme to correct the problem are significantly less.

The final point to understand is that when a dog has learned to use aggression, even though they may have started reluctantly, some dogs may actually enjoy being aggressive.

We can divide aggression into different categories to find a reason for the behaviour but this still does not get away from the two F words in aggression: fear and frustration. Some of these categories are:

- Territorial aggression
- Fear aggression
- Possessive aggression
- Dominance aggression (using aggression to influence an owner)
- Protective aggression
- Predatory aggression
- Food aggression
- Redirected aggression

We can also roughly divide dog-to-human aggression into three basic categories:

1. Dogs that are aggressive towards their owners or family
2. Dogs that are aggressive to frequent visitors or acquaintances
3. Dogs that are aggressive to strangers or infrequent visitors.

I could go on but that will only over-complicate things so I will stick to these categories to show you some of the ingredients required and to give you a framework of how to change your dog's behaviour.

43
Aggression Towards Family Members

Lots of people believe that a dog will never bite the hand that feeds it but sadly this is not always the case. Sometimes it is only the family that get bitten by their companion dog. Take the case of a miniature poodle that will not allow its owners to groom it but the groomer reports that there is never a problem. So why would a young puppy grow up with a desire to bite the very people it shares its life with? The pattern is almost always repeated in this manner.

REQUIRED INGREDIENTS

When the puppy was acquired it was not with the intention that it would be shared equally between all the members of the household. It was acquired with just one person in mind. So we have at least two people living in a house but the responsibility for looking after and educating it is not going to be shared equally. It would be a better ingredient if one of the adult household members did not really want to get a dog in the first place.

Now take a look at the rules set for the puppy's education. We have at least two people who share the house with the dog and each has their own ideas on how it should be raised. In effect, we have one person trying to set some basic rules for the dog and the other not really backing up these rules or, worse, they have their own set of rules. Now dogs are very adaptable and it is not beyond the realms of possibility that this dog is able to learn two different sets of rules dependent on any one particular circumstance. So let's take a hypothetical look at how things can easily go wrong.

The husband of the couple has always wanted a dog of this breed and the time is right for him to fulfil his desire. By choice, his wife would not really want to get one, but she has been persuaded to accept a dog in the house because her husband wants one. The puppy arrives; she does not actually dislike it but lacks the enthusiasm of her husband. Now let's look at how the relationship develops.

The puppy is settling into the house well and becoming the best friend of the husband. His wife does interact with the dog but not in the same way or for as long as her husband. Both husband and dog are building a good bond through the way that they interact. The husband tolerates more play biting, puppy chewing and overexcited play behaviour than his wife. As the puppy grows, it begins to try and get on the couch to sit next to husband, who does not mind it being alongside him. On occasions he will even lift it up onto the couch. The dog has started to notice it is getting preferential treatment over his wife and his wife has started to notice that as well! She does not like the dog being on the couch and when her husband is not at home she will always insist that it gets off by either yelling at it or dragging it off by the collar. When her husband is home alone, however, the dog is allowed unrestricted access to the couch and may even be encouraged to get up and lie on it.

If the young dog picks up something it is not supposed to have (such as a scrap of paper), takes it to a place of safety (underneath or behind something) and begins to chew it, the husband will smile as he approaches and turn the whole thing into a game, maybe even trying to get his dog to bring the paper to him. His wife, on the other hand, will shout 'Bad dog! Leave it!' and remove the trophy with a scowl of disapproval on her face.

So the dog learns that there are two acceptable forms of behaviour, depending on who is in the house. If the husband is with the dog by himself then playing with paper is a fun thing to do and there is never any confrontation. Getting up on the couch is allowed as well. When his wife is home alone with the dog the rules are different. The dog is not allowed on the couch and the dog is confronted when it picks up something it is not supposed to have. But what happens when both partners are at home with the dog at the same time? This is now where we can add words like confusion, frustration and conflict – three of the ingredients that are required for aggression to occur.

So this dog is now around ten months of age (it depends on the breed when this will first happen), and the husband and wife are in the house together. The wife is in the room with the dog and the husband is present but probably not in the same area of the house. The dog gets on the couch and she tells it to get off. This causes confusion in the dog's mind because its attachment figure is present and this behaviour is surely allowed. The dog is now in conflict and emits a low growl at the person trying to impose their authority. His wife immediately backs away and goes to find her husband, complaining that the dog has growled at her. He does not believe it and is convinced that she must have done something to provoke the dog.

For the first actual bite to occur the circumstances have to be similar. What has happened is that as the dog starts to mature, it sees itself as having a high status which has been elevated by being the best friend of the group leader. Aggression is almost always then reported as:

- 'Becomes aggressive when I try to make him do anything he does not want to do.'
- 'Becomes aggressive when I try to move him from a resting area.'
- 'Becomes aggressive when I try to take anything away from him that he does not want me to have.'
- 'Becomes aggressive if I try to restrain and inspect or groom him.'
- 'Becomes aggressive when I try to get hold of his collar.'

All this is regardless of the breed of dog. No breed of dog exists that has been bred exclusively to become aggressive towards the people that it lives with, so this has to be a behaviour that has been learned in the environment where the puppy was raised. This type of aggression always starts with just one person but when most owners try to correct the problem, they do so by the other partner joining in the confrontation. After practising on the first partner and flushed with success that aggression works well, some dogs progress to using the same strategies even on the person that they originally looked up to.

Just imagine a young dog getting a scrap of paper and taking it underneath or behind something and then starting to chew it. When one owner approaches, the dog growls and they back off. They then complain to their partner that *their* dog has growled when they tried to take the item away. The other partner then tries to approach and the dog bares its teeth and growls at them as well and backs them off. What the couple did not realise is that if, in the early stages of this problem developing, they had both approached and removed the offending item, the dog would have let them take it! The dog has become aggressive because they do not work to the same set of rules, because they put a lot of confusion in the dog's mind, and because the dog has had its status raised by being given preferential treatment over the other partner.

Some dogs even progress to allowing one partner to sit next to them on the couch but not the other. They may even object to the two partners showing any affection to one another. In short, at the beginning of the problem it is easy for the dog to mistakenly believe that one human partner does not like the other – they seem to argue a lot and there is a great deal of unrest. It seems to me that some dogs then agree to help get rid of the offending partner and there is evidence of this being successful on many occasions. Do any of these words sound familiar? 'You think more of your dog that you do of me.' 'It's *your* dog and you should stop him doing that.' 'This dog arrived at the shelter because of a marriage break up.' (It was probably the dog that caused it!)

PREVENTION AND CURE

To prevent this problem from occurring in the first place it is important that you:

- Do not give the dog the idea that it is more important than your partner or your children – it is not.

- Agree on a set of rules that are fairly and evenly applied by everyone in the house equally.
- Back one another up. If you want your dog to learn rules, you have to help one another enforce them and appear as a united front.
- Remember that persuasion is often better than force.

What if you already have a problem with your dog becoming aggressive towards you and/or your partner? Assuming that you have things in life that your dog cannot get without your help, all you need to do is write up a list of behaviours that you want and then give your dog something from his list whenever it does anything you want. So dealing with this type of problem, this is what you need to write up for your dog.

- A set of rules under which it gets fed each day. This could be that no one is now allowed to feed the dog from the table. It might mean that for a few weeks all the food the dog is given, it has to earn by doing what you want.
- There is no free love or affection because you are going to set rules under which your dog gets affection love and attention.
- The big one: a set of rules for playing with your dog.

This is an important set of rules, so when playing with your dog maybe the rule has to be that no one is allowed to play individual games where the dog can compare its strength against you and your family. From now on we may need to set the rule that the dog is only allowed to play retrieve games (the concept of sharing – see page 40). We may need to set a rule that says the dog must only play with toys when there are two people present and all games have to be played with the dog on a house line (light nylon cord attached to its collar). For larger, stronger dogs we can tether the toy that the dog is playing with so that the dog has to play under the rules set by the owners.

We also need to establish rules that govern touching, handling and grooming the dog. If you want to teach your dog to fully accept being groomed, this is how to do it.

First pick a location that gives you the maximum amount of control. For small breeds this will probably be up on a table or raised platform, whereas for the larger breeds it will probably be standing on the floor. You will need to use a lead to tether your dog, one end being fastened to a secure, correctly fitting collar and the other end to a fixed tether point approximately in line with your dog's neck. The distance between the fixed tether point and your dog's collar should be around six to eight inches. Stand or kneel behind and to the side of your dog and support him by placing your arm under his tummy.

Using a soft brush you should now commence gently grooming down his hind legs. Make sure there is a small amount of slack between your dog and the tether point so the dog is not being strangled against the pressure of the lead when you start grooming. As the grooming continues, keep talking to your dog in a reassuring voice. If your dog starts to struggle, simply ease him away from the tether point to slightly tighten the lead, but stop speaking. The important thing here is to just keep quietly grooming so that your dog learns that struggling or having a temper tantrum no longer works. As soon as the dog relaxes, make sure that the pressure that it is exerting on the lead is reduced and then praise lavishly with your voice.

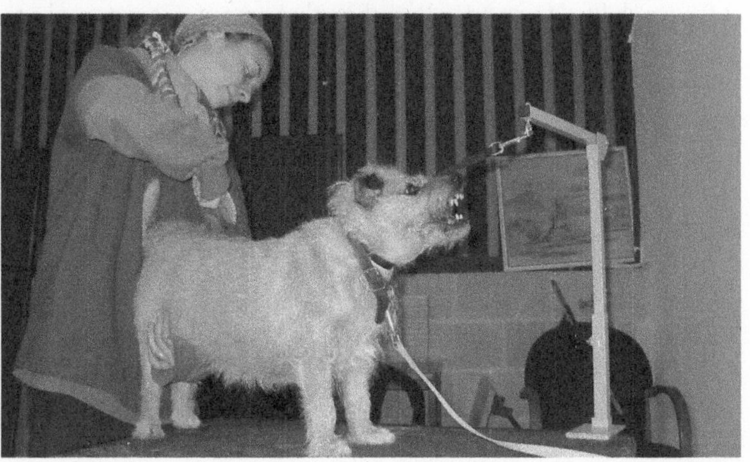

The correct way to groom

You should continue your grooming in the confidence that you are going to succeed and in the knowledge that your dog cannot possibly bite you. You also have two hands free to restrain, groom and stroke him as appropriate during this time. In the early stages it is better not to try to bribe the dog to stand still and accept being groomed, as offering rewards usually results in the dog becoming over-aroused, which is the opposite of what you want. When your dog has completely and totally accepted the grooming procedure for around 20 minutes, you can release him from the restraint.

For the first few sessions you will have only groomed down the dog's hind legs and possibly his back and tail, as these are the areas furthest away from his teeth! As you progress with each session you will extend the grooming further until you can groom his front legs, chest and head. After a week of daily grooming sessions, when your dog is fully accepting the procedure, you can start to link grooming to rewards such as going out for a walk or being fed.

If you are in any doubts about being bitten then using an Elizabethan collar should minimise any risk. You could use a muzzle but this over-complicates the procedure as you will first need to get your dog used to wearing a muzzle! So if you feel worried about grooming your dog because of the possibility of aggression then the only course of action would be to take your dog to a professional groomer and watch to see how it is done.

Remember that throughout your programme to re-establish yourself as your dog's role model, when you ask your dog to do something for you it is important to let it know you are pleased with it before you give it a reward. If your dog does not do as you ask, it is also important to walk away in disgust, thereby removing the reward from the situation.

For example, when you are going to take your dog out for a walk, get to the front door and ask your dog to sit. When he does so, gently show your appreciation by saying 'good dog' and smiling. Now count to 50 and if he is still sitting, attach the leash and take him out for a walk. If he moves before the time is up, walk away in disgust and hang the lead up, remove your jacket and go and sit back down. Wait for at least ten minutes (this is called latent learning time) and try again. Your dog should quickly get the message. Remember that you *asked* for a sit. If the dog gets to the door and sits automatically then ask it to lie down instead. Don't be fooled into allowing your dog to 'oblige' you to take it out for a walk by offering a sit when it has not been asked for!

With this type of relationship problem, training your dog to understand a few basic commands really does help as well. (See the section on basic training, page 97.) By setting and applying rules to the dog's life which are carried out consistently by all members of the family you should end up back in control of your dog.

One promise I will make you is this. If you and your partner are not fully committed to working with your dog jointly in any kind of behaviour programme and you do not agree on the rules or to give one another full backing, no programme ever devised will offer the result that you are seeking.

In trying to establish if a behaviour programme is going to work, we often have to take a close look at the owner and their ability to work to a given training (behaviour modification, rehabilitation) programme. Unfortunately, some dogs with problems that are not insurmountable live with owners who are just not capable of devoting the time or energy needed to make things work and receive no support from their family.

If you or anyone in your family has actually become frightened of your dog then I am afraid that the relationship is probably at an end in terms of your being able to fix the problem. No one should be asked to live in fear.

But don't despair – there is one solution that is not the final one of having the dog put to sleep. You could always get a secure compound built in your back yard and provide your dog with a shelter that simulates the type of environment he is looking for – a couch of his own, unlimited supplies of water, food and things to be possessive over, and no one to ever confront him. You become the keeper of a dog. This is no different to what some animal charities do with dogs they keep for life and *some* of these dogs do live out a happy and fulfilled life and never put anyone at risk.

You could also pay money to a trainer or a behaviourist but remember that they cannot change your dog's attitude towards you and your family. At the end of the day, it is up to you.

44
Fear and Aggression

It has always appeared to be a little strange to me that these two words often appear together in the world of companion dogs. By nature, if a dog feels threatened by something it is unsure of then surely the best strategy is to stay away from it. So perhaps the reason that fear behaviour ends up as fear aggression is because at some stage that option has been taken away from it.

If we start with fear and remove the escape, then we can then add the word aggression. So if we work to remove the fear, we have a confident biter, right? Dogs that are confident at biting do it better than dogs that lack confidence – and it is a much harder problem to correct. So surely to remove the aggression, we have to reintroduce the escape. It has always astounded me why anyone would want to teach a fearful dog to approach people. Isn't it wiser to teach the dog that it's OK to stay away? That way no one ever gets bitten.

Now let me take you through the ingredients for fear and aggression.

THE INGREDIENTS AND PATTERN

A puppy who lacks confidence with people may well have learned this behaviour from its mother who was also apprehensive of people she did not know, or it may have stemmed from a breeder who did little to expose puppies to lots of people early in life. It can also come from the fact that the new owner, maybe because of the veterinary advice, did not take the puppy out until it was fully protected by a vaccination programme. It can also start because a puppy has been kept with its littermates or another dog for far too long, so it learns good social behaviour around other dogs but humans are a mystery to it because it does not live in a world with much human contact.

We start off with a puppy that is apprehensive of people that it does not know. It is fully relaxed around its owners but when the dog is exposed to visitors to the house it backs away from them, for the most part seeking a safe place to escape to, which is usually somewhere close to the owner. At this stage what we see is a mild fear response and the puppy choosing flight behaviour as the best strategy.

Let's take a look at how the visitor comes to the house. They knock on the door or ring the bell first. The door is opened and a person unknown to the dog then enters after the owner (role model) has greeted them briefly. The stranger then comes into the house and is invited to take a seat. The owner also takes a seat a short distance away in a chair directly facing the stranger and then they began a conversation. The puppy – acting on the role model's (owner's) signals – also takes up a resting position at a distance from and facing the stranger.

During the conversation the stranger keeps looking in the direction of the puppy and making weird baby noises, holding out one hand as they do so. Feeling threatened by this, the puppy gives a few woofs almost under its breath. The stranger then intensifies the conflict behaviour by beckoning the puppy over, encouraged by the owner. Realising the puppy is showing fear and avoidance behaviours, the quick-thinking owner then approaches the visitor and gives them a few food treats to entice the puppy to go towards them. After delivering the food treats the owner then immediately backs away to return to their chair.

On smelling the food, the puppy is tempted to go in the direction of the stranger. It is still in a state of fear arousal and is now going to link this fear of strangers to the smell of food. It finally plucks up the courage to get close enough to take the food but then immediately retreats to a safe distance, just as its owners had demonstrated. (This is called allelomimetic behaviour under stress.) Instead of teaching the puppy that it's OK to stay away from people it is worried about, the puppy is learning to approach people it is worried about in the expectation of getting some food. Not really a clever thing to do, is it?

If the owner was a strong role model for their puppy, the best thing they could have done is to sit next to the visitor and give them a big hug! This has the effect of demonstrating that this is a person you really like and it also puts your scent all over them, making them more familiar and less frightening.

The next part of the progression is when a stranger 'who knows about dogs' tries to approach the puppy when it is at a distance and showing fear. The owner urges their puppy towards the stranger, who now manages to get close enough to touch it and stroke it. The puppy's eyes roll and it looks for an escape route but none is available (this stage usually takes place when the puppy is on a lead). So then the behaviour changes and now when a stranger approaches, the puppy begins to bark to warn them away.

This bark has a particular kind of sound. It is explosive, and as the puppy barks its front feet almost leave the ground. To look at it you could easily get the impression that the dog is lunging at the stranger. In fact it usually either stands its ground or moves backwards – it is fear-based, remember. At this stage the stranger will often make things worse by trying harder to get a good interaction when what the puppy is asking for is no interaction.

Now all we require is an owner who believes that their dog needs to be exposed to lots of different people to socialise it. Wrong! If you try this, you will discover that your dog is eventually fine when you walk it in a crowd of people. But after walking in a crowd with no reaction, you will walk past someone standing alone at a bus stop and as soon as they look down at your dog, it will immediately explode into barking. Common sense should tell you that if your dog is not happy about people it does not know, then exposing it to lots of people that it does not know will not be helpful.

What the dog needs when it has reached this stage is multiple exposures to the *same* person until its fear subsides. This can only happen by giving the dog distance and time. Only when your dog is behaving acceptably with one person – who after multiple exposures is no longer a stranger – can you start with a second person, thereby slowly increasing the dog's circle of known people. After reaching a certain number – around 20 – one at a time, your dog should start to generalise this to everyone it meets and should become more relaxed in the company of strangers. Providing your dog is showing an improvement each time, you are on the right track.

Only when your dog shows no fear reaction might you consider rewarding the dog with a treat. This is always carried out with the visitor throwing the food treat over the dog to land behind it. That way, if things go wrong at least the dog will learn to stand back from the person it was worried about and not to rush up to them. The last thing you want a fearful dog to do is rush up to someone in the expectation of food. If you take that line, then what usually happens is that your dog will approach people it is worried about to see if they have food. The dog will approach with caution and when close enough will sniff in the direction of their hand. On realising they do not have food in their hand, the dog glances up to look at their face and then explodes into barking.

As the young dog grows and starts to mature, the behaviour often gets worse to the point where it will nip at strangers when they get too close. Once a dog has bitten and received the result it had been trying to find for months, this behaviour will be the one of choice and we end up with a dog that is fear-aggressive. What was the good result that the dog got from its aggression? The person backed away and stayed away from the dog, giving it distance and time!

All a fearful dog ever asks for is distance and time to make a decision. Listen to your young and fearful dog and you will never have to deal with the problem of aggression being added to fear.

Unfortunately, there are times where the puppy has had fear of humans, other than those that it lives with, so imprinted by its mother that it is impossible to correct the problem. How would you recognise this? Let's do a test.

I am going to come to your house, where your fear-aggressive dog is. I am going to come in and completely ignore your dog. That means I do not want your dog to come to me and say hi. How long do I need to be there before your dog treats me as if I am of no consequence to him at all? An hour? Two? Three, four, five? The point I want to reach is where I can move around your house and your dog accepts and ignores me. (I am still not interested in your dog being friendly and approaching me.) Let's say it is five hours.

Now I am going to leave and return in two days' time. I am going to enter as before and totally ignore your dog. Do we still have to wait for five hours before your dog relaxes enough to ignore me? Maybe we have to wait even longer this time. So I repeat this four times over one week. If the dog is still ultra suspicious of me, even though I have presented no threat at all, and does not have the capacity to make good decisions based on its memory of me, then I am afraid that I cannot offer a solution and I know of no one who can. Your dog is fear-imprinted to any human it does not live with.

Bonny's bad behaviour

Bonny, a White German Shepherd, was bought in for a behaviour consultation by a mother and daughter who lived together. She came from a breeder who kept the father as a guard dog and the owners never got to meet him. Bonny's mother was extremely fearful and barked and lunged so much she had to be removed by the breeders so that our two buyers could look at the last remaining puppy in a litter of nine. They tried to stroke the terrified fear-imprinted puppy and it snapped at them. The breeder suggested that the introduction would best be carried out in the prospective owners' home, so mum and daughter went home followed by the breeder with the puppy. They were told to let the puppy settle in the house for a few days to build up its confidence in them. Bonny settled in just as the breeder had suggested and quickly bonded to the people she shared the house with.

The owners quickly noticed that their puppy barked at and ran away from anyone who came into their house. So they took Bonny to puppy socialisation classes at the age of 12 weeks (too late by then anyway) and food was used extensively to teach her to approach people. After several weeks they had succeeded in teaching Bonny, who used to back off and bark at people, to approach and bark at people. They then went to regular dog-training classes, from which they were expelled because Bonny bit a person when they put their hand out to stroke her.

Bonny was then packed off to a dog-training facility for two weeks of boarding and training. After one week the trainer reported that Bonny had settled in well and was working well in all the basic obedience commands. She would be ready to collect in a week's time. Excited at the prospect of getting back a more obedient dog that understood all the basic commands, mum and daughter arrived at the training facility where they got to see the trainer working with Bonny. They viewed this on a TV screen in an office and were pleased with the results, so they parted with their money and were reunited with Bonny, who entered the office with her trainer. Immediately she ran towards them and bit them both before breaking into a really frenzied barking episode. Only trust the people that you share a house with!

If you think about it, you will realise that trying to correct this dog's problems would have been absolutely impossible. It could not even recognise the people it had lived with for a year and did just what her mother had taught her. The only solution I was able to suggest was a correctly fitting basket muzzle, to be put on all the time the dog was out in public, and an indoor kennel or an area in the house that the dog could be placed into when visitors arrived. Needless to say the owners were very disappointed that I could not 'cure' their fear-imprinted dog that had been practising aggression for the past 16 months!

If your dog has not been fear-imprinted by its mother, like Bonny, with my one-week test you would notice that, with time and repeated exposure to the same person, the dog eventually chooses to ignore them. You would also see that the time it takes to make the decision to ignore this person is definitely reducing each time they come into the house.

Now let's have a look at things you can do to fix the problem. How you weave these ideas into a programme is up to you.

Remember that the two things that benefit a nervous dog the most are distance and time. So please do not be tempted to start getting people to bribe your dog to come to them by using food. It makes little sense because it is really easy to classically condition a dog to show a fear response when a certain type of food is presented. It works like this. Stranger equals fear response. Stranger paired with cooked liver also equals fear response. After a short period the smell of cooked liver now produces a fear response (see the section on classical conditioning, page 79).

Let's start by looking at what starts the dog into fear arousal. You are a human being and when you go into your house the dog greets you enthusiastically. I am also a human being but when I try and enter your house your dog shows fear and barks at me, backing away as it does so. So how does the dog discriminate between you and me? I smell different, look different and sound different. If I get close enough I may also touch your dog in a different way from how you do.

But the barking started even before you opened your door to me. Why? Because when you enter your house you put your key in the lock and turn it. That gives your dog a signal that the person about to enter is a friend and lives there. When I arrive at your house I ring the doorbell. That gives your dog the signal that I do not live there. This signal applies equally whether we are dealing with territorial or fear-based behaviour. So there are two ways that you can at least reduce your dog's level of arousal – you can either ring your front doorbell each time before you enter (to remove the signal that the person on the other side of the door is scary) or you can give everyone in your neighbourhood a key!

Breaking down the problem even more, you could also leave your dog at home and arrange to meet someone away from your house. Take one of your dog's favourite toys with you and ask your friend to rub their hands all over it and to rub it all over their body. Now put the toy into a zip-lock poly bag and take it home. After you have rung your front door bell and entered the house, take the toy out of the poly bag throw it over your dog's head so that he turns around and picks it up. You may find that he views it suspiciously at first but with a bit of help and encouragement he should lose his apprehension. Repeat this twice a day for three days. Then when I arrive at your door and ring the bell, as soon as your dog smells me what should he make an association with? He should back off and wait for the toy to be thrown.

Getting the dog to back off people when they enter the front door is absolutely the best strategy you could use for a dog that is fear-aggressive. There are many ways you could achieve this. Teaching your dog to immediately go to a safe place that is well away from the front door not only gives your dog distance and time but also makes it easier for anyone to get through the door.

Try putting all the things your dog values at a point as far away from the door as you can, preferably up on a shelf so the dog cannot get them by himself. Now each day as often as you can, ring your front door bell and enter the house. Do not greet your dog anywhere near the front door but walk straight past and head for this secure area where all the resources are. When you get there, ask your dog to sit and keep him waiting for approximately two minutes before giving him something from the shelf. If you do this around ten times each day for a week – 70 repetitions in all – your dog should make an association between the doorbell ringing and the anticipation of a reward at the desired location away from the front door.

Make sure that this is a location your visitors are not allowed to go. The idea is to give your dog a secure area to run to when people enter your house and it is not secure if visitors are allowed to go there. You are always the one who will reward your dog for reaching this area, not your visitor. Ah, you say, but I want my dog to be friendly towards visitors. Wrong! You want your dog not to bite people who visit your house. Using this method means more people are likely to come to the house, so you have more people to help your dog eventually overcome its problems.

You might try teaching your dog to go and lie in its bed in the kitchen on your command. This is known as teaching an incompatible behaviour, because if you train your dog to lie in its bed when you tell it, and no one is allowed to go near the dog's bed, you can effectively solve your dog's problem by teaching it to stay away from people it is worried about.

How about desensitising your dog to strangers by getting a big bag of old clothes from a charity shop? Keep them in a shed or garage and put on a different item – which has the smell of a stranger on it – each time you enter the house, thus getting your dog used to different smells, each of which ends in a good consequence – you.

Recording friends in conversation and playing this for a few days before the person visits the house will make your dog less sensitive to the sound of your friend's voice before they arrive.

In any programme to reduce fear you have to make a decision – do you want your dog to ignore people or pay attention to them? If you want your dog to pay attention to people then link the sight, sound and smell of visitors to rewards. If you want your dog to ignore visitors then do not use any rewards: simply teach your dog that visitors are of no consequence. Your friends will usually thank you for taking this approach especially if the dog has shown fear-aggression in the past.

If you own a dog that is fear-aggressive to people when you take it out for a walk, make sure you teach it to always switch sides when anyone is walking past so that you are always between that person and your dog. Never insist that your dog approaches anyone it is telling you it does not want to. If you take avoiding action as your dog is asking you to, then you will never have to deal with the aggression.

45
Territorial Aggression

All dogs are territorial by nature in the same way that we are. In nature, territorial behaviour has the effect of dispersing a species across the widest possible habitat so the available resources are not depleted to the point where the species dies out. So in an environment where resources are plentiful, aggression to defend that territory is reduced. In an environment where valuable resources are scarce aggression increases to defend the territory from intruders. Also, in a dispute over territory it is usually the occupant that wins as it puts up more of a fight since he or she has more to lose if they are defeated.

Territory has to do with resources. If you keep your front door to your house locked, you are just as guilty of territorial behaviour as your dog. We humans are fence-builders and boundary-markers. Dogs do not build fences to mark out their property lines. Also bear in mind that some breeds have been developed to guard property, so they have had their basic territorial instinct heightened by selective breeding. Most dogs will warn of the presence of an intruder by barking and this barking is territorial in nature. It is designed to give information to the possible intruder that this territory is occupied and to warn the rest of the group occupying the territory of the presence of a possible intruder.

There is also something known as territorial marking. There seem to be two reasons for this behaviour (as distinct from urinating). One is to warn away possible intruders and to give them the information that the area is occupied. The other is to invite 'guests' on to the property. Thus a bitch will usually start to increase her territorial marking around the time she is about to come into season to invite possible suitors. Territorial marking in dogs is just like us leaving written information for anyone that might wander past our property. If the written notice says 'no trespassers, this building is alarmed, keep out', it tells us that the occupant feels very insecure. If the notice says 'good looking 35-year-old male with good sense of humour seeks a female for outings and friendship', that conveys a very different message!

If it is only the actual marking behaviour that is a problem because your dog has started doing it in your house, the 'cures' are very simple. Castrating a young dog or spaying a female should stop territorial marking that was designed purely to attract a member of the opposite sex. The results should be seen within a few days of the operation.

For marking out of insecurity, simply take a piece of cloth and rub it vigorously around your dog's ano-genital region, thereby transferring the glandular secretions (scent) from that area onto your cloth. Then rub this cloth on every spot in the house your dog has marked. Repeat the treatment every day for at least a month and once a week thereafter and, like a miracle, your dog will no longer need to mark in your house. What you have done with your cloth is to put your dog's scent on to the spots it needs to mark. Your dog does that by using urine as a propellant. Don't worry – your friends will not notice any difference in the smell in your house, other that the smell of dog urine has now disappeared!

If you have a dog door that lets your dog out into the outside world, then replace it with a solid one. Dog doors (from the dog's perspective) also let the big wide world in to where the dog lives, thereby increasing its sense of insecurity. Putting in a dog door for a dog that already feels insecure is like leaving your front door open when you go to bed at night if you live in a bad neighbourhood.

Territorial marking to warn away intruders tells us a great deal about the dog, the relationship it has with its owners and how it views other dogs (and people) in the environment it is laying claim to. In very general terms the greater the number of important resources in the area the dog is kept in, the less you will see extremes of territorial behaviour. The larger the physical area the less extreme the territorial behaviour is going to be. Dogs that show the most extreme territorial behaviour tend to be ones who feel very insecure.

If the owner is present in the area and the dog still displays uncontrolled territorial behaviour by excessive barking or displays of aggression, that would tell me that the owner lacks influence over the dog. The dog possibly believes that he (or she) is the one who has the responsibility to decide who is allowed to enter.

So your framework for dealing with the problem includes:

- Teaching your dog some simple obedience commands and practising these near the entrances to your property. You could also teach your dog to go and lie in its bed, which should be kept as far away from the front door as possible. (Check out the section on training for tips on how to do this, page 160.)
- Reviewing your relationship with your dog and establishing yourself as the owner of the property with the right to decide who enters it. This simply means putting yourself in more control by using the strategies outlined in regaining control.
- Increasing the resources within the territory – two water bowls, more food available, two sleeping areas, more toys etc. By increasing the important resources you should see a decrease in extremes of territorial behaviour.
- Not allowing your dog to occupy areas close to entrances. This certainly means not allowing your dog to have a resting or sleeping area near to where visitors enter your house. This is because it is often thought that the sleeping area represents the centre of the dog's territory.
- Never inviting guests into the house where they are put in a position

of having to walk past the dog to get in. Again this means that there should be no introductions in a narrow hallway.

- Having your guest meet the dog on neutral territory before entering the property. To do this, simply arrange to meet your visitor with your dog at least a hundred yards from your property and allow them to walk back to the property together, letting your visitor enter first.
- Never leaving your dog unsupervised in a back or front garden where people and dogs are likely to walk past. With dogs that show a high level of extreme territorial behaviour, consider spending some time in your garden with your dog to establish you as the owner of the property. Simple daily obedience sessions in these areas should help to establish your influence over your dog.
- You could also have the dog in a secure area when guests arrive and only introduce it to them after they have been in your house for at least 20 minutes, so your dog walks into an area they already occupy.

Other things that you can try are removing *all* valuable resources from your property each evening. Throw away all your dog's food so that there is none for him in the house. Throw away all his toys. Throw away his lead if he likes going out for a walk. Then tomorrow have a visitor arrive and deliver just enough dog food for that day. Have them return to their car and then deliver a set of toys, then repeat with a lead and any other resources that the dog needs. Within three days the dog should see this visitor in a completely different light. The person arriving each day is now someone who benefits the dog's survival in that territory.

Bank tellers at drive-in banks in the USA learned this trick a long while ago. Put your hand into someone's car where there is a territorial dog and you are likely to get bitten when you take cash from the driver. Put your hand in with a dog biscuit that was not available before the hand went in and suddenly the hand going in represents adding a resource to the territory, so there is no aggression!

The case of Mischief, the Jack Russell Terrier

One day I received a call from a woman called Sally saying she was having an aggression problem with her Jack Russell Terrier. Mischief was just ten months old and slept in his owner's bedroom. Every morning when the postman arrived Mischief leapt out of bed and jumped up and down, scratching at the bedroom door. Sally would then get out of bed, put on her dressing gown and try to grab Mischief by the collar while she opened the door. There then followed a frantic race to get down the stairs and at the mail first. Often Mischief would wriggle free by spinning around and if he managed to get to the letters first he would grab as many as he could carry and then rush past Sally. When he got to his spot at the top of the stairs he would then shred the letters and if Sally went near to him there was no doubt in her mind that he would bite her.

I told her I was amazed that she was having this problem because not ten minutes earlier I had received a telephone call from a Jack Russell Terrier called Mischief who said he was having an aggression problem with his owner. Every morning when the postman put the letters through the letter box, his owner would become excited, get out of bed and race him to the bedroom door. Then she would race him down the stairs, trying to hold him back. If she got to the letters first, she would pick up as many as she could carry and take them into her spot in the kitchen and shred them. There was no doubt in Mischief's mind that if he tried to take them from her that she would get really aggressive!

There are several things I could have told her to do to solve the problem. One management solution would have been for Sally to buy an American-style mailbox and put it outside the front door. A second management solution would have been to fit a wire mesh cage to the back of the door. There is usually a management solution to almost every behaviour problem.

Another thing I could have told her to do was this. Every day for the next two weeks get an envelope, address it to yourself and put a stamp on it. Just before you seal it, put in a teaspoon of the hottest chilli powder you can find and mail it to yourself. When the postman arrives you let your dog rip up the letter and have a very disagreeable experience, which should then make the behaviour self-correcting.

This is an aversion solution and relies on the dog finding the chilli powder unpleasant enough to stop the behaviour in really short order. With this solution Mischief would never associate Sally with the burning sensation in his mouth and therefore not blame her for it. But there is always the risk, especially with terriers, that they will actually like the chilli powder and develop a taste for it. Aversion should only be considered when all other avenues have been exhausted, as it can easily lead to a dog losing all trust in its owner.

I also could have told her to record the sound of the postman arriving and putting letters through the letterbox and then play it over and over at ten-minute intervals throughout the day. When Mischief hears the postman coming and the letters falling through the letterbox, he'll race up to the door only to find that there are no letters. After a day of this, Mischief will think there is no point in racing up to the door because there are no longer any letters associated with the sound of the postman. This is known as habituation. It is the same as repeating a cue where the dog expects a result, but over a period of time comes to change its expectations and then finally treats the initial cue as if it is of no consequence.

Yet another approach could have been for Sally to have split Mischief's food into ten equal portions and then, ten times each day, play the recording of the postman arriving and lead Mischief into the kitchen and give him a portion of his dinner. After repeating for around a week there is a good chance that when the postman arrives, Mischief will run into the kitchen, expecting to be fed. This is known as counter-conditioning and simply teaches the dog a different response to the sound of the postman arriving.

Another way this could have been resolved would have been by Sally teaching Mischief to sit and stay at the top of the stairs while she went downstairs to retrieve her letters. This is known as teaching the dog an incompatible behaviour, as sitting at the top of the stairs is not compatible with grabbing letters at the front door.

I then asked Sally if Mischief had ever received any letters of his own. She said he had not. I then told her that Mischief's problems were probably down to frustration. Every morning she was to set her alarm for half an hour earlier than the postman was due to arrive and then attach a house line to Mischief's collar. When the postman arrived, Sally should lie in bed for ten minutes and relax, using the line to prevent Mischief from scratching at the bedroom door. When she was ready, she could hold the line, walk calmly down the stairs and into the kitchen. She should then let Mischief out into the back garden and make herself a cup of tea. When Mischief came back in, she should go to the letterbox and pick up the letters. Most people get junk mail every day, so when she came across a piece, she could pick it up and say, 'Oh, Mischief, this one is for you' and give it to her dog. Then she could go about reading one of her letters. If she didn't want to keep one after reading it, she could give that one to him as well.

To this day she continues to do that. Every morning when the postman comes, Mischief will calmly walk down the stairs with his owner and go out into the back garden while she makes herself a cup of tea. When his owner picks up her mail, he will wait for his letters and then proceed to rip them up. I didn't change the behaviour; I changed the way she viewed the behaviour and gave her a means of managing it that was suitable for both of them, while eliminating the aggression.

46
Aggression Towards Children

I thought long and hard before writing this section of the book as it puts me in a no-win situation. If I advocate no contact between children and dogs then you could argue that no child ever gets bitten. But then where will our next generation of dog owners come from? Will owning a companion dog become a thing of the past? So I decided to include this section, not to try and convince anyone that you should attempt to 'cure' a dog that has bitten a child, but to show how to recognise the warning signs and prevent these problems from occurring in the first place.

Statistically a child is more likely to get bitten by a dog in its own household than by a dog they do not know. So let's begin by looking at how much the child's age plays a part when a dog becomes aggressive to it. Again, remember that a dog does not suddenly wake up at the age of two and suddenly decide to bite the child it has lived with for two years – there has to be a reason.

I divide children into different categories based on their age.

NEWBORN TO EIGHT MONTHS

Usually the family dog has few problems with the arrival of a new baby. Dogs are creatures of habit, so if the routine changes dramatically when the baby arrives, often the dog will react to this changed routine. This is usually a change in the amount of attention given to the dog, resulting in the owners describing the dog as jealous of the new baby. Students of animal behaviour will not agree that jealousy applies in the dog world but I think it is a great way to describe what is going on. So if your dog's behaviour changes after your new baby arrives, it usually takes the form of an increase in attention-seeking behaviours.

To prevent this happening, try writing down the total amount of attention your dog gets from you on an average day for two months before the baby arrives. All you need to remember is that although you might want to rearrange when your dog gets attention from you, it is important to ensure it still gets the same amount after the baby arrives. Providing the amount of attention is the same each day your dog should remain content. If you then go about your daily duties as if nothing has changed you should find – apart from looking puzzled when the baby cries or moves – the dog accepts it without any problems.

For the next few days, try to link one or two pleasant associations with the baby, like going out for a walk or a game with a favourite toy when the baby has been put to bed, and you should find your dog soon grows to enjoy the new arrival. Avoid trying to speed up the process by carrying the baby towards the dog to introduce it or by insisting that the dog goes over to say hello. When the baby is being held or cuddled, give the dog a chew bone or toy to play with as a special treat to help prevent it feeling unwanted and trying to push in for attention. The vast majority of pet dogs soon accept and enjoy the company of a new addition to the family.

It should go without saying that even if your dog is of impeccable temperament, it should never be left with the baby without adult supervision, even for a moment. Although it is extremely rare, it has been known for a dog to become over-aroused by the cries of a very young baby. We can only imagine that with some dogs these cries switch on a predatory instinct where the dog simply sees the baby as a prey. Parental supervision at all times is therefore essential, especially with some of the terrier breeds. You can always test for this by switching on the taped sound of a baby crying and watching for the dog over-reacting and becoming very aroused. You can also make your dog less sensitive to baby cries by playing a recording of babies crying.

I often get asked questions about dogs that suddenly start territory marking in the house after the arrival of a new baby. The main reason for this is insecurity, as after the baby arrives the dog's whole world will change forever. Even the smell of the house and its occupants changes as the odours of baby oils and powders now permeate the building. Again, the answer is to use these preparations at least two months before the baby is due to arrive to habituate the dog to these smells.

ONE MONTH TO 18 MONTHS

If your dog is going to have problems with your child then this is when it is most likely to happen. Obviously, parental supervision is required, which means that any free interactions between the child and the dog should be closely supervised – meaning being in the same room and paying attention.

In the unlikely event that your dog starts to show aggression towards your child it will most likely be when they get to the crawling and walking stage. I am sure that, from the dog's perspective, the toddler is neither canine nor human as it manoeuvres around the floor. The typical pattern of behaviour is that the child crawls towards the dog and the dog, which has no escape route, growls out of fear to warn the child not to come any closer. The child fails to understand the growl as meaning 'keep away', so they continue to crawl towards it.

If parents are present then they will often physically or verbally challenge their dog for growling. This is now a no-win situation for the dog. The effect that punishment has on the dog's behaviour is that it will either cause the dog to growl much earlier when the child is a greater distance away, or the punishment will remove the warning growl and the dog then snaps at the child when it gets too close.

Look at it this way. You are frightened of spiders and you learn that if you stamp your feet they go away. Then you come across a spider that keeps on coming towards you, so you intensify your stamping in the hope that if you do it loud enough it will go away. Then when you do this someone hits you and screams 'No!' Does this make you less frightened of spiders? Something is now likely to happen as a result of a simple set of associations but we don't know what it is until it happens.

If you had made the link between stamping your feet and the smack and you wanted to avoid the smack, you would not stamp your feet the next time you saw a spider. But what happens if you don't stamp your feet? The spider keeps on coming! So just wait until it gets close and then stamp on it to solve the problem. Well, at least you did avoid getting smacked, right? Wrong, because in this example you could end up being put to sleep for making this choice.

If you had made the association between me the spider and my smack, you would learn to run away from me and stamp your feet at a distance from the spider.

The lesson here is never to punish your dog for letting you know how he feels. I would much rather hear a dog growl – so I can understand that he has a problem and solve it for him – than stop him telling me how he feels so that the only indication I get is when it is too late to take avoiding action – the bite has already occurred.

So the strategy is to always leave the dog with an escape route and teach the dog to use it whenever necessary. The escape route should allow the dog to leave the area without the child being able to follow. A baby gate or barrier in a doorway that you teach and reward your dog for jumping would be just fine. Alternatively a barrier in a doorway that the dog can squeeze through would also work. If you had a length of light nylon line attached to your dog's collar when the child approached the dog, you could quickly pick up the line and teach your dog how to exit the room. As your dog's confidence at being able to get away increases, it should tolerate more intrusions into its space, knowing that if it wants to leave, it can. Once the child is walking, this fear problem usually goes away.

EIGHTEEN MONTHS TO FOUR YEARS

If you are unlucky enough to have problems between your dog and your child, the problem will most likely be over toys and possessions. This is why when you get your dog as a puppy, it is so vitally important to get it playing games of retrieve. This teaches the concept of sharing, which is essential for our family companion. It is also a valuable concept to teach a child.

You have to make a decision about rules for playing with toys. The safest way to do this is to provide both child and dog with their set of own toys and not allow either to play with the other's. Or you can teach them both the concept of sharing, which I think is a better if riskier approach. If your dog will not return with one of his own toys or one of your child's toys when you ask, you either have to go through the section on how to get your dog to play or ensure that all contact is supervised. This type of supervision includes teaching the dog not to play with the child's toys and teaching the child not to play with the dog's toys.

FOUR YEARS TO EIGHT YEARS

This is the age at which it is more likely to be a visiting child that gets bitten. These bites are usually more serious as they fall into two main categories: territorial and protective aggression. Experience shows that usually it is not on the first visit that a child is likely to be bitten but the third visit. The very first time one of your child's friends visits your house, their approach is likely to be more cautious because they are unknown to the dog. There is also probably more parental supervision on the first visit to oversee any dog and child interactions. By the third visit there is probably less parental supervision and maybe the child, by now thinking they know the dog, is more likely to take risks.

It seems the majority of children get bitten under one of two circumstances: either when they approach the dog in its resting area or when they are playing an exciting and often physical game with the resident child. Remember the saying, let sleeping dogs lie!

Remember too that if you have always allowed your dog to jump up at you when you came in through your front door, this can be a terrifying experience for a child who may not be used to dogs, even though the dog is only being friendly. Once the dog starts to realise that the child is frightened, it may well begin to bully them.

Prevention is always better than cure so my suggestions include:

- Have a dog-proof room in the house where the children can go to play but the dog is physically prevented from entering.
- When the dog is allowed to interact with the children there should be parental supervision at all times to protect the visiting child from the unwelcome attentions of the dog and vice versa.
- Do not allow the visiting child to go into the area where the dog sleeps and teach the dog to sleep in an area away from where the children play.
- Don't allow the visiting child to help itself to food and drink from cupboards or the refrigerator (especially if the dog sleeps in the kitchen) as it may see the child as removing resources.
- Make sure that any child that visits regularly sometimes brings resources into the house (see territorial behaviour, page 269).
- Don't allow the children to play physical, competitive games with the dog present or your dog may be forced to take sides if it believes that your child is being threatened.

Providing you are sensible, there is no reason at all why your dog should not accept and enjoy the company of any child your son or daughter brings home to play with. Generally dogs and kids get on well together and with a bit of thought and good planning on the part of the parents, there is no reason why a child cannot continue to get pleasure and learn a lot about life from their family companion.

TEN YEARS ONWARDS

If you have never experienced any behaviour problems with your dog relating to the child, it is normally perfectly safe to allow them increasing amounts of unsupervised time together without worrying that either will come to harm.

It is not advisable to leave a dog you have taken in for re-homing within the previous six months any free access to a child until you are absolutely certain of its temperament. Depending on the breed, you should also be in a position to allow short excursions when the dog may accompany your child to a friend's house, or out on a walk with friends. It would also be acceptable to allow your child some responsibility in the dog's formal education under the guidance of a training instructor. It is possible for a child of ten or over to compete successfully against adults in any of the sports associated with dogs, such as obedience or agility.

Some of the more enlightened people in education and animal welfare are now starting to introduce the concept of pet education into the school curriculum. The children of today are the dog owners of tomorrow and the future of the pet dog as we know it is in their hands, so it is up to each and every one of us to ensure that we teach them the basics of responsible pet ownership. If we teach our children how to care for a pet dog that is almost entirely dependent on us for survival, perhaps that will, in some small way, prepare them for their eventual roles as parents themselves.

47
Food Aggression

Almost all food aggression begins at the breeders where competition over food resources is created by feeding a number of puppies out of just one food bowl (see the section on puppies, page 19). So if you have a problem with your dog being aggressive over food it was almost certainly there before you got it.

If your dog came primed for this behaviour, then you will notice a pattern. The first stage is usually the owner noticing, their puppy starts to eat its food faster when they approach. This tells us that this young puppy is already trying to protect its food. The problem with modern, complete, high-performance packaged dog food is that it is fed in ridiculously small quantities. So when a puppy is gulping down its food there is not enough time for the owner to linger near the food bowl. The idea is to teach the puppy that your presence at the food bowl does not in any way reduce the amount of food it gets to eat. If owners see their puppy bolting down its food so fast it coughs up pieces of food, most will try to get it to eat it more slowly, often by picking up the food bowl or holding on to the puppy's collar to slow it down. As soon as this happens the puppy perceives the owner as competing over the food and it is pushed into the second stage of food aggression.

The second stage is that when anyone approaches, the puppy now puts its head further over the bowl, looking out of the corner of its eye and emits a low growl. As soon as this happens and the owner shouts at the dog and verbally or physically threatens it, they push it into the third stage of aggression.

The third stage is when anyone approaches the food bowl and the puppy now turns its head away slightly. As the owner gets near, the puppy snaps at their hand. As this behaviour is almost always challenged by the owner who has just been snapped at, this youngster moves on to the fourth stage of food aggression.

This is where the young dog, now confident at using aggression to maintain control of the food bowl, faces the owner as they approach. The dog then growls, shows its teeth and launches an attack when the owner is still a distance away.

Whatever stage of food aggression your dog is at, there are various strategies you can employ to resolve the problem.

First, it should stand to reason that if you feed your dog a brand of food that nine out of ten dogs prefer, then because of this higher value, your dog is more likely to guard it than the brand that only one out of ten dogs prefer!

Next look at how many times each day you feed your dog. If it is just once a day then your dog will be extra hungry around the time leading up to being fed and so is more likely to become highly competitive around the precious food. So if you feed your dog four times each day he will be less hungry at meal times and therefore less likely to be aggressive.

You should also think about feeding your dog randomly during the day. If you feed it at exactly the same time each day, it will get into the routine of expecting food at that time and start to get into a higher level of arousal up to half an hour before the meal is due. If you mix up your dog's food in the morning and divide it into the number of portions you are going to feed it that day, you can randomly surprise it with a portion when it is relaxed and not highly charged with expectation.

If your dog has a pre-existing condition of food guarding then I would not recommend spaying or neutering until the aggression problem has been resolved. Spaying or castrating a food-aggressive dog almost always results in the behaviour getting worse. Why? Because after the operation the dog's appetite usually increases at the very time when your veterinarian will recommend you cut down the quantity of food you feed your dog. You now have even better ingredients for food aggression to develop further.

The sure-fire way of preventing your dog from biting you when you give it a bowl of food is to confine your dog to a large indoor kennel or isolate it in a room or area of your property while it is eating, only letting it out of the confinement when it has finished all the food. Any other procedure increases the risk of aggression by your dog to guard its food.

With any programme to correct food bowl guarding, you may want to start shortly *after* your dog has eaten a light meal. If your puppy is just at stage one then your goal is to teach it that your presence around the food bowl does not, in any way, decrease its intake of the available food. On the contrary, your dog should soon come to welcome your presence around the food bowl. To achieve this there are several alternatives that you might try.

You could moisten the food and then pop it into your freezer to chill. Then sit on the couch to watch your favourite TV programme with the semi-frozen food bowl between your feet and allow your dog to eat. There is no need to do anything, just sit there and let your dog eat its food and it should learn quite quickly to take no notice of your presence near its food bowl. All attempts to swallow the food in the shortest possible time should disappear.

Alternatively, you could put a length of large link chain in the bowl. Your dog will now have great difficulty in gulping down food because of the chain and this should slow its ingestion down considerably. You could also put some large stones in the bowl for the same effect. You could also feed the food dry or throw in a large handful of dry bran, which again has the effect of slowing down the consumption rate. The idea is to spend as long as you can near the food bowl when your dog is eating, hopefully around ten minutes or more.

Another strategy is to scatter-feed your dog. This is carried out by scattering all its food around a large area such as a back garden or yard. Let the dog watch the food being thrown all over the area and then release it to find and eat it. Stay in the area and help your dog find the food by calling him to you and pointing to as many morsels as you can. You can also occasionally call your dog over to where you have secretly dropped a few extra tasty dog treats such as chicken or cooked liver. If the area is reasonably large then it should take your dog around 20 minutes to find and eat its food with your help, or longer if he is left by himself.

If you are at stage two where the dog is freezing and growling but not biting, try this. Each time you feed your dog, place an equal amount of food into three separate bowls, spaced at least six feet apart. Slow down the rate that your dog eats by using one of the techniques described above. Now whichever bowl your dog starts to eat from, simply go to one of the other two, pick it up and place some extra tasty food on the top. Now put the bowl back down on the floor and your dog should come over, attracted by the smell of the food treats, and eat from this bowl. Then walk away and pick up one of the other two bowls, add the food treats and put this bowl back down. Keep repeating this all the time there is food in any of the bowls.

Within a few days your dog should watch you approach and leave the bowl it is eating out of to see which bowl you are going to pick up and put some more tasty food into. When this happens and your dog leaves the bowl he was eating from, pick that one up and put the tasty treats in it. Once the food aggression problem has been resolved in this way, I am often asked when the owner can go back to feeding the dog out of one bowl. You can't. Once you have changed your dog's behaviour there is often no going back. Your dog will now eat out of three bowls for the rest of its life.

For stages two or three, where the dog is actually snapping, try this. Fasten your dog on a tether no longer than four feet. Now get your dog to lean forwards to the extremity of its tether and mark a line on the floor where its nose can reach. Fix a large-diameter food bowl so that one half is on your dog's side of the line and the other half is on your side. Make sure that the tether is strong enough so that your dog's nose (and teeth) cannot get to your side of the bowl. Now put a quantity of ordinary dog food onto your half of the bowl and walk away. You may well have to fasten the bowl to the floor so your dog cannot pull it towards him. When you are a short distance from the bowl, turn around and walk back to it. Now put your hand in your side of the bowl and flick a few pieces of food to your dog's side of the bowl then retreat again. Keep repeating this until all the food is eaten.

The first time you carry out this procedure you should ignore any growling and keep on approaching and flicking food to your dog. The growling should cease within one or two days as your dog starts to realise that your approaching the food bowl results in him getting the food that he now cannot get for himself. If the growling has not subsided after a few days, simply walk away from the bowl without putting your hand in to flick food across to your dog. Once he realises that his growling removes the possibility of him getting the food, he should make the correct association.

You should find that within a week your dog now actually wants you to approach the food bowl and will wag his tail as soon as you walk towards it. The next stage is to fill the bowl with the same ordinary dog food fed dry but when you approach the food bowl have some tasty food treats concealed in your hand. Put your hand in your side of the bowl and lay the treats on top of the dog food on your side, then flick a few pieces across to your dog. Again, after a few repetitions your dog should welcome your hand coming into the bowl. The final stage is to switch to feeding your dog out of three bowls placed at least six feet apart.

If your dog is at stage four, try repeating the treatment for stages two and three above but in addition to having your dog tethered, you will also need to use three large-diameter food bowls spaced around three feet apart on the circumference of your dog's tether. Each bowl must be half on your side of the line and half on your dog's side. The procedure now is to place food on your side of each bowl and then approach any bowl your dog is not trying to guard and flick some food across for him to eat. While he is eating this, go to one of the other bowls and flick some food across for him. Keep moving around the bowls until all the food has been consumed.

When your dog is happily wagging his tail when you approach one of the three bowls, switch to one bowl as in the solution for stage two and three aggression. When you have finished that stage, switch to feeding out of three bowls with the dog untethered. The idea is that when you start the programme you have a dog that does not trust you near the food bowl when it is eating. What you end up with is a dog that desires your presence around the food bowl.

However, that does not cover the problem of what to do if your dog starts to guard other food items. One way of preventing this is to manage all food so that your dog gets only what he is given. Some owners complain that their dog is only aggressive when it is eating food it has stolen. Again this has to be a behaviour that has been trained by the owner, because if the dog is not aggressive over food that it has been given, that tells me that either the stolen food is perceived as being of greater value than the food he is given every day or that the owner has artificially raised the value of the stolen food by competing with the dog for it.

John Henry's disgusting habits

Take a look at this case of John Henry, the miniature poodle. John Henry's owners complained that he would pick up disgusting things when out on a walk, and when they tried to remove the offending food item he would become very aggressive. What finally prompted them to come and see me was the time John Henry picked up a rotting rabbit carcass and refused to drop it. He then carried the trophy all the way home and all attempts to bribe him to let go of it by offering other tasty morsels failed. Eventually Joe, John Henry's owner, donned a pair of heavy-duty gardening gloves and while his wife Helen held the dog on the lead, proceeded to try and prise the rabbit leg out of John Henry's mouth using a set of fire tongs!

Joe and Helen told me that John Henry would happily let them approach when he was eating his normal everyday food out of a bowl – it was only when he picked up any other type of food that there was a problem. The most annoying part of this behaviour was that he was particularly partial to the most disgusting food items. I had to explain that they were obviously not disgusting to John Henry or he would not touch them in the first place. I then asked them what they did with the offending item when they had managed to get it from him and they said they threw it into the bin.

I then tried to get them to see things from John Henry's perspective. He is fed the same food day in and day out and even leaves some uneaten food in his bowl on most days. So when the chance of something much more exciting comes along, something that smells and tastes amazingly good compared to the rubbish he usually gets, then any dog would seize the opportunity to eat it for fear the chance might never come again. Then, once he's started to devour this exciting food, the owners begin to get really competitive over it and behave as though it is the most valuable food they have ever come across as well. After succeeding in gaining control over the gourmet item, they then refuse to share it and bury it in a bin for later consumption! As far as John Henry was concerned, his owners were guilty of exactly the same crime as they saw him committing.

What could they have done to solve this problem? There is a whole host of solutions:

- They could have managed food in their house so that John Henry never had the opportunity to steal anything.
- They could have fed him things like rabbit, chicken, pizza crust and all the exciting things he craved so he did not have to steal and fight for them.
- Out on walks they could have put a basket muzzle on John Henry so he could not pick up anything they did not want him to have.
- They could have used the reversal principle to get him to drop anything that he was carrying.

What is the reversal principle? Read on...

48
The Reversal

This is the process by which we are able to rapidly change or reverse what goes on in the dog's mind. For it to work properly the dog should get the exact opposite of what it has come to expect. So let's imagine a dog that becomes really aggressive when it is given a prized possession such as a bone. The dog takes the bone away from its owner to an area that is easy to guard and lies down to enjoy it. Its owner approaches and from its easily defended position, the dog manages to get the owner to back off, using either an aggressive display or by lunging out and snapping.

What are the dog's expectations? That's easy. The dog expects that he will have access to a secure area. He also expects that when the owner approaches, his enjoyment of the bone will be called into question by the owner, who also appears to want the bone. So the dog may well expect to be verbally challenged over the bone and has therefore learned that giving an aggressive display is the surest way to retain possession of it.

You could make sure that the dog was never given a bone in the first place or you could give the dog a safe area to take it and never approach that area. Using either of those two strategies will avoid confrontation and the subsequent aggression that accompanies it. Or, although there is a risk attached, you could try the following.

Attach a lead or length of line to your dog's collar. Now find the biggest bone that your dog could possibly hold on to. Keeping hold of the lead with one hand, hand your dog the bone. Your dog should take it eagerly and turn to take it away but should find immediately that this is not possible as he is attached to you by the lead or line. All you now have to remember is not to look at your dog and don't let your dog lie down. To eat this bone your dog has to lie down and put one foot on it to hold it in place. So keep your dog standing – it's also OK if he sits but do not ask him to sit. You should be turned slightly away from your dog as he works out what to do next. As the bone is heavy and getting heavier by the minute, his head will slowly lower and he will drop it to the ground. Now walk away from the bone – your dog has to follow because he is attached to you.

When you are around ten feet away from the bone, turn around and walk back towards it. When you do this, make sure you keep yourself between the dog and the bone. Now at arm's length, pick up the bone and give it back to your dog. He still has the same problem as he cannot take it away and cannot eat it, so you should find that he will drop it a little quicker than he did the first time. Repeat the walking away and returning to pick up and hand your dog the bone until you have done it ten times.

On the tenth repetition you should find that your dog now drops the bone really quickly. On the next repetition you should hand your dog the bone but hold on to your end of it for around a minute. Your dog should now be able to chew on the bone for the time you are holding it. When the minute is up, let go of the bone and your dog will very quickly drop it on the floor and look at you to pick it up. When you do this, again hold on to your end for a minute or so and then let go again. The bone should again drop to the floor.

After you have repeated this five or six times, hand your dog the bone and let go. Your dog should now turn towards you, look up and wag its tail asking you to get hold of the bone. Why? Because in the space of around 20 minutes your dog will have learned that your hands are much better tools to grip the bone while he gets the pleasure of eating it. It should convince him that you want him to eat the bone and are there to help him. One of the drawbacks of this system is that you can end up with a dog that now brings its bones for you to hold whenever he wants to eat one!

You can use this principle of reversal on anything that your dog is possessive over, to change what is in his mind and teach him that far from being his worst enemy, you are his best friend.

49
Possession Aggression

One of the most common problems raised when I work for the military organisations or dog-sport enthusiasts who teach their dogs bitework, is that when their dog is biting a protective sleeve, he will not let go. Before we decide to do anything we need to look at what is going on inside the dog's head.

First of all, the person has clearly begun this training without having sufficient control over their dog. Bitework training should only start when a dog is around 18 months to two years of age and when the handler has gained complete control of the dog. We could view a dog that will not release its grip on a protective sleeve in the same way as a dog that will not release a toy or any other trophy.

I was once consulted about a police dog in Cyprus that would not release a sleeve on its handler's command. I asked to see the dog and put on the protective sleeve that was being used. The dog was Duke, a six-year-old German Shepherd, who obviously lived to bite people. Biting gave him a reason to get up in the morning and nothing excited him more than seeing someone who might be presented as bait. The dog was brought out into the training compound and knew why he was there – to bite someone. As soon as he spotted me with the sleeve on he immediately started to bark in excitement and lunge towards me. His handler gave him the command to attack, which was completely unnecessary as the only thing on Duke's mind was biting me – and released the dog.

Duke launched himself at me and immediately grabbed my right arm, which was protected by the sleeve. No sooner had Duke gripped it than his handler shouted, 'Duke, leeeeave!' Duke immediately gripped harder. Froth from his saliva was now all over the sleeve and I was being pulled around like a rag doll. Something strange about military and police training is that when the dog disobeys a command the handler simply repeats it but much louder. So once again I heard a deafening 'Duke, LEEEEEEAVE!!' As soon as the command was given Duke again tightened his already vice-like grip.

I told the handler to be quiet and say nothing. Duke was a fit dog but the good thing about aggression is that it is quite tiring and even trained athletes cannot maintain this level for too long. Plus the more competition over the possession of the sleeve, the more Duke would be encouraged to fight for it. Duke was shaking my arm from side to side and growling constantly as he did so. About a minute later Duke was still gripping my arm but the growling and shaking had reduced considerably. Two minutes later there were only occasional growls and shakes interspersed with much panting. This was mid-afternoon in August in Cyprus, so after five minutes Duke was exhausted and barely gripping my arm.

I then asked his handler to get Duke to sit. The handler bellowed 'Duke, sit!' but Duke continued to stand. I asked if Duke was deaf and was told that he wasn't. So I asked the handler to tell Duke to sit but without shouting. The handler said 'Duke, sit' in a normal spoken voice. Duke sat but in doing so let go of the sleeve. I told the handler I wanted Duke to sit but also keep a grip on the sleeve, so we got Duke back on to my arm. When he was gripping it, his handler once again asked Duke to sit. He did so but again let go of the sleeve. So we did it again: Duke gripped my right arm and then the handler told him to sit, quickly shouting the command 'hold' as Duke went into the sit position. Duke still let go of the sleeve!

Now I pulled the sleeve off and asked the handler to get Duke to sit and hold it. Duke sat and the handler tried to get him to hold the sleeve but Duke did not want to. I asked the handler to try and put the sleeve in Duke's mouth while he was sitting and get him to hold it for 30 seconds. The more the handler tried, the more Duke turned his head away and refused to cooperate. I then asked the handler what the problem was with Duke. 'He will not let go of the sleeve,' was the reply. 'It seems to me like he will not bite the sleeve at all,' was my observation.

Trying to get Duke to let go of the sleeve while he was in an incredible state of arousal was not a very smart idea. By lowering Duke's level of arousal we could get him to listen more easily, but to Duke the sleeve was a prized possession. Very early in his training he had been encouraged to become very possessive over it without his trainers first ensuring that there was sufficient control. The handler's very forceful and excruciatingly loud command only served to hype Duke up even more. Duke also knew that when he released the sleeve he would be put back into his kennel until the next training session. What's more, he rarely got to bite more than once at each session because he was so difficult to control.

It is also difficult for any dog, even a highly trained one, to multi-task – do two different things at once. Look at it like this. The handler throws the article and the dog runs out to pick it up. The handler then commands the dog to hold it. The dog now picks up the article and the handler gives the command to come. The dog now drops the article and returns without it.

Or the handler sends the dog to fetch an article and then gives the 'hold' command to get the dog to pick up the article. The dog returns automatically with the article and gets all the way back to the handler, who then commands the dog to sit. The dog then drops the article and sits, much to annoyance of the handler who wanted the dog to present the article in the sit position. But in training, the dog had been conditioned to obey single-action commands such as 'come', 'sit', 'down' etc. So if the dog was left in the sit position and trained to hold that position, then it would have also learned to move only when the handler released it from that position or gave it an alternative action to carry out. So each command superseded the previous one.

Thus telling a dog to sit and then, after a few seconds, to lie down, conveys the message that the sit behaviour is no longer desired and the down position now is the correct one to adopt. So you can see why, when the handler gave the dog a command to sit when it was holding an article, it (correctly in its mind) dropped the article.

I have watched people trying to train dogs for competitive obedience all over the world make this simple mistake. Dogs cannot multi-task without huge amounts of understanding and careful training. Duke was no exception and neither is your dog. So, using the reversal principle and knowing that dogs cannot multi-task, you can now see why it is easy to teach any dog to release an article, toy or trophy.

For toys you have to ensure that your dog cannot self-reward by sitting and chewing it. Heavy toys or ones that are heavy at one end work best in teaching this principle. If you fully understand and can apply this principle, then you are one step nearer to understanding the code.

50
When Enough is Enough

Sometimes, even though it is usually possible to change a dog's behaviour, the risks involved are so great we have to look for other possibilities.

Jason

Dear John,

The consensus of all the dog people who've seen Jason is that he has a problem with life. He is a multiple biter who bites hard. A number of non-doggie friends find him incredibly frightening. He is a lunger and snarler who tries to push me out of the way to try to get to anyone on our street.

Jason is always on red alert looking for a problem. His body is always tense to the touch. He is ultra suspicious, particularly of people. He doesn't trust anyone, he doesn't sadly completely trust us, nor we him and, in a nutshell, that is possibly the biggest problem.

Our social life is zero. We cannot go on holiday. There is literally no one he can stay with. We are both exhausted.

Prior to his second inoculations I carried him out in my coat but he growled continuously at any strangers in and out of the house. I found this odd behaviour in such a little pup. He screamed and chattered his teeth if picked up by strangers.

At 14 weeks a number of attempts to socialise Jason with a toddler were thwarted as Jason darted in and out growling like a manic snake. I feared the toddler might get bitten.

To date I have had about 30 biting incidents. The bites are multiple attacks up and down the body. I would call them hysterical and out of control. Jason does not growl or warn. The closer we are to the house the more likely he is to lunge and try to bite passers-by.

Jason attended a weekly obedience class until nearly two. Eventually he became bored and disruptive and I stopped because I felt we were regressing. He was easily the quickest learner but also a troublemaker who would take a dislike to certain dogs as well as people.

He dislikes teeth being looked at, ears and paws being touched, and screamed when a friend put nail clippers next to his paws. A few weeks later he went for me when I attempted to put prescribed eye drops into a slightly infected eye.

He also has a really nasty attitude to dogs and puppies and attacks them aggressively if they get in his space, even off the lead.

After seeing a behaviourist we spent about four weeks trying to get Jason used to a muzzle by getting him to take food from it in a game. Finally he flew at my face. We never actually managed to get it on him.

Jason takes treats very gently and has been taught not to snatch. However, combining treats with behaviour training is still a bit risky, in my view. On advice we asked some trusted friends to do some treat/touch training with him – he was fine but then bit each on the hand when they withdrew it.

What should we do?

It is so easy to let your heart rule your head in this situation, so what is required is a look at the hard facts. Jason appears to have had this problem ever since the owners got him from the breeder at seven weeks of age. These are not first-time owners. They had previously successfully raised and trained one dog, and adopted a second dog with a few problems that they managed to sort out. So in disagreement with the famous trainer Barbara Woodhouse, I am going to say that these are not bad owners but they do have a bad dog!

With more than 30 biting incidents in a variety of situations by two years of age, it is unlikely that even with expert help, Jason's aggressive behaviour would not change quickly. That means that any behaviour or training programme would carry the risk of repeat attacks. So what could be done to help Jason's owners?

There are three possible solutions to his problems. The first is that the owners could put a secure kennel and run in their back garden, where they could keep Jason in the way a zoo keeps a wild animal. Maybe Jason really does not like people and just wants to live the life of a hermit! If you think that's a bad idea, then think about some of the rescues that adopt a non-destruction policy. Some of those shelters do successfully keep dogs in kennels for the rest of their lives while providing them with a reasonable quality of life.

The second strategy could be to keep Jason safe by making sure his owners only ever took him out with a muzzle on, keeping him on the lead at all times. The problem with this plan is Jason's associated aggression when they attempt to put the muzzle on him. This alone would probably make this a non-starter. They could also confine Jason in an indoor kennel before they opened the front door when letting visitors in.

There is a third strategy that might result in a change in Jason – a behaviour modification programme. But given his case history, it appears other trainers and behaviourists have already been unsuccessful in this and have maybe even inadvertently made some procedures worse for his owners. And we don't want owners to go through the rest of their lives being frightened of the dog they acquired as a companion.

So we are left with very few options other than the first one above. Passing the dog on to a rescue is not an option, as the liability for Jason's behaviour rests with his owners. Plus no rescue organisations I know have lists of pet homes wanting aggressive dogs!

My advice in such cases is to place the dog in a boarding kennel for a period of two weeks, during which time they can get their life back in order. They can spend two weeks not having to be concerned about their dog, can invite friends round and recover the social life that has been absent since the arrival of the nightmare puppy. After two weeks they will be in a better position to make a rational judgement on the alternatives.

In Jason's case the owners decided to have their dog humanely put to sleep, to end the dog's apparent torment and their own. There are many tens of thousands of nice dogs sitting in rescue centres that have to die every year because suitable homes cannot be found and space is limited, so sometimes, when all possibilities to change aggressive behaviour have come to nothing, ending the life of an aggressive dog to save that of a dog that deserves a second chance is the best outcome of all.

Section 7

Dog-to-Dog Aggression

'Common Sense is that which judges the things given to it by other senses.'

- Leonardo da Vinci

51
Aggression Towards Other Dogs: An Overview

It is late afternoon and my telephone has just rung for the twentieth time today. On the other end of the line is a very well-spoken lady who lives around 250 miles away. 'I am ringing about a problem that I have with my dog,' she tells me. 'He is dog-aggressive and I have to keep him on the lead because he runs up to other dogs to fight with them. He is getting difficult to hold on to as he lunges and barks whenever he sees another dog even if it is in the distance, so I want to make an appointment for you to come and help me.'

I ask her to tell me about her other, older dog, because she must own another, older dog, right?

'Gosh! How did you know that?' she asks in a very surprised tone.

'Because you must have another dog to have the type of problem you describe,' I tell her. There is a stunned silence as I go on to explain exactly how her dog developed the problem. I then ask how many hours out of every 24 her two dogs spend together.

'Twenty-four,' she replies.

'And how many hours do you spend with your younger dog without the other dog there?'

'About 20 minutes,' is her reply.

'Who is the role model then for the way your young dog behaves?'

'Me?' she answers hesitantly.

'It has got to be your other dog,' I reply. 'If you want to make an appointment then I can't see your dog for five weeks, during which time I am going to ask you to separate them so that they do not have any access to one another, and I want you and your problem dog to have as close to 24-hour access to one another as you can get. The reason you are having a problem with your dog is because he likes to play aggressively with other dogs and cannot communicate with you. It is like having a feral dog living in your own home. He has no reason to listen to you when he can hold a conversation all day long with your other dog. Ring me again in five weeks when you have done this and if you still need to we can make an appointment. Most people who make this appointment for five weeks hence then phone up and cancel it because they no longer need to see me as they no longer have the problem.'

'My God!' she exclaims. 'That just makes so much sense – you are absolutely right. I never realised.'

Whenever I receive a telephone call about dog-to-dog aggression, the owner is almost always amazed at how I know that they have another, older dog. Sometimes I can even tell them that it is the same breed, sometimes the opposite sex, sometimes the other dog is very old, sometimes it is very young, sometimes a littermate.

For a dog to exhibit aggression there has to be a learning process. This is usually in the form of another dog to practise with. Most times this occurs in the way the two dogs play and interact, and these interactions need not be physical. To be able to hold a conversation with another dog all day long is sometimes enough, because the more that they practise communicating with one another, the less your dogs will be able to communicate with you.

Look at it like this. If you moved to a non-English-speaking country at a very young age, but you lived in an English-speaking household and community, would you ever really need to learn and be fluent in the language native to that country? Not really, as you would have daily opportunities to practise English and, provided there was someone there 24 hours a day who could translate for you, the requirement to learn this new language would be virtually zero. It's common sense really.

Let's look at the most common patterns of dog-to-dog aggression with a view to either preventing them from ever occurring, or trying to repair damage that has been done by allowing a dog to become dog-aggressive.

As we have seen, to be able to correct a problem there has to be a pattern to it. It has to be predictable. It needs a set of ingredients. Dog-to-dog aggression is no exception, so what we are going to examine is why one dog would ever want to attack another. We can divide dog-to-dog aggression roughly into three basic categories:

1. Towards the other dog that they live with
2. Towards dogs that they know and meet frequently
3. Towards dogs that they do not know or see infrequently.

Categories two and three are by far the most common types of aggression, so let's now look at the reasons why dog-to-dog aggression has increased dramatically over the past few years around the world.

If you look at the traditions in any culture and their view of companion dog ownership, you will see that many changes in behaviour patterns in both dogs and people come about because of a change in that culture.

A traditional family dog in England would always have been an only dog in that family. It would be purchased as a six-week-old puppy and raised in the family home as part of the family unit. When the family went out visiting friends the dog would go as well. When the family went on vacation the dog would often be taken along. Going out for a day at the beach, the dog would be taken along. Going to the pub in the evening, you would often see dogs with their owners. If the children went to the park to play the dog would be taken along. In short, the dog would share in much of the family's day-to-day life.

Then we had a rapid change in our culture. Property prices soared to unimaginable levels. Suddenly the traditional family where one person, usually the male, went out to work each day leaving their partner at home to look after the house, raise the kids and the family dog was lost. To be able to afford to their own property, both partners now commonly go out to work. This now leaves us with a slight problem – who is going to raise and train the family dog? No problem. Breeders came up with the perfect solution – buy a second dog to keep the first dog company or buy two puppies out of the same litter!

OWNING MORE THAN ONE DOG

Training becomes difficult when a young dog prefers to be with an older canine companion as it drastically reduces the effectiveness of positive reinforcement or reward training. Just imagine tying up the older dog to a fence or leaving it in the car while you attempt to train the younger one. Every time the pup obeys a training command and you try to praise it, all it wants to do is run over to the other dog as it is almost uninterested in the praise you have to offer. If you try to regain control by shouting at the young dog or by dragging it away from the other dog, this serves only to make you less attractive to your puppy. The more you try to gain the pup's respect, the more you reinforce the older dog as the more pleasant in the relationship.

If you want to find out whether your young dog's relationship with you is better than that with the other dog(s), try this simple test. Leave the older dog at home and take the youngster out for a walk for half an hour or so. When you return home, walk into the house alongside the pup and note whom the older dog greets first. If the older one was the only dog in your household when you acquired it, it will greet you before turning its attentions towards the young dog. Now leave the young dog in the house while you take the older one out for a walk. When you arrive home, enter the house as before and watch to see if your young dog says hello to the older dog before it greets you. If this is the case, in order to correct any behaviour problems – particularly those involving aggression – it is essential that you improve your relationship with the young dog so it sees you as the most important member of the family. It is almost useless to attempt to teach correct behaviour to a dog that views its owners as merely incidental to its relationship with the other dog.

PREVENTING DOG-TO-DOG AGGRESSION IN THE FIRST PLACE

If you are contemplating purchasing a puppy and already have an older dog in the family, then observing a few guidelines will make the whole process a great deal easier. First, you need to decide whether you want a dog or a bitch. Although a dog and a bitch is undoubtedly the best combination to keep in the same house, you will have to give careful consideration to preventing unwanted litters of puppies by having the bitch spayed or the dog castrated before breeding age is reached. Two male dogs are the next best combination, although in some specific breeds males have a reputation for not getting along very well together. Check with the breed society concerned before making a decision.

Two bitches can usually live together perfectly happily under the same roof, but it has to be said that if they take a dislike to one another it can often lead to serious injury or even death. Two male dogs that start to fight are usually fairly easy to cure.

How old should your older dog be before you consider getting a second one? It is best to wait until it is fully mature, reasonably well behaved and under proper control. Seven years of age is a good guide. If your dog is out of control, is difficult to handle or you are experiencing any behaviour problems with it, then you should devote all your time and effort towards improving it rather than considering adding to your problems by getting a second dog.

You should never even contemplate buying two puppies from the same litter. This is almost always doomed to disaster because the two pups will already have such a strong bond that it is unlikely, unless you are very experienced or exceedingly lucky, that you will end up with any form of control over either dog's behaviour.

If you already own a dog that is quite dominant, try to pick a puppy that appears to be submissive. Do not confuse submissiveness with nervousness! Conversely, if you already own a submissive dog then it would be better to pick a more dominant puppy because there is less likelihood of rank-related friction developing as it grows.

For the first six months it is important that the puppy learns to enjoy playing more games and has more fun with you than it does with your older dog, and that any games it plays with other dogs are not allowed to get to the point where teeth are used.

Look at it like this. Why is it important that your young puppy learns that playing at biting your hands, arms and fingers is to be discouraged? It is because if we give any sign that we approve of such behaviour, your puppy may well think that biting people is acceptable. So when it is playing at biting your older dog, surely the same rules apply. If your puppy thinks it is acceptable to bite your other dog then it may well go on to do this to other dogs it meets. If you must allow your puppy to play with your older dog, encourage them to play with big toys so they can put their teeth into a toy and not one another.

Do *not* leave any toys lying around for both dogs to play with, and when you produce a toy, make sure the pup is isolated from the influence of the other dog. You should also try to ensure that the two dogs sleep apart and have no unsupervised access to one another when you are not there. This does not mean that they cannot be in the same room as one another; all you have to do is purchase a wire mesh indoor kennel into which you can place the pup whenever you have to leave the dogs alone for short periods. It will still have the company of the older dog but will not be in a position to play any games that may get out of hand.

If you see the puppy approaching the other dog and trying to play games that involve the use of its teeth, then quickly reprimand it verbally, isolate it for a while (disassociation time) and then play with it yourself. If you only allow your puppy to be with your other dog when it is tired, it will not want to play much in any case. It must learn that it is never allowed to use its teeth on anything but a toy. If the puppy appears to be in a playful mood then it is up to you to play with it yourself so you are in a position to introduce some education and control into such games.

You can allow and encourage correct non-aggressive interaction between the two dogs, such as gentle games that do not involve physical strength, and there is a lot to be gained by allowing gentle play to develop between the two of them when the older dog initiates it. You should never allow your young puppy to pester the older dog to play. By the time the pup is seven months of age you should be able to call it away from your other dog, even if it is playing, as it should prefer to play games with you rather than your older dog or, for that matter, any other dog. Education and training now become much easier because of the bond you have built with the pup through play.

At around six to eight months you can allow the pup to sleep with and spend some time with the other dog unsupervised. The two dogs will now be company for one another but each will prefer to be with and to play with you. The added bonus is that your dog will also have learned to approach other dogs in a non-aggressive manner that is very unlikely to be seen as threatening.

CONTROLLING TWO DOGS

If you are the one who controls the games your dogs play, you should have little in the way of problems controlling both dogs. If, on the other hand, you are unable or unwilling to control both dogs when they are playing, you will be the owner of a pack of dogs that do not really see you as a member at all, and you will be unlikely to exert any control should your dogs decide, for instance, to chase other dogs, people, livestock, etc. If you are unlucky enough to be the owner of two dogs that are dominant over you, particularly if one is a nervous dog, you need to get help fast, as everyone in the family and the community will be at serious risk until you regain control of your dogs.

Formal training must initially be carried out individually until you obtain a good measure of control. You can then, by degrees, introduce the distraction of bringing both dogs together to continue this training. If you have carried out the early socialisation process between you and your dogs correctly, you will be the greatest distraction around with the result that you will have two dogs that respond to you more than to one another. The pleasures to be gained from owning more than one dog more than repay the time and effort expended, but never underestimate just how much of a contribution you will have to make to their early education and training.

Finally, if the idea of spending a large amount of time playing with two dogs individually for the first seven months does not appeal to you, then please do not even consider getting a second dog. If you have acquired a second dog as a playmate for your first dog because you yourself do not have the time to play with it, perhaps you should never have owned a dog in the first place.

INGREDIENTS IN AGGRESSION

The main ingredient for dog-to-dog aggression is to own a second, hopefully older, dog. If you want to give yourself the best possible chance of having a dog-to-dog aggression problem, the dog you already own should be around ten months to three years old when you get your new puppy. It would also help if the new puppy is the same breed as the dog you already own and even better if it is the opposite sex. But why is this?

Well, if you already have a very young dog why would you want a second dog? Unfortunately you probably got your new one as a pet for your first dog because your time for it was limited. This begs the question: if you did not have enough time for one dog, what were you thinking when you decided to get a second that would take up even more of your non-existent free time?

The effect of a second dog arriving into a house where there is already a young dog in need of your attention and education is dramatic. So getting a puppy when you already have an immature dog that is still learning about life is not the most sensible thing to do. Also buying a puppy of the same breed gives your puppy the opportunity of learning something called breed discrimination. Watch what happens when two Staffordshire Bull Terriers that have been raised together meet a young Boxer in the park for the first time! Getting a puppy of the opposite sex also gives the opportunity for protective aggression to develop, as the male may well have a deep-rooted bond with its housemate that prevents other males from getting anywhere near his female. What you are in danger of ending up with are two feral (street) dogs that happen to live in your house.

Let's look at what typically happens when you acquire a puppy when you already have a young dog in your house. The young puppy is taken away from its littermates, with whom it has built up a very strong relationship, and arrives at its new home, where it feels worried about entering this new environment. There are humans available and another dog for company. It will immediately relate to the other dog rather than its new owners. Over the next few weeks the relationship between the two dogs will strengthen, often to the point of the younger dog becoming far more interested in playing with the other dog than it with its owners.

The contact the owners have with the puppy now centres around correcting bad behaviour, such as chewing, house-soiling etc. We now rapidly reach a point where the puppy takes more notice of the older dog than it takes of its owners because interactions with other dogs are generally pleasant while the owners, in the dog's eyes, become mildly unpleasant because of the discipline they try to impose. The good social contact through play that will build a relationship is now becoming the responsibility of the other dog.

If the owner tries to encourage the puppy to play with a toy with them, it will not be particularly interested. If the owner throws the toy, the pup will probably pick it up and take it to the other dog to play with. Once the pup starts to exclude its owners from games it also starts to exclude them from its life. The rules under which it plays games are dictated by the puppy and the older dog: the owner loses all control of these games and therefore begins to lose control of the puppy. Any attempts to stop the pup from playing, or attempts either to enforce control or to administer correction, result in the pup running to the older dog for comfort.

When exercised outside the house the young pup will follow the older dog rather than the owner, and all its interaction with other dogs or people will be influenced by the games and contact it has had with the older dog. If at the age of around seven months the young dog is taken out by itself and is approached by a person, it will often become agitated and appear uneasy as it is unable to cope with the situation without the reassuring presence of the other dog.

The reason is that the puppy cannot understand human language and does not have the older dog there as a translator. This is why the most common breed-show problem dog I see, related to aggression towards judges or ring shyness, is the younger of more than one dog living in the same environment. That dog has built up a relationship with another dog and cannot cope with any stress while in the company of its owner, with whom it has little or no relationship at all. The owner, in fact, is viewed in the same manner as a piece of furniture.

The problem of correcting bad behaviour also becomes more difficult when two or more dogs are owned, simply because any verbal correction applied to the puppy for its misdemeanours will also be inflicted on the older dog as it will be confused as to just who is in trouble. Suppose you arrive home to find the carpet has been chewed. If you apply the popular 'Who did that?' to the puppy, it is likely that your older dog will start to become apprehensive because of its prior association with the tone of your voice. Praising and rewarding either individual dog for good behaviour will create excitement and interactions between them. This usually results in the two dogs getting more excited with one another than either dog is with their owner. These interactions between the two of them will again often exclude their owner.

In order to socialise and train a young dog correctly, it is important that the relationship between dog and owner is stronger than the younger dog's bond with the other dog in the family. If the owner takes the responsibility for education, mainly through games, rather than leaving this to the other dog, then problems can be minimised. If we take a look at the games played between a puppy and an older dog, we get several clues as to the puppy's future behaviour.

If you allow your young dog unrestricted and unsupervised access to an older dog, it is inevitable that the younger one will want to play all the same games that it played with its littermates. These games will consist mainly of chasing and wrestling, which become very enthusiastic on the pup's part. During the game the pup starts to bite the older dog around the neck and ears which, if the older dog is of a very soft nature, it will tolerate. The owner does nothing to stop these games and is actually quite pleased that the two dogs are getting on so well together.

The games quickly develop to the point where the puppy will not leave the older dog alone when it is feeling playful. The bites become harder and the puppy may actually start to break the skin of the older dog and start to growl and bare its teeth in play, in a similar manner to a pup that has been allowed to play at biting its owner's hands. By the time it is old enough to go out to exercise areas with its owners (with whom it does not play much, if at all) it will become excited at the sight of other dogs and will want to play with them. Its approach towards other dogs will now be influenced by the games it has played with the older dog. Most other dogs it meets will accept the fact that it is still a puppy and tolerate its bullying behaviour to a certain extent.

As the pup grows it becomes obsessed with playing with other dogs when exercised and will often cry and whine when restrained on the lead if there are any other dogs about. The owner rightly believes that the young dog wants only to play with the other dogs, but we know by now the type of biting and wrestling games that it finds exciting and wants to play. When it gets to about seven months there will come a time when it approaches another dog in the manner to which it has become accustomed and the other dog will no longer see a puppy but a maturing dog who is rapidly becoming a threat, and it will attempt to deal with that by using aggression. In a few seconds we have the word aggression added to the game.

The problem is that the young dog is very well practised in the game of aggression and is now perfectly well equipped to defend itself, having spent the whole of its life practising its fighting techniques on the older dog.

After this first serious confrontation, the owners will be aware of a change in their young dog's behaviour that they often find puzzling. The dog will still get excited when it sees other dogs and will give the appearance of wanting to play, but when it is allowed off the lead it will approach the other dog and quickly attack it before it has a chance to weigh up the situation. The owner is soon left in no doubt as to the dog's intentions because, after a few repetitions, the young dog will chase and attack dogs and bitches alike when released to play the aggressive games it has learned, thanks to its older companion.

It may well be that when the puppy was first taken home and tried to play with the older dog, it was growled or snapped at for its undesirable behaviour. Here the owner would step in very quickly and chastise the older dog for showing aggression to the new pup. Unfortunately the owner would not be aware that he is reinforcing the pup's behaviour so that it will quickly learn that the owner will back it up in aggressive games with other dogs. Thus when the owner is present, the pup will learn to growl at and bite the other dog, safe in the knowledge that the older dog dare not retaliate. We now have the problem that as the puppy grows it becomes increasingly aggressive towards other dogs when the owner is present, even though other people can walk it past other dogs without difficulty. This is because it has learned that the owner, who has supported it in games of aggression with other dogs, is on hand to assist it in fighting every dog that comes into sight.

In general, dog-to-dog aggression problems are less easy to correct than the corresponding dog-to-human aggression problems. This is mainly due to the fact that in a dog-to-dog encounter you cannot use a cure such as getting the other dog to squirt water at your dog or throw a toy for it or feed it. It is therefore the owner who must always take the initiative in applying corrective measures to prevent aggression from succeeding.

As mentioned earlier in the section on owning more than one dog (page 306), the majority of dog-to-dog aggression problems are learned through early games. By allowing a young dog to play aggressive games with another dog to the point where the owner has no control over the games, you are sowing the seeds for the possibility of dog-to-dog aggression as your puppy starts to mature.

How do you go about trying to change your dog's behaviour towards other dogs? Well, if you only own one dog then the fix is relatively easy, but the chances are that if you have a dog-to-dog aggression problem then you are one of the 90 per cent of owners with this problem who own a second, older dog.

The very first thing to do is to separate your dog from all unsupervised contact with your other dog(s) for at least five weeks. You will also need to prevent all contact with other dogs outside of your home for five weeks. You can't do that? Then I know of no way you can really solve your dog's problems. So I ask that you separate your dogs for five weeks in the following way. They are to be allowed no unsupervised access to one another, and that means they are not even allowed to see one another when you are not present. If you are now going to say that they will pine for one another, what does this tell you about their relationship with one another? This means that when you arrive at the place where your young problem dog is it will actually be pleased to see you. You have to spend much of your time over the next five weeks trying to get your dog to play with you with a toy (see how to get your dog to play, page 111).

You will also need to spend time learning how to communicate with your dog. At the moment it does not understand your language at all. If it did, it would not be dog-aggressive, would it? It would also help if you trained your dog to understand a couple of simple commands such as coming when called, sitting and lying down when told. The ultimate command to teach a dog-aggressive dog is a 'hold' command, where the dog learns to hold a toy in its mouth. This strategy is then used in the presence of other dogs and works on the principle that a dog cannot bite another dog if it already has its mouth full.

Your dog is allowed no more than two 30-minute periods each day in the company of your other dog(s) but this *must* be closely supervised. The reason you are going to supervise these interactions carefully is so you are in a position to teach your problem dog *not* to play in any way at all with your other dog(s). Simply do not tolerate any type of interaction other than mutual grooming or licking behaviours. You must immediately stop your dogs chasing, bullying, intimidating, wrestling, biting or bumping into one another. If you were to do this for the next five weeks your dog should start to get the message. You cannot operate a double standard and give your problem dog permission to do these things to your other dog(s) at home all day long but then tell it that it is wrong to engage in the same behaviour but with aggression added when it meets other dogs outside.

Imagine I own two dogs, a two-year-old Labrador and a ten-month-old

German Shepherd. Both dogs live in my house and ten times each day I let them out into my back garden. Each time I do, the young Shepherd barges past the Labrador on the way out and turns to face him. When the Labrador walks out of the door, the playful young Shepherd suddenly leaps forward and playfully grabs the Lab by the back of the neck and the two run off around the garden, playing a game where the Shepherd tries to wrestle the Lab to the floor. The Shepherd practises this behaviour each time I let them out but I do nothing to stop it, believing they are only playing.

Then I notice that my Shepherd is becoming unpredictable with other dogs outside the house. When I take him to the park for exercise he keeps a close eye on the park gates and whenever he sees another dog coming through them he charges up to it and tries to grab it by the neck. Of course I find this unacceptable behaviour and try to stop it without realising that he does it many times each week in my own home right in front of my eyes and I never do anything to stop it!

So you can see where this is going: control the games your dog is allowed to play with your other dog and it goes a long way to being able to control him around other dogs. All you are doing is returning to the time that you first got your problem dog as a puppy and doing the things that you should have done in the first place.

Of all the dog owners who make an appointment with me five weeks in advance to find a cure for their dog's aggressive behaviour around other dogs, around 60 per cent phone back to say they no longer need to see me because their dog's behaviour has subsided. There has been a miraculous turn around, almost as if the dog has suddenly become very obedient around other dogs. So a 60 per cent success rate and I have not given any advice other than to stop owning a feral dog, to teach your dog some of your language, and that playing games with other dogs is no longer allowed – but playing with you is to be encouraged.

What about the other 40 per cent? They need to show up for the appointment so that I can take a closer look at the problem. Once again we must talk about aggression by prefixing the word with another, such as fear, territorial, possessive etc.

If you have a problem with your dog starting to show aggression to other dogs, it is best to seek professional help from a dog trainer or behaviourist. The first thing that he or she should do is to conduct a series of tests to find out what type of aggression it is and what is in your dog's mind at the point that he makes the decision to behave aggressively towards other dogs.

The tests

Behaviour testing and observation are a way to determine the possible reasons why a dog may act aggressively and the likelihood of behaviours being repeated. Behaviour testing is now widely used in rescue centres to determine a dog's likely behaviour when placed into a new home.

To carry out these behaviour tests the owner arrives at my house with their dog-aggressive dog. After seating them at one end of the room I first of all check the dog's collar to make sure that it is fitted correctly and the dog cannot escape out of it. I also take a look at the leash to make sure it will hold the dog if it decides to lunge forwards. I am going to bring in a number of different dogs so my instructions to the owner are as follows.

Keep a tight hold of your leash but do not use it to try and pull back on your dog if it pulls forwards – simply brace yourself and only allow your dog to reach the end of the leash. At no time do I want you to speak to, look at or touch your dog – just look at the pictures of dogs on the far wall. The idea behind this is to remove the owner's actions from the dog's behaviour without removing their presence or influence for the time being.

The door of the room that I use creaks as it is opened – something that could be cured by a drop of oil but it has remained the same for 25 years as it is part of a sequence of events that will form a pattern in the dog's mind. The door creaks open and my assistant walks in with the first of our dogs, a small terrier crossbreed called Gina. Gina enters the room and turns away from the problem dog to face the person who has brought her into the room (food treats help here!).

I watch the problem dog carefully for any indication that it is becoming aroused and for signs of how this dog recognised the fact that another dog has entered the room, usually a sniff in the air. Assuming that we get a display of aggression, I now start a stopwatch to find out how long it is before the problem dog realises that its aggressive display is not achieving anything at all. This is probably the first time in its life when it has displayed aggression but nothing has happened as a result. The owner does nothing, the person who entered with the other dog has done nothing, the other dog has done nothing, neither approaching nor leaving. We simply wait and observe.

I expect that within the first two minutes of the encounter the problem dog will have stopped its aggressive display and looked up at its owner's face. If it does not do this then it tells me the owner has not in fact separated their problem dog from any other dog that they own for the five-week period – the first part of the programme for putting right a problem of dog-to-dog aggression.

In other words, I am looking at the relationship between the owner and their problem dog. When we have changed the dog's expectations in this type of encounter, it should look to its owner for guidance. If it fails to do this, it cannot have the correct working relationship that would allow the owner to cure the problem.

Just by making this observation we can tell a large amount about how the dog has learned to become aggressive and the role that the owner has unwittingly played in the act. What if the problem dog bursts into aggression as the other dog enters the room and then after around 30 seconds it suddenly breaks off, looks at its owner, wags its tail, sits and looks at the handler's pocket?

I see this pattern of behaviour a lot where dogs have started to show aggression and the owner has tried to solve the problem by pulling their dog away, getting it to sit and then rewarding it with a food treat! After many repetitions the dog learns the most reliable way to get food treats from the handler's pockets is to lunge out at other dogs with an aggressive display!

What about a dog that keeps on interrupting its aggressive display by glancing at the owner over its shoulder and cowering for a few seconds before repeating the aggressive display? The likely scenario is that during previous aggressive displays the owner has struck out at their dog.

I wait until the aggressive display has subsided. Aggression is very tiring and there is a big clue here in devising a strategy to reverse dog-to-dog aggression. When the aggressive display has ceased, which usually results in the problem dog lying at the feet of its owner, our little terrier Gina is taken out of the room. If the aggression problem was rooted in fear, the problem dog should show signs of being relieved that Gina has been removed from the room, usually signalled by a slight wag of the tail. If the dog explodes into aggression as Gina is removed, it is more than likely to be a bullying type of frustration problem. In other words, the problem dog likes to play games of intimidating other dogs and is disappointed and frustrated when Gina is removed from the room.

After two minutes Gina is brought back in. Again I watch carefully as our problem dog sees Gina come in. Does the dog have the capacity to remember that this is the same dog that entered before? How long will it be before the problem dog ceases the display when it realises that there will be the same outcome? When the aggression ceases for a second time and Gina is removed, how many repetitions will it take before there is no aggressive display when she enters or leaves? What I am trying to establish is how quickly the dog learns that an aggressive display has no effect on its owner, the handler of the other dog or the other dog. This will give us an insight into how easy or difficult it is going to be to change the problem dog's behaviour.

As soon as I reach the point of no aggressive display I switch to having a different dog enter the room. I usually have at least eight dogs at my disposal which range from large dogs to small dogs, hairy dogs to smooth-coated dogs, castrated males to uncastrated males, and spayed females to unspayed females. Sometimes the sex of the other dog makes a difference, sometimes size.

After being exposed to a large number of dogs, sometimes with multiple exposures, the owner is finally given a new set of instructions. This time when we bring in a new dog the owner is to drop their leash to the floor. Many owners are reluctant to do this as they are worried that their dog will attack my dog. I usually have to reassure them that my dog can take care of himself and anyway the responsibility for what happens is entirely mine. So the door creaks and the dog's leash is dropped as my assistant pulls my dog into the room. He is always reluctant to come in as he has been attacked many times, twice requiring stitches. We then sit and watch the attack, which will be a carbon copy of how the dog has learned to be aggressive during early play with other dogs!

Oh, don't worry – the dog that has just entered is not a real dog! It is a lifelike stuffed toy dogs but remember the creaking door and the pattern that we put in the problem dog's head? Our problem dog *assumes* it has to be another real dog as he has no reason to suppose otherwise. So at last, without having to put any other dogs at risk, we have a vivid display of what is driving the aggressive behaviour and how the dog has learned to become aggressive.

A fearful dog will simply rush up to my stuffed dog, nip it on the back of its leg and run back to the owner, barking and continuing to warn the stuffed dog to stay away. A bully will grab my stuffed dog and pin it to the ground, then stand over it growling and almost willing the other dog to try and move. Dogs that are leash-aggressive only usually run up to my stuffed dog and signal that they want to play, although the display they gave on the leash was that they were wanting to fight. So this is aggression born out of frustration that they cannot get to the other dog.

It has to be said that most types of dog-to-dog aggression involve a great deal of noise but rarely do they result in actual bodily injury. The display and threat of aggression are usually enough to provide a satisfactory outcome for our problem dog. More serious types of aggression would be indicated by a dog that grabs and violently shakes my stuffed dog, or by a dog that flips my stuffed dog over onto its back in a heartbeat and grips and shakes it by the throat.

Some owners, to their credit, have never allowed their dog to get close enough to another dog to see what would happen, so this test is a revelation to them about what their dog is actually likely to do if given the chance.

Let's now examine each category of dog-to-dog aggression to try to understand how the problems are caused and consider the guidelines to use in modifying any aggressive behaviour.

52
Nervous Aggression

There are three possible causes of nervous aggression towards other dogs. By far the most common is a young puppy being attacked by an older dog while out exercising. The pup does not need to be physically injured for this to occur: the shock of being bowled over is usually quite sufficient to leave the pup mentally scarred. If this happens only on one isolated occasion, the resultant problem will often be breed-specific, which means that if the young dog was attacked by a black Labrador then it may never tolerate the presence of a black or chocolate Labrador again. Occasionally the problem may also be related to the area where the attack took place, so the dog will not accept any Labrador near it in the park but will be completely at ease if it encounter a Labrador in a dog-training class.

If the young dog is attacked or intimidated on several different occasions by different breeds of dog, the puppy may well become nervous and aggressive towards any other dog that comes near it. The aggression towards other dogs will have become more generalised.

The second type of nervous aggression is caused by depriving a puppy of social contact with other dogs during the critical early period in its life, from four to 16 weeks. This problem has increased over recent years since the onset of parvovirus, which is particularly lethal to puppies. The average owner will generally have been advised, by the breeder or vet, to avoid all contact with other dogs until it has developed full immunity after a course of vaccinations.

While this may be the correct advice for disease prevention, it is not conducive to good socialisation. When the pup is finally taken out to socialise with other dogs, the ageing puppy will usually feel frightened and intimidated by them in early encounters and unable to cope with the situation. It then clings tightly to its owner, often not even daring to peek out from behind its owner's legs.

The aggressive side of its nervous nature starts to develop at around seven months, when the owner decides to socialise it with other dogs in an attempt to improve its behaviour. Believing that what the young dog needs is more social contact with lots of unknown dogs is the first mistake. What the dog actually needs is some good multiple exposures to nice dogs one at a time. Until your dog has learned to be less afraid and trust one other dog, it is pointless to expose it to lots of them.

Usually three to five weeks of trying to expose a youngster that is fearful of other dogs will see a dramatic change in behaviour. This is particularly apparent if most of these encounters take place on a leash. Free-running encounters at least give a fearful young dog the opportunity to run away; being restrained on a lead does not. The owner will see a transition from fear to fear and aggression when another dog comes within the dog's critical distance (usually the length of the lead they are on). With no means of escape, our fearful dog will lunge forwards and bark at the other one. As soon as this happens it immediately gets two big rewards. One is that the other dog's owner pulls it away, thereby removing the offending dog from within the nervous dog's critical distance. The second reward is that the owner pulls the nervous dog away, which also serves to remove the offending dog from within its critical distance. Remember, a nervous dog *does not want* another dog to approach too closely! It is asking to keep its distance from other dogs it is worried about.

Some owners make the mistake of taking fearful young dogs into a dog-training class, where the whole experience of being thrust into what it perceives to be a pretty hostile environment proves extremely frightening. Maybe other dogs are barking in the hall and the poor dog, having no visible means of escape, becomes more and more withdrawn, sometimes trying to hide under the chairs.

It is usually around the third week of attendance that owners start to notice a sudden, often dramatic change in their dog's behaviour. Now, whenever another dog approaches, the nervous pup starts to growl, turning its head away from the offending dog but still maintaining eye contact. By the fifth week of attendance, it only takes another dog to approach and our nervous youngster will fly out to snap at it, dog and bitch alike. The aggressive phase of the nervous behaviour is now complete.

The nervous dog could equally well be exposed to other dogs in the local park in an attempt to socialise it and the end result will be the same; it is just accelerated by exposure to a large number of dogs in a closed environment.

The third major cause of nervous aggression towards other dogs comes when a bitch that is nervous-aggressive towards other dogs has a litter of puppies and is then aggressive towards other dogs in the presence of her puppies. They then not only grow up learning to be frightened of other dogs but also their mum's aggressive techniques for regaining control of the situation. This learned type of nervous aggression need not be confined to exposure to a nervous mother. If a puppy is taken away from its littermates at between six and 16 weeks and homed where there is another dog that is nervous towards other dogs, then the pup can easily pick it up from that dog. This is why it is so important to make sure any dog you already own has no behaviour problems related to nervousness before you buy a young puppy.

So how do you go about trying to change your dog's attitude towards other dogs?

That depends on a number of factors, such as the age of your dog and the history of the problem. Sometimes, with an older dog (i.e. over the age of 18 months), it is better to give the dog what it is asking for, which is to stay well away from other dogs.

Strategies for older dogs that are dog-aggressive would include the following. Multiple or continuous exposures to known dogs, one at a time, that are not only good at communicating with other dogs but have also been trained to a high level of control. Basically what you are looking for is a dog trainer who has a well-behaved, laid-back adult dog that has little interest in other dogs. By exposing our fearful and aggressive dog, either muzzled and/or held on a lead, to our trained dog several times each week (or continuously for several days), there should be a significant reduction in fearful behaviour and a corresponding lessening in its aggressive displays.

Sometimes you have to accept that rather than trying to reduce a dog's fear of other dogs, it is easier and safer to retain the fear but to teach a flight response to replace the fight one. To do this, you again need to seek out a trainer who has not only the correct dogs to use but understands the 'burning bridges' procedure.

This is set up in the following way: The nervous and aggressive dog is held on a lead and also has a light line around 15 feet long attached to its collar. The owner holds the lead and the line is stretched out in front of the dog. The trainer now enters the area with their own non-aggressive dog on a leash and they walk towards the nervous dog. As they get to within 15 feet, they simply pick up the trailing line. Then the trainer continues to walk towards the nervous dog, watching for any signs that the dog is going into fear or aggressive arousal. Signs would be an increase in focus, the dog holding its breath, the hackles on its back rising (pilo erection), a slight turn of the head showing the whites of its eyes etc.

At the first sign of arousal – not when the aggressive display has started – the trainer tugs on the line to pull the nervous dog towards his own dog. At the same precise moment the owner throws his lead to the floor and storms away in disgust – maybe even getting into their car and leaving. This is the reversal principle described earlier. What the dog expected from its experience was that the trainer would pull his dog away and its owner would do likewise. In fact the reverse has happened, leaving the dog abandoned in no man's land. The dog has 'burned his bridges' and finds that there is no way back to its owner.

The effect is usually very dramatic as the nervous dog immediately turns away from the trainer and his dog and focuses on the escape route that its owner and role model took. This escape route is not available to the dog, who has been deserted by his owner. When the owner returns into view after a couple of minutes, the trainer releases the line to let the dog run to him. It is important at this stage for the owner not to praise the dog or get excited: he should remain calm and collected. The trainer then picks up the end of the line and the owner should then pick up the lead and slowly walk towards the trainer and their dog. Any signs of arousal on the nervous dog's part are dealt with by the trainer putting a slight amount of pressure on the line to pull the dog forwards away from its owner. The dog will resist and hang back behind its owner.

The owner is now asked to walk past the trainer and his dog. The nervous dog should cross behind the owner's legs to stay away from the trainer's dog, and this avoidance behaviour should be gently rewarded by the owner. Remember, we are trying to remove the aggression. By rewarding any signs that the nervous dog is now actively avoiding other dogs while on the lead, and by always allowing it the option of moving away from other dogs, you may increase its fear of other dogs but there is no doubt at all you will remove the aggression. This process now needs to be repeated in six different areas using six different dogs, and the nervous dog should learn to rely on the strategy of avoidance working better then the previous strategy of conflict.

With young dogs that have not yet added aggression to fear, there is a better solution. First I need to emphasise that this strategy is for young dogs that are merely worried about the presence of other dogs, not aggressive towards them. Go along to your local rescue and ask about the possibility of short-term fostering. If the staff can identify a suitable friendly dog and introduce it to your dog in a neutral area, all you need to do is take the foster dog home and, by allowing your dog continuous and supervised exposure to another friendly dog, it should habituate to it within a few days. By careful and expertly controlled multiple, or better still, continuous exposure to other known dogs from a rescue centre, not only can you teach your young dog to trust other dogs but you also carry out a valuable fostering service for your local shelter.

53
Leash Aggression

This category of bad behaviour was first observed in the USA and describes a dog that becomes very aggressive towards other dogs when restricted by a lead. So we come back to our two F words: fear and frustration.

To deal with the fear aspect first, we can recognise the aggression as being purely defensive, which means that the dog only exhibits it when the other dog gets within a certain critical distance. The reason behind that aggression is that the dog, knowing it is restricted by the lead, cannot escape and therefore has to use aggression to remove the threat of the other dog coming closer. For a dog to become leash-aggressive through fear one of two conditions has to apply.

The first of these is that dog has been traumatised by being attacked by another dog or dogs when being walked on a lead. In this case we need to look at various possible fear associations to work out a framework to retrain the dog. So let's imagine I take my young Springer Spaniel puppy for a run in my local park. When the exercise is finished I put it on a lead to walk it back home but as I set off my puppy gets mobbed by two Labradors. My puppy is not injured but has had a really frightening experience.

Later that day my wife takes our puppy out and reports that she has no problems. Two days later I am out for a walk with my puppy and as we walk past a house, the resident Dalmatian races out and wrestles my puppy to the floor. Again my puppy is not injured but is clearly upset by this unpleasant experience. For the rest of the week my wife takes the puppy out and reports no further incidents. At the weekend I take the puppy for another walk and it gets attacked by an Airedale Terrier.

What my puppy may now start to learn is that when he is with me he is liable to get attacked by other dogs, so he becomes defensively aggressive. When my wife walks him she never encounters any problems. Off the lead there are also no problems because he has never had any unpleasant experiences – they have all been when I have been walking him on the lead.

But probably the more common reason is frustration. It invariably starts by giving a young dog the impression it is allowed to go up to and meet any other dog it encounters being taken out for a walk. Some dog-training classes teach something called a meet-and-greet behaviour on the lead, where dogs are encouraged to approach each other to say hi. Also, if you allow your dog to play outrageous games with other dogs whenever you take him out and let him off the lead, guess what will happen when he then sees another dog and is not allowed to go up to it, either on or off the lead? That's correct – he will become very frustrated and pull harder to get to the other dog. The more frustrated the dog becomes, the worse the behaviour gets and the more that the owner starts reprimanding the dog. This only serves to make the other dog more and more excited.

This is a particular type of aggression, as the resultant grip-and-hold bite that the dog carries out if it manages to get close enough is inadvertently trained the same way as a grip-and-hold bite is trained by a police dog trainer (see the section on aggression, page 245). Basically, if you had trained your dog to walk correctly on the lead in the first place and taught him that he was never allowed to approach and greet a dog when on the lead, the problem would not have arisen.

I approach almost all problems of leash aggression by simply teaching the dog to walk properly on the lead without pulling, because if your dog fully understands that he is not to put any pressure on the lead then his bad behaviour towards other dogs will subside. As we saw earlier on page 120, teaching a dog to walk properly on the lead is really easy and it is better to teach your dog what you want him to do than try to teach him what you don't want him to do.

There is more you can do to teach your dog to walk correctly and reduce aggression on the lead. For instance, you could use any one of the many specially designed head collars which will give you more control. You could also put on a correctly fitting basket muzzle if you must take your dog out around other dogs, but remember that even if your dog has a muzzle he can still intimidate and traumatise other dogs. It is for this reason that if you need to muzzle your dog, you should never allow it off the lead around other dogs.

54
Territorial Aggression

When I'm in the USA I am often asked, how can I stop my dog from guarding its crate (travel kennel) when at a dog show? I usually answer the question by asking some of my own. Is the physical size of the crate big enough to support two dogs? How about the water supply – how many bowls of water are in the crate? How about chews or toys – just one or lots? So it stands to reason that if you double the size of the crate, put in two water bowls, several dog treats and toys, you will at least reduce the dog's aggressive display. Also remember that to teach your dog not to guard its territory, you need to be there in attendance.

What about the dog that starts to defend not only the property in which it lives but the surrounding area? The worst thing you can do in this case is take the dog out for a regular walk using the same short route around your neighbourhood. This effectively extends the dog's idea of territory and is likely to culminate in the dog throwing out challenges in the whole area that surrounds your house. It would be better to take the dog out in a car to reach an exercise area. Also, if your dog begins to become territorial and aggressive in the area in which it is regularly exercised, you should find at least five different exercise areas and make sure you do not exercise your dog in the same area more than two days running. By taking your dog to the same area each day, especially if the dog is allowed to mark this area multiple times, you could be setting the scene for your dog to start warning off other 'intruding' dogs!

What to do about a dog that fence fights with a neighbour's dog? Again, I would normally ask where are you when this is happening? If you are inside your house then of course you will have no influence over the way that your dog is behaving. Also, if the two dogs only ever meet up at the boundaries of their respective properties, then it is understandable that they may want to warn each other away from the fence line which delineates the properties.

There are three ways that you could handle the situation. One is to make sure you are always present whenever you let your dog out into your back garden, so you are there to educate him about what he is and is not allowed to do. The second way to handle it is by good management and coming to an agreement with your neighbour on a timetable for letting both dogs out so the situation does not arise. And thirdly you could again talk to your neighbour and both take your dogs out for walks on regular occasions so they have the chance to meet up on neutral territory and socialise with one another. When this has been accomplished, and providing the two dogs have taken a liking to one another, you could remove a panel of the fence to allow the dogs to interact more socially when they are let out.

55
Frustration and Intimidation

If you have a problem of dog-to-dog aggression, it is probably down to the fact that your dog enjoys playing fighting games with other dogs or is frustrated by the fact that it cannot get at the other dog to play such games. If your dog would willingly leave your side to run more than 20 yards to engage in acts of aggression towards other dogs, I think we can rule out fear as a motive!

If you have read the section on why dogs get involved in aggression (page 303), it should be no surprise that there has to have been another dog involved in early games of mock fighting. So in all probability these two categories occur when there are two dogs sharing the household. So how would you go about trying to resolve the problem?

Many strategies have been tried with varying degrees of success. The first one is the use of food to distract the problem dog from other dogs. The owner is instructed to take tasty treats in their pocket and as soon as another dog is spotted, they are simply asked to distract their dog using the food.

A more powerful version of this is to use all the dog's dinner instead of food treats. So for a period of around two weeks the only food the problem dog is allowed to eat is when out on a walk when the owner spots another dog. Sometimes you would start this programme by taking the dog out for a few days to a place where you are unlikely to encounter other dogs and get it used to being fed its dinner on a walk, before progressing to walking where there might be other dogs. Carried out correctly, this should move the dog's focus further away from the other dogs and centre it more on the owner, who is providing all the food the dog needs in order to survive.

Some of the more modern trainers also advocate the use of a clicker to mark the point at which the dog receives the food treat. This system is certainly worth a try but if you attempt it and do not see any improvement – i.e. the dog is too aroused by the presence of the other dog to eat, then abandon this idea within three days or your dog will get very thin!

A second strategy would be to enrol in a dog-obedience class to teach your dog a series of control commands. By teaching your dog to focus on you using a competition command ('heel') and the commands 'sit', 'down' and 'stay', it is sometimes possible to have much more authority over how your dog behaves around other dogs. Barbara Woodhouse was known worldwide for using these techniques to modify the behaviour of aggressive dogs and many trainers still use this approach. The downside of this system is that it requires the average owner to be as good as a dog trainer who competes at the highest level. There is a body of opinion that believes there is no such thing as a behaviour problem but merely dogs that are very disobedient, and that by a correct and thorough schooling in formal obedience, any problem can be resolved, particularly dog-to-dog aggression problems.

A recent addition to the strategies that exist to solve these kinds of aggression problems was the 'growl' class. The idea is to get all the dogs with aggressive tendencies together in a specialised class environment under the control of a professional trainer. All the dogs wear muzzles and are basically allowed freedom to interact with one another and sort out their differences without the possibility of actual bodily harm. Usually after several weeks of such a class, dogs that previously seemed to hate one another often started to tolerate one another.

It is easy to understand how this might be effective for a fixed group of dogs that meet up regularly but more difficult to see how it would work when any of these dogs meet up with unknown dogs away from the class. Many people who have attended this type of class with dogs that either get frustrated around other dogs or like to try to intimidate them confirm there are limited benefits to be obtained from it. In the better growl classes the emphasis is on control exercises as well as freedom to interact.

My own strategies differ from all the above by first dramatically reducing the dog's exposure to other dogs for around five weeks, thus removing all opportunities the problem dog has to practise fighting behaviour. When this period is over and hopefully a more meaningful relationship has developed between dog and owner, they can start on the second part, which involves teaching a simple behaviour that can be used in the presence of other dogs. This can be a 'sit' command or whatever the owner finds the easiest to train. Ultimately the best behaviour is to teach your dog to hold on to an object in its mouth. If it is concentrating on holding something in its mouth then it cannot attempt to lunge and bark at or bite another dog. Unfortunately, as with most Barbara Woodhouse techniques, this requires a level of training skill well beyond most dog owners. Once we have picked the desired behaviour, we need to find a suitable reward to use for its correct completion and a suitable penalty for non-compliance. We will also need the services of another dog and handler for practice.

If this seems quite complicated, it isn't really, as most people with a dog-to-dog aggression problem already have most of the ingredients necessary to correct it. For instance, you could use your partner or friend and your own 'other' dog for the practice sessions. The choice of behaviour, reward and penalty is up to you, but let's say the chosen behaviour is a sit and stay, the reward is giving food along with lots of verbal and physical praise, and the penalty is withholding food in a particular manner and a display of emotions from the owner. It starts like this:

For around one week, mix up your dog's food each morning and divide it into ten equal portions. No other food is to be made available for the next few weeks. At any time of the day while in the house, put your dog on a leash and get him to sit. This can be carried out by luring him into the sit, bribing him to sit by holding out the food bowl or by gently and physically guiding him into the sit. When he is sitting, count to five then smile, gently stroke him and use your voice to tell him what a great dog he is. Then give him a portion of food. If he moves out of the position before the five seconds are up then give a big display of disgust as you drop the leash and turn away from him. Put the portion of food away so he cannot get it.

Now wait for at least 20 minutes before trying again. During this first week it is important that he gets as many opportunities as he needs to get his food each day. You are *not* to withhold food but use it to teach him what is required to get what he needs to survive. If you have difficulty, contact an accredited trainer to help you achieve this.

For the second phase, pick any number between one and 50 each day and, as before, have ten portions of food available. You are still going to get your dog to sit and stay but now the length of time he does it becomes more variable. After having been successful 70 times the previous week (ten food portions each day over seven days equals 70), your dog should realise the behaviour required to get his food. So now the penalties become more severe. If your dog moves within the random time you chose that day, then in addition to expressing disgust and walking away, this portion of food is actually thrown away rather than put away for a later try. If you find that after two days your dog is getting very little to eat then return to phase one of this programme for a further week before starting phase two again.

After a week you should be able to move to phase three, which repeats weeks one and two but adds the distraction of another dog. In all probability this is your own other dog as around 90 per cent of all dogs with this type of aggression problem are the younger of two or more dogs that share the same household! For this phase we also need to increase the rewards on offer and the penalty for non-compliance. So fill two containers with something extra special, such as cooked chicken, but the other eight only with your dog's normal daily food. Now when you ask your dog to sit, you need to get someone to walk into the room with either your own other dog or another known and friendly dog on the lead.

Remember that you have asked your dog to sit and he has two choices – to comply with what you want, in which case wait for a few seconds then reward him with one of the containers of chicken, or to break the position to say hi to the other dog. If he breaks the position then immediately give your expression of disgust and lean forward to give the container of food to the other dog before leaving the room with your dog on the lead. This usually has a profound effect on your problem dog and the way he now views failing to carry out the behaviour you have painstakingly taught him when other dogs approach.

Progress by having him sit for longer, having the other dog walk past him and so on for a further week. Week four should see you start to take him out for walks but for the first few excursions you should arrange to meet up with your assistant either with your own other dog or their own friendly dog and repeat the training.

Ultimately, the hold behaviour is the best one to use with a favourite toy, the penalty being if he drops it to lunge or bark at the approaching dog that the toy is thrown to the other dog to walk off with! The end result of this should be that whenever other dogs approach, he should turn his head away from the other dog to protect the toy in his mouth. Reward this behaviour with lots of physical and verbal praise and you should see a significant improvement within a couple of weeks.

56
Aggression between Dogs Sharing the Same Household

Before examining any strategies that might prove helpful in prevention and possible 'cures', we need to take a look at why dogs in the same household might fight.

If you have two or more dogs that live together, then fights between them would usually occur initially when one dog is in close proximity to food and the other dog tries to approach or even steal it. This can even happen over a water supply. The same is also true for toys or other possessions, where one dog tries to approach or remove a toy or trophy from the other, and sleeping areas, where one dog approaches or tries to displace the other. But by far the most common thing that will provoke this kind of aggression is the presence of the owner.

The worst possible set of ingredients if your two dogs fight one another is a mother/daughter combination. The next worse set is two sisters, then father and son, and finally two brothers. If a breeder sold you two brothers or two sisters, this is where your problems first began!

So how does the first fight start? Let's take a typical case of mother and daughter. They have been together since the puppy was born, they have played a great deal together and, during these games, the daughter finds she is a close match for her mother in terms of strength. Things are usually fine until mother starts to see her daughter as more of a threat – this will usually be around the time her daughter comes into season for the first time. Now, with the effect of hormones on behaviour, there will be an incident over a resource that had previously been shared or when the two dogs get overexcited. Mother believes she is being challenged by her daughter and so a fight ensues.

This first fight will be intense in terms of the amount of noise that is used and there may even be some minor injuries, but to minimise the risk of serious injury this first fight will almost exclusively take place in the presence of the owner – the one particular person that they both look up to as a role model. Why? Because the probability of the owner stepping in before it gets out of hand makes this first fight safer. Pack leaders are remarkably efficient in dealing with trouble from within the ranks.

The problem is that most owners tend to side with the wrong dog! So with two evenly matched dogs and an owner who seems to artificially favour first one dog and then the other, we have all the ingredients for the fights to worsen. The process of siding with one dog when you are the role model for both is known as 'status by association'. Simply stated, this means that if you are of fairly low rank but you are the best friend of someone with a very high rank, your association with that person raises your status within your social group.

Unfortunately it is not really possible to raise two evenly matched dogs as equals. If you try then often you will have to deal with the fights that will start between them, which results in the fights being sustained over a very long period. For this reason I discuss how and why to select a second dog in the next section.

So to understand the concepts involved in stopping the problem developing and/or trying to cure the problem, we again take a look at basic dog behaviour – in this instance dogs living in small social groups.

The hierarchy or pecking order that dogs place themselves in is by no means static. It depends on three important factors, namely:

1. Where the dogs are: the territory that they are in, including available resources

2. What is happening at that particular time in terms of levels of arousal
3. Who in the group is present or absent at the time.

Each dog's position in the dominance hierarchy is related to status. This simple fact is usually completely overlooked by most owners of more than one dog. The subsequent disagreements and fights are usually the result of the owner's ignorance in trying to bring up both dogs as equals instead of understanding that there is no such thing. What often confuses the owners is that the two dogs will often share the same bed at night and can be left alone without problems.

To understand this more fully let's look at a common area of conflict when a young dog is just starting to challenge the older dog for dominance. The older dog is sitting alongside the owner being stroked and the young dog enters the room and stares at the older dog. The older dog takes this stare as a challenge and growls to warn the younger dog away. The owner immediately reinforces the younger dog's position by either physically or verbally chastising the older dog, thus making the younger dog more confident about his status when the owner is present. It is easier to understand if we apply the same logic to two children.

If my youngest son Matthew enters my eldest son Marc's bedroom and starts to play around with his stereo equipment then Marc, being ten years Matthew's senior, will challenge and possibly try to assert his authority over him. If Matthew then comes to me and tells me that Marc has threatened him and I go storming in and reprimand Marc, I am bound to increase the conflict between them because Matthew will start to take advantage of the fact that Marc is powerless to take control while I am in the house. If, on the other hand, when Matthew came in complaining about Marc's threats I chastised him for entering Marc's bedroom and touching equipment that does not belong to him, end of problem. Matthew would very quickly learn the limitations of his status and territory.

If we reinforce the more dominant dog's status by giving it the preferential treatment commensurate with its status, then it is possible to reduce or even eliminate any growing conflict between them. Preferential treatment would be simple things like putting the more dominant dog's food bowl down first, patting it on the head first when entering the house, putting on its lead first when going out for exercise etc. All these actions serve to remove the confusion that might otherwise exist in the company of the owner.

The idea of giving one dog preferential treatment may not appeal to many owners but it is the natural way of life for any dog within a pack. They will readily accept and enjoy living like this rather than go through life in constant conflict with their owners and one another. If you feel sorry for the underdog, remember the saying 'every dog has its day.' This means there will often come a time when the older dog has to give up its privileged position to the younger dog. This time comes when the young dog has started to win most of the possession games it plays with the older dog, and the final takeover comes when the younger dog gains total control of the other dog's sleeping areas. When this happens, you can make the transition much smoother by transferring your allegiance from the older dog to the younger. This may seem hard on the older dog but it is a way of avoiding serious confrontations between them. Remember that ultimately you are the figure that both of your dogs should look up to, so you need to make sure you hold the position of top dog in your household.

Now some tips on how to reduce the possibility of your two dogs beginning to fight.

1. Avoid situations where you are playing with both dogs together and they become over-aroused. It is better to play individual games if you find that trying to play with both together results in friction between them.
2. Try to avoid the dogs being together in areas of high excitement, such as the front door when you have visitors.
3. When feeding your dogs try not to have a set meal time. If they know they are going to be fed at 6pm every evening, then at 5.30pm they start to look forward eagerly to being fed. At 5.45pm they begin to get

excited. At 5.55pm they can hear their owner preparing their meal and start throwing out challenges to one another. Then at 6pm, when their owner walks into the room with their dinner, they start fighting as the first bowl is placed on the floor.

4. Make sure the dogs are not confined to very small areas when you leave the house. The bigger the area they have in your absence, the less chance of friction. Ensure that your dogs have more than two of everything including food bowls, water bowls, toys etc.

If fights have already started between your two dogs, we need to look at what you can do to fix the problem. To begin with, you have to firmly establish the correct pecking order for your dogs. You need to work out which dog you believe to be the more dominant and which the more submissive. Generally speaking, the more dominant will be able to retain possession of a favourite resting area and will be able to displace the more submissive dog if he wants the spot. He will also be able to retain possession of a toy and food such as chews.

Also, take a look at the more submissive dog for tell-tale signs. It will generally not try to take a possession away from another dog and will move out of a resting area when the other dog wants it. A submissive dog will often show lots of appeasement behaviours, often licking the other dog close to the mouth particularly when greeting the other dog after a short absence.

Having identified the dog you believe to be the more dominant, with two males you should have the more *submissive* dog neutered. If you have both neutered then you will see no change and if you have the more dominant dog neutered then the friction will in all probability get worse. If you are really not sure which dog should be neutered then contact your veterinarian with a view to starting one dog on hormone therapy, sometimes called 'chemical castration'. If this works in the short term then neutering will almost certainly work in the long term.

With females the rules are reversed and you should consider having the more *dominant* female spayed. This is due to the effect of the chemical testosterone on the behaviour: spaying an already dominant female often makes her dominant behaviour more of a factor.

If your two dogs then start to fight when they are being fed, you will either have to feed them separately or in the following way. Use three food bowls instead of two and the biggest area possible in which to feed your dogs. Place the bowl for the dog that you are promoting and maintaining as number one on the floor first, telling your number two dog to sit and stay. As soon as you have placed this first bowl on the floor you can now immediately put the second bowl down for your number two dog. In this bowl, you will have placed a rock or length of chain on top of the food to slow down the rate at which your dog is able to consume the food, ensuring that he finishes last.

Now place the third bowl on the floor at a short distance away from where your two dogs are eating. When your number one dog has finished eating, call him away from your other dog, who should still be eating, and guide him to where the third bowl is. Allow him to eat a few mouthfuls before removing him from the feeding area and allowing your number two dog to finish his meal. If you are in doubt about your ability to call your number one dog to you, you could attach a light line (around six feet in length) to his collar before he starts eating and use it to teach him to do what you want.

The idea behind this food programme, which should always be fully supervised, is to teach your number one dog not to try and intimidate your number two dog into leaving his food bowl. By teaching him to finish his food and then move to the third, full bowl, you are thus rewarding him for leaving the other dog to finish his meal.

You will also need to increase the number of water bowls so there are at least three available at all times. And increase the number of dog beds in any one area to three.

When you arrive home after a short absence, try to greet your number one dog first, insisting that number two dog stays a short distance away. After briefly greeting number one, tell him to stay while you briefly greet number two. Similarly, always put number one dog's lead on first when you take them out for walks.

You can also tie a light line to your number two dog's collar to teach him how to move out of a bed or resting area if your number one dog wants it. Always remember to reward your dogs, one at a time, for doing what you want.

The above procedures should let both dogs know you are giving your chosen dog the status as your assistant pack leader. This has the effect of reducing the number of challenges your number two dog throws out as he now has a bigger problem to solve. In his mind you are now forming a coalition with your number one dog, so it is easier for him to opt for a quiet life and not run the risk of upsetting you both!

If your dogs do begin a fight, never try to grab at either dog's collar. Because of the high level of arousal it is likely that your hand will be seen as a threat by one or both dogs and you are likely to get bitten. Throwing water over them or, better still, an old blanket, will usually get them to stop, allowing you to regain control. Remain standing and as they come apart you might need to shout to get both dogs' attention and respect.

Finally, if your two dogs have reached the point where they are damaging one another even when you are not present, then you may have to accept that they are telling you they do not want to be made to live together. In this case it is far kinder to find another home for one dog than to ask both to live in fear of being seriously injured or even killed by the other.

Epilogue
A Vision for the Future

'Anyone who in discussion relies upon authority uses, not his understanding, but rather his memory.'
– LEONARDO DA VINCI

Dogs have come a long way since the humble beginnings of our relationship. They are now under increasing pressure as they are being left behind in our modern world of technology. Unless as dog owners and enthusiasts we are able to change the modern trend which sees more and more restrictions on ownership, then companion and working dogs will become a thing of the past in much the same way as we saw the decline of the horse when cars, modern warfare and farm machinery removed the need for horses. Foxhunting bans and even the possibility of banning horseracing mean that a child being able to see or touch a horse is becoming less and less likely, especially if they live in a town.

If we take a look at what is happening with dogs, it becomes very worrying indeed.

For many dog owners, the decline in their access to public areas hit a milestone in 1979 in the city of Berkeley, California when the world's first dog park opened. This was the breakthrough that most anti-dog people seemed to have been waiting for. At last a model existed for removing dogs from parks and recreation areas and restricting them to an incredibly small area, effectively segregating them from the public. Many other states in the USA quickly followed, as did other countries, and as a result, specific dog classes were set up to cater for this dramatic change in social skills that are required to enter one of these parks safely.

Trainers set up classes so pet dogs could learn to be part of a large and changing feral pack, describing these as 'socialisation classes'. This changed the emphasis on dog-training, which had previously centred on getting the dog to understand, communicate with and obey its owner. Many dogs in classes were now learning to better understand, communicate with and obey other dogs. Once a dog park becomes established in a community, either off-leash bans or completely banning dogs in any other public area become almost a formality. Increasing a dog's access to other dogs in a community while restricting its access to people is certainly no help as an aid to correct socialisation.

It was then noted that some owners were taking advantage of dog parks by dropping their dogs off before going to work and then collecting them on the way home. Realising the potential for a new business, several enterprising trainers then started doggy daycare or the dog crèche. So now an owner can turn their dog over to an organisation so that it can become part of a feral pack five or more days each week.

We also have the problem of an increasing number of animal charities that have a policy not to send a dog for adoption to a family if there is a child in the house under the age of ten. So it is hard to see where our next generation of dog owners is going to come from. Will future generations continue the trend of becoming the keeper of a dog? Will the only place a child ever gets to see a dog be in a dog park or in a zoo? Are the days of seeing a family having a picnic on a village green with their faithful companion enjoying the outing with them going to become a distant memory?

The difficult thing for most dog lovers to understand is that if you are a dog owner you are in a minority. The majority of people in any country do not own a dog and many of these people do not care for dogs at all. They do not want to hear dogs barking, be threatened by dogs or have to deal with dog excrement. So how are we going to change things so our children and grandchildren can still experience the pleasure of growing up with a canine companion?

Let's start by looking at a model that breeders, owners and trainers can use to try and get back on track. Many non-dog-loving people admire the work carried out by service dogs such as guide dogs for the blind.

To become a service dog, a dog should have undergone a certification process approved by Assistance Dogs International. It will also have undergone regular health checks and be structurally sound. In short, the dog should end up being an ambassador for the canine world.

The following public-access test extracts are reproduced by kind permission of Assistance Dogs International. For the full set of tests please contact Assistance Dogs International.

Public Access Test

Purpose: The purpose of this Public Access Test is to ensure that dogs who have public access are stable, well-behaved, and unobtrusive to the public. It is to ensure that the client has control over the dog and the team is not a public hazard. This test is NOT intended as a substitute for the skill/task test that should be given by the program. It is to be used in addition to those skill/task tests. It is expected that the test will be adhered to as closely as possible. If modifications are necessary, they should be noted in the space provided at the end of the test.

Dismissal: Any dog that displays any aggressive behaviour (growling, biting, raising hackles, showing teeth, etc.) will be eliminated from the test. Any dog that eliminates in a building or shows uncontrollable behaviour will be eliminated from the test.

Bottom Line: The bottom line of this test is that the dog demonstrates that he/she is safe to be in public and that the person demonstrates that he/she has control of the dog at all times.

Testing Equipment: All testing shall be done with equipment appropriate to the needs and abilities of the team. All dogs shall be on-lead at all times except in the vehicle at which time it is optional. This test is to take place in a public setting such as a mall (shopping centre) where there are a lot of people and natural distractions. The individual will handle the dog and can use any reasonable/humane equipment necessary to ensure his/her control over the dog.

The evaluator will explain the test thoroughly before the actual testing, during which he/she will follow discreetly to observe when not directly interacting with the individual on a test-related matter. The only things an evaluator needs are a clip board, an assistant, another dog, a plate with food, and access to a shopping cart.

Commands: Commands may be given to the dog in either hand signals or verbal signals or both.

Controlled Unload out of a Vehicle: After a suitable place has been found, the individual will unload the dog and any necessary equipment (wheelchair, walker, crutches, etc.) out of the vehicle. The dog must wait until released before coming out of the vehicle. Once outside, it must wait quietly unless otherwise instructed by the individual. The dog may not run around, be off-lead, or ignore commands given by the individual. Once the team is out of the vehicle and settled, the assistant should walk past with another dog. They should walk within six (6) feet of the team. The Assistance Dog must remain calm and under control, not pulling or trying to get to the other dog. The emphasis on this is that the Assistance Dog remains unobtrusive and is unloaded in the safest manner possible for everyone.

Approaching the Building: After unloading, the team must manoeuvre through the parking lot to approach the building. The dog must stay in a relative heel position and may not forge ahead or lag behind. The dog must not display a fear of cars or traffic noises and must display a relaxed attitude. When the individual stops for any reason, the dog must stop also.

1. **Controlled Entry Through a Doorway**: Once at the doors of the building, the individual may enter however he/she chooses to negotiate the entry safely. Upon entering the building, however, the dog may not wander off or solicit attention from the public. The dog should wait quietly until the team is fully inside then should calmly walk beside the individual. The dog must not pull or strain against the lead or try to push its way past the individual but must wait patiently while entry is completed.
2. **Downs on Command**: The down exercises will be performed in the same sequence as the sits with the same basic stipulations.

   The first down will be at a table where food will be dropped on the floor. The dog should not break the down to go for the food or sniff at the food. The individual may give verbal and physical corrections to maintain the down. There should not be any extraordinary gestures on the part of the people approaching the dog. Normal, reasonable behaviour from the people is expected. The second down will be executed, and then an adult and child should approach the dog. The dog should maintain the down and not solicit attention. If the child pets the dog, the dog must behave appropriately and not break the stay. The individual may give verbal and physical corrections if the dog begins to break the stay. The third down will be accomplished, and then either a stranger or the assistant will be asked to step over the dog. The dog may not break the stay to solicit from the stranger. The individual may give corrections as indicated above.

3. **Restaurant**: The team and tester should enter a restaurant and be seated at a table. The dog should go under the table or, if size prevents that, stay close by the individual. The dog must sit or lie down and may move a bit for comfort during the meal, but should not be up and down a lot or need a lot of correction or reminding. This would be a logical place to do the food drop during a down.

Now if you contrast this standard of behaviour to the standard that used to be applied in public dog-training classes in the 1960s, you will see where we perhaps started to get things wrong. Training classes were based very heavily on competitive obedience. The first obedience tests in the USA were devised in New York in 1933 by Helen Whitehouse Walker to showcase the training and intelligence of her poodles. In the tests the dog was (and still is) required to walk to heel on the lead on the handler's left-hand side. Take a look at a small part of the competition requirement for a dog walking to heel and you will notice that what is required bears no relationship to training a dog to walk with you along the road.

Competition requirements for walking to heel
The dog should start off by sitting straight at the handler's side.
On the command 'forward' given by the judge or steward, the handler should walk briskly forward in a straight line with the dog at heel. The dog's shoulder should be approximately level with, and reasonably close to, the handler's leg at all times when the handler is walking and the lead must remain slack at all times.

On the judge or steward's command of 'left turn' or 'right turn' the handler should turn smartly at a right angle in the appropriate direction and the dog should maintain its position at the handler's side.

There is a big difference between what was – and sometimes still is – trained in a typical public dog-training class and what is actually required in real life when you take your dog out for a walk.

The same is true for the competition recall exercise. Again this bears little or no relationship to getting a dog to come when called in the local park, unless you are lucky enough to have your dog sitting and facing you waiting to be called!

These competition obedience tests often also include sit stay, down stay and a retrieve on a dumbbell of all things. Now while many thousands of trainers and dogs get a huge amount of pleasure by training and competing in these tests (I did them myself for many years), they were not exactly designed to help a pet owner gain more control over their dog where it was needed – out in public.

So we give credit to the American Kennel Club (AKC), which in 1989 adopted an idea put forward by the first training organisation in the world to get dog trainers together under one umbrella, the National Association of Dog Obedience Instructors (NADOI). They devised a new series of more realistic tests, which they called the Canine Good Citizen tests.

This evaluation consists of ten objectives. All parts of the test must be completed satisfactorily for the dog and handler to pass.

Canine Good Citizen Tests

1. Accepting a friendly stranger
2. Sitting politely for petting
3. Allowing basic grooming procedures
4. Walking on a loose lead
5. Walking through a crowd
6. Sitting and lying down on command and staying in place
7. Coming when called
8. Reacting appropriately to another dog
9. Reacting appropriately to distractions
10. Calmly enduring supervised separation from the owner

Many other countries soon followed suit. In England the tests were first presented by Roy Hunter at a course in Lincolnshire. Soon afterwards they were revised and finally adopted by the British Kennel Club in 1992. Unfortunately, little has changed since then and the tests, while a step in the right direction, no longer reflect what is required by modern communities.

Breeders need to focus more on producing dogs of outstanding temperament and free of genetically inherited defects. Poor temperament should be a disqualification in all dog sports.

Kennel clubs should change all breed standards to reflect what is required in society – nice dogs. Maybe a starting point should be to take a look at the breed standard for Labrador Retrievers. This is about the same in every kennel club in every country and includes the following:

'True Labrador Retriever temperament is as much a hallmark of the breed as the "otter" tail. The ideal disposition is one of a kindly, outgoing, tractable nature; eager to please and non-aggressive towards man or animal. The Labrador has much that appeals to people; his gentle ways, "kind", friendly eyes, expressing character, intelligence and good temperament; intelligence and adaptability make him an ideal dog. Intelligent, keen and biddable, with a strong will to please. Kindly natured, with no trace of aggression or undue shyness. Good-tempered, very agile. Excellent nose, soft mouth; keen love of water. Adaptable, devoted companion.'

Now for us trainers! For far too long we have probably been guided in our training classes by what dog owners seem to have wanted. Maybe the way ahead is by asking people in our communities who do not like dogs what training we should be carrying out to make dogs more acceptable in society? I think that every non-dog lover would agree that all they want is for the owners to be responsible and train their dogs so that they do not bother people. Contrast this with some puppy socialisation classes where young dogs are actively encouraged to approach and bother people in the expectation of being fed! Or how about resurrecting the exercise of teaching dogs to eliminate on command so they do not foul public areas? Guide dogs seem to achieve this with remarkable success! What about a system that will allow an owner access to a local recreation area with their dog only if they pass an annual test?

Maybe instead of thinking of more ways that dogs can be eliminated from areas and owners who allow their dogs to misbehave punished, we should use a system of rewarding the best and most responsible owners who have taken the time and trouble to train their dogs.

We also need to touch the hearts and minds of more children by putting a specially trained, good-natured therapy dog and its handler into every children's play area in the country. This should not be difficult to achieve as well-trained therapy dogs are now being accepted more and more into hospitals and nursing homes for the benefits they provide to the patients and residents.

It is the responsibility of all us to ensure that our relationship with our dogs is not broken irretrievably by the irresponsible few. If we succeed in our quest to learn the code and understand, communicate with and train our dogs, then the future looks very bright indeed. We have more individual people and organisations who are committed to making a difference, ranging from animal charities, assistance dogs, search and rescue dogs, cancer detection dogs, seizure alert dogs etc. etc. – all of whom portray the best side of the bond between ourselves and our friend the dog. We now need more companion dog owners to follow their lead and ensure that we guarantee our dogs remain part of our heritage and way of family life.

A dog and its owner in a pub

If by reading this book you have been inspired to learn more about your dog's behaviour, then by contacting one of the many dog-behaviour groups or universities offering courses on dog behaviour you can have access to a huge amount of information on the subject. If I have inspired you to want to go out and train your dog, there are many organisations involved in the training and certification of dog trainers, such as the Association of Pet Dog Trainers (APDT) or the National Association of Dog Obedience Instructors (NADOI).

As for finding a good instructor, the most comprehensive, and in my view the very best, international dog-trainer accreditation is run by the Kennel Club in the United Kingdom. Contact them to find an accredited trainer near you.

With behaviourists the picture is less clear, with many organisations claiming to be the best, all of them having different criteria by which they assess applicants for inclusion in their groups. Again the UK Kennel Club is the world leader in the field of accrediting dog behaviourists, so if you want to find a trainer or behaviourist that can produce results with your dog, look for one that has the letters KCAI (Kennel Club Accreditation scheme for Instructors in dog training and canine behaviour) after their name.

If I have inspired you to want to become a dog trainer or behaviourist, you could not do better than to sign up as either a student or a member of the KCAI programme. Gaining an accreditation will lead you on your path to unravelling the ultimate Dog Vinci Code and keeping it alive for future generations.